WIVES, MOTHERS, AND THE RED MENACE

WIVES, MOTHERS, AND THE RED MENACE

CONSERVATIVE WOMEN AND THE CRUSADE AGAINST COMMUNISM

MARY C. BRENNAN

UNIVERSITY PRESS OF COLORADO

Published by the University Press of Colorado
5589 Arapahoe Avenue, Suite 206C
Boulder, Colorado 80303

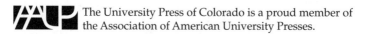 The University Press of Colorado is a proud member of
the Association of American University Presses.

The University Press of Colorado is a cooperative publishing enterprise supported,
in part, by Adams State College, Colorado State University, Fort Lewis College,
Mesa State College, Metropolitan State College of Denver, University of Colorado,
University of Northern Colorado, and Western State College of Colorado.

∞ The paper used in this publication meets the minimum requirements of the
American National Standard for Information Sciences—Permanence of Paper for
Printed Library Materials. ANSI Z39.48-1992

Library of Congress Cataloging-in-Publication Data

Brennan, Mary C.
  Wives, mothers, and the Red Menace : conservative women and the crusade
against communism / Mary C. Brennan.
     p. cm.
  Includes bibliographical references and index.
  ISBN 978-0-87081-885-1 (hardcover : alk. paper) 1. Women conservatives—
United States—History. 2. Conservatism—United States—History. 3.
Communism—United States—Prevention. 4. United States—Politics and
government—20th century. 5. United States--Social life and customs—20th
century. I. Title.
  HQ1236.5.U6B76 2008
  320.52092′273—dc22

                                                                    2007043582

Design by Daniel Pratt

17 16 15 14 13 12 11 10 09 08   10 9 8 7 6 5 4 3 2 1

For
The Emperor of the Galaxy
and the
Queen of the World

CONTENTS

ACKNOWLEDGMENTS

These ladies have been with me a long time. They've seen me through tenure and marriage and a baby. They've taken me to archives across the country and introduced me to interesting people. They helped me earn promotion. They have also refused to fit neatly into any of the preconceived packages I created for them. Every time I thought I had a handle on how to get their story out, they wouldn't quite cooperate with my methodology. Finally, I had to give up and let them have their say.

Along the way, I have accumulated debts too numerous to mention, but I will try. When you work on a project for over a decade, you have to have a significant support system holding you up and keeping you going. The administration at Texas State University–San Marcos provided both financial assistance with a Research Enhancement Grant and departmental travel funds as well as much-needed

time for research through a developmental leave. The Margaret Chase Smith Library also generously awarded me grant monies for two visits to their beautiful facility. Archivist Angela Stockwell deserves special mention for her willingness to share her time and memories with me. I was also privileged to receive a travel grant from the American Heritage Center at the University of Wyoming. Wherever I traveled I was fortunate to encounter archivists and librarians who were generous with their time and knowledge. I especially appreciated their willingness to chat with a lonely stranger. Dawn Letson of the Woman's Collection at Texas Woman's University floored me by sending unsolicited information she found that she thought would be useful for my study. Back here in Texas, I was fortunate to work with the ever-ready and amazingly diligent Margaret Vaverek, reference librarian at the Alkek Library. Margaret never found my requests for obscure information anything but challenging.

As always, I have benefited from the help, support, and advice of colleagues across the country and here in Texas. Historian Thomas Reeves graciously allowed me access to his notes from the extensive interviews he conducted for his biography of Joseph McCarthy. William H. Moore offered me advice and a tour of Laramie during my visit to the American Heritage Center at the University of Wyoming. Richard Fried and Leo Ribuffo offered advice and encouragement. Perhaps most important, I have been blessed with that rarity in academia: a department of true colleagues. They go far beyond the normal polite queries of "what are you working on?" They sit through countless brown-bag discussions, asking pertinent and probing questions; they lend sympathetic ears to rejection notices and send heartfelt e-mails of congratulations. Moreover, their ability to produce top-notch work while teaching large numbers of students has continually inspired me. In particular, I thank Gregg Andrews for his ever-ready editor's pen, Jimmy McWilliams for his incisive comments, and Frank de la Teja for his tech wizardry and determination that I would finish this project.

Two of my colleagues deserve special thanks. Vikki Bynum has been colleague, mentor, and friend as well as ruthless editor. Perhaps most important, she started all of this in the first place when she suggested I investigate Joe McCarthy's wife. If Vikki initiated the project, Ken Margerison provided the final push to get it done. As I struggled with revisions, he volunteered to read through the entire manuscript, giving up a good part of his summer to work with me. Ken's and Vikki's thorough editing, insightful questions, and relentless pursuit of clarity are responsible for much that is valuable in this work. I accept responsibility for all the mistakes.

After wandering lost in the publishing jungle, I lucked upon Darrin Pratt and his associates at the University Press of Colorado. They have proven wonderful to work with. I especially appreciate their patience and senses of humor.

Lastly, I must thank my family and friends. Nancy Scott Jackson worked hard for years to keep me focused on the project. Trace Etienne-Gray and Jo Snider willingly listened to various versions of the book. My cousins in Cincinnati and my in-laws across Texas showed interest and offered encouragement. The continual support of my sisters Brigid and Patty, my brother-in-law Jack, and my nieces and nephews sustained me over the years. None of this would have been possible, however, without the efforts of my husband, Alan Apel, and our daughter, Riley. Alan impressed me at our first meeting by asking questions about this project. Almost ten years later, he told me he was taking over full-time parenting for the summer so I could finally get the manuscript sent off. He never doubted the project or me. As for Riley, her sweet voice asking me "so, how was work?" made me double my efforts so I could get home to her.

WIVES, MOTHERS, AND THE RED MENACE

INTRODUCTION

A man walks into his kitchen and greets his wife after a hard day's work. As he sniffs the pots boiling on the stove, she reminds him that he has a union meeting that night. He says he told the guys he had something else to do. She asks if he will go to the PTA meeting with her. Again, he begs off. She sighs, knowing he is making a mistake. He goes to bed later, content with his uninvolvement in his world. He wakes in a nightmare world. His happy household is gone, his family replaced by automatons he recognizes but does not understand. His loving, supportive wife has become cold, calculating, and demanding. His oldest daughter has been transformed from a boy-crazy teen into a zealot who moves away to work on a government-sponsored farm. His younger children threaten to turn him in to the authorities for violating rules he does not even know exist. Placed on trial, he is sentenced to death. Before his punishment can be meted out, however, he awakens from his "Red nightmare," shaken but with a renewed dedication to family and community.[1]

This scenario from a 1961 Department of Defense film looks corny today, but it epitomizes the way anticommunism had permeated American society in the years after World War II. The blue-collar worker, who makes enough money—thanks to defense spending—to live a middle-class lifestyle, takes his good life of peace, prosperity, and freedom for granted. As a result, the film shows, he could lose everything. Vigilance, the government warned, was necessary at all times. Interestingly, the person who seemed to understand the need for caution was the wife. Although she is portrayed as a typical housewife who nags her husband to become involved in his union, his church, his children's lives, and his community, she recognizes the importance of participation in these activities as a way to protect their way of life. She is going to the PTA meeting. During the nightmare, however, communism turns the wife into a hard, authoritative figure, completely unlike the warm, soft American woman she had been previously. The communist woman is obsessed with the party, whereas the American woman's activities are centered around her home, family, and community. The filmmakers clearly intended to show how communism would destroy the American family. Probably unconsciously, they also indicated the essential role women played in the struggle against communism.

The relationship between women and postwar anticommunism is the subject of this book. At a time when governmental, religious, and social authorities encouraged women to fulfill themselves only as wives and mothers, millions of women expanded their notion of household responsibilities—at least temporarily—to include the crusade against communism. Some participated in traditional "womanly ways" by writing letters or hosting teas. Others took up the banner and ran for political office. Most did not see their participation in the war against communism as anything profound or controversial; they were simply doing what needed to be done to protect their families. In joining the ranks of male anticommunists, however, these women challenged existing assumptions about women as political players. Additionally, their view of the crisis, their methods of confronting communism, and their actions affected the overall tone and success of the movement. Women helped mold the domestic Cold War into a much broader and more encompassing crusade.

The fight against communism dominated American politics, economics, and society for almost fifty years. It colored Americans' views of the rest of the world, led them into two wars, and generated numerous military actions. It fueled the prosperity of the postwar years and, later, economic instability. It fostered an atmosphere of suspicion that at times threatened to undermine basic American civil liberties. It leached into society and culture, affecting in a multitude of ways Americans' thoughts, purchases, and leisure activities. It spawned both an anticommunist movement carried out by a variety of individuals and groups and an anticommunist mind-set that permeated the image Americans had of themselves and others. It permanently altered the way Americans and the rest of the world view the United States. Understanding the depth, breadth, and longevity of anticommunism is essential to comprehending late-twentieth-century America.

Responding to this imagery as well as news reports from the media and speeches by politicians, a vast majority of Americans said they viewed communism as evil. They might not have been able to explain communism as an intellectual theory or an economic system, but they perceived it to be a threat to America's international position, the country's national security, and even the internal stability of their local communities. Many accepted the government's rationale for taking steps to protect Americans from military threats abroad and subversion at home. For most Americans, however, their acknowledgment of the existence of the dangers of communism manifested itself infrequently in dinner conversations, in voting for "patriotic" Americans, in signing petitions, or in waving the flag on the Fourth of July. Most were more concerned about paying bills, saving for a new car, or going to a ball game than they were about eternal vigilance against the Red menace.

Other Americans understood that the danger was imminent. Ignoring ideological and geopolitical issues, they saw communism as a direct threat to their personal freedom. They believed the communist system forced everyone under its jurisdiction into a singular mold, depriving individuals of choices regarding religion, lifestyle, and employment. They feared what they perceived would be the inevitable destruction of family life as communist leaders sent fathers to factories or the army, mothers to work outside the home, children to indoctrination schools, and babies to communal care centers. Communism, in their minds, deprived its victims of control over their finances, their families, their futures. This perfidious ideology would, they argued, ultimately enslave all Americans.

As a result of their deeply held fears, these Americans did not trust government officials and politicians to end the crisis. These anticommunists remained constantly on guard, scrutinizing official actions, educating the public, searching out new encroachments against their version of democracy and free enterprise. For these anticommunists the fight against communism took on the language and urgency of a crusade. Some formed committees, both local and national—sometimes with thousands of members, sometimes with a handful of like-minded souls—to do their part in protecting the American way of life. Others worked on their own, writing books, articles, and newsletters. The memberships of these committees often overlapped, with the same names appearing on numerous boards of directors and mastheads of magazines. Anticommunist crusaders corresponded with one another, comparing notes, discussing strategies, looking for volunteers or funds.

Although they shared a common loathing of "the Left," they did not always agree on the specifics of what that term meant. Some only reacted vigorously to card-carrying members of the Communist Party USA or to the geopolitical threat posed by the Soviets and Chinese. Others widened their lens to scope out fellow travelers, people who either consciously or indirectly helped the "real" communists. True zealots went even further, arguing that Americans faced a wide variety of threats from groups ranging from liberals to those who supported social welfare programs, Democrats, civil rights activists, feminists, homosexuals, and, for some, Jews. For the purposes of this book, this divergent group of organizations and individuals constitutes the anticommunist movement. When I write about anticommunists, I mean these activists.

These anticommunists also constituted an important component of the evolving conservatism of the postwar period. Throughout much of the twentieth century, men and women espousing very different views thought of themselves as "conservatives." Thus, some conservatives were classical liberals who desired limited government intervention, especially in economic affairs; others were traditionalists who advocated government support of Judeo-Christian values. Because they fought as much with one another as they did with their more liberal opponents, they lacked the unity or the numbers to challenge progressives within the Republican and Democratic parties. Although the New Deal policies of Franklin Delano Roosevelt, which increased the federal bureaucracy and the presence of women and minorities in

Washington, D.C., had galvanized conservatives of all varieties, it took the threat of communism to bring them all together. Both economic and social conservatives hated communism, so the crusade provided them with common ground. Consequently, many of the most fervent anticommunists shared not only a loathing for the Soviet Union but also a deep distrust of the federal government in general and Democrats in particular.[2] For these reasons, conservative anticommunists conflated their two enemies: communism and the American political Left. In fact, while anticommunism helped unite conservatives, it also served as a convenient platform from which conservatives could advocate for a right-wing agenda along with hatred of communism.

By placing women at the center of the struggle against communism, this book enhances our understanding of the Cold War in several ways. First, it shows the way women translated the key political and ideological issues that fueled the anticommunist campaign for the general public. Frequently describing communism as a personal threat, the words of female activists paint a striking portrait of America in those years—simultaneously belligerent, arrogant, and frightened. Their actions as well as their writings helped mold the overall tenor of the campaign. Second, an emphasis on women's participation shows the depth of the fear and paranoia communism created in Americans. Despite idealized mores of the era that discouraged middle-class women from entering the political sphere, male anticommunist crusaders recognized that all citizens, including traditionally nonpolitical women, must unite to battle this enemy. Third, many women acted at a local level, indicating that this struggle went all the way to the grass roots. Political leaders pursued the diplomatic policy of containment at the national level, but concerns over brinkmanship in a nuclear age spread throughout the populace, drawing average citizens into the war against the Red menace. Finally, the gendered language and imagery used to describe the Cold War frequently reinforced the connection between a complicated diplomatic and political situation and the reality of everyday life for American men and women.

Anticommunist activity provided women with a way to involve themselves in the politics of the day. At a time when the image of female domesticity smothered most women's career aspirations, women found few outlets for their political ambitions. Because almost all Americans believed communism was evil and must be stopped, however, working against communism afforded women the opportunity to jump into a national political struggle without having to justify their actions, as might be required of women who supported women's rights or unionism or any number of left-wing causes. These anticommunist women could engage themselves in politics while espousing the female domestic virtues endorsed by mainstream society.

Female anticommunist crusaders built on a historical tradition of American women's participation in politics, especially when danger threatened home and family. For example, in the years preceding the American Revolution, women found themselves drawn into political debates that affected them through their roles as household managers. Colonial boycotts against English goods transformed shopping into a political exercise that turned women into active participants in the rebellion. Later, intensifying hostilities forced women to play roles usually forbidden: soldier, businesswoman, head of household. Although most men and women viewed these actions as temporary, a significant change in gender relations did occur in the aftermath of the Revolution. The development of the ideal of Republican Motherhood created a way for women to participate in the political process without appearing to undermine the traditional political role of men. Educated and informed about local and national concerns, the Republican Mother served as teacher, guide, and role model for her children. She showed them how to be good citizens, no matter how large or small their role in the body politic might be. Maintaining their primary function as wives and mothers, American women during this period nevertheless broadened their sphere of activity, if only slightly.[3] Their domestic responsibilities were now invested with political significance.

The industrialization of early America similarly brought changes to women's lives. As men's labor began to shift from the farm to the factory and from rural to urban areas, women—especially middle-class white women—were increasingly inundated by advice manuals, novels, and religious sermons that emphasized what historian Barbara Welter called "the cult of true womanhood." A woman, according to religious and social leaders, should be pious, pure, domestic, and submissive. Too delicate to perform any "real" (i.e., paid) labor, women were directed to focus on home and family, providing a safe haven for husbands and children against the dirty, dangerous world of industry. Women, according to this view, utilized their natural moral superiority to balance men's more aggressive and sinful tendencies. This image also served as a way to distinguish between the classes; many immigrant and black women hired themselves out as wage laborers, while proper middle-class white women did not. For all its hypoc-risies, the cult allowed middle-class women to cloak themselves in respectability.[4]

Some women took advantage of the ideals of Republican Mother-hood and the cult of true womanhood to operate outside their normal boundaries. Domestic reformer Catharine Beecher accepted the premise of separate spheres and worked to carve out a unique place for women within that system. Rather than seeing the cult as a limita-tion, she empowered women's position within the home by redefining domesticity and motherhood as a vocation that preserved essential American values. Other women, working within their proper area of domesticity and piety, involved themselves in church and reform activities, carefully selecting those that conformed to their assigned sphere. Thus, women worked for missionary societies, joined ladies' clubs organized to save children and fallen women, and tried to eliminate the evils of alcohol. Once they became involved in public activities, women might move beyond such "womanly" reforms to embrace much more overtly political concerns such as abolition and suffrage. By the mid-nineteenth century, women had created a unique political role for themselves. In addition, by expanding the boundaries of home, women expanded their sphere of influence to include "anywhere women and children were [located]." In the process of redefining their sphere, they created a "distinct . . . political culture."[5]

This expansion was perhaps most evident during the Progressive era around the turn of the twentieth century. Unmarried, educated middle- and upper-class women found new opportunities to broaden their activities. Like their earlier sisters, these women joined reform societies that fought alcohol, moral decline, and child labor. They went further, however. Taking their cue from European women, Jane Addams and Ellen Gates Starr founded Hull House, a settlement house in Chicago. Their aim was to help immigrants in surrounding areas cope with the adjustment to life in America. Other such enterprises followed, providing needed help to the poor and working classes and creating a new profession for women: social work. Since these women acted as nurturers and caretakers, many Americans tolerated the fact that the settlement house workers exhibited nontraditional female behavior. After all, they were just cleaning up the mess left by male politicians and businessmen who welcomed the immigrants' labor but ignored their troubles.

As women pushed the limits of accepted behavior, however, they met with opposition from both men and other women. In particular, the suffrage issue caused problems. Ironically, both sides fell back on the "cult" imagery to make their arguments. While suffragists often used the language of moral superiority as a justification for granting women the vote, those opposed claimed women were moving too far outside their domestic sphere. Anti-suffragists feared that if women entered the male world of politics, all women would lose the protections and privileges the ideology of separate spheres had afforded them.[6] Recognizing that they would have to move into the political realm to fight their enemies, anti-suffragists rationalized their behavior. They told themselves that their foray into politics was just temporary, designed to achieve a higher purpose, and that it would have no lasting implications for women's social role. Once they had achieved their goal, they would gladly go back to the responsibilities of home and children.

Throughout much of American history, both advocates of women's political participation and those who opposed it have used the image of woman as housewife to benefit their cause. Colonial women boycotting English goods, abolitionist women protesting the degradation of slave women, and Progressive women setting up kitchens in settlement houses discovered that their normal duties could take on a political meaning. Similarly, anti-suffragists used their desire to preserve women's housewifely role as a justification for their political activities. These early-twentieth-century women so successfully incorporated the concept of "municipal housekeeping" into the image of the lady that future generations assumed "good" women could be active in certain areas of the "man's world." Clearly, the image of the homemaker-mother was fraught with political overtones.[7]

The idealization of the housewife image, however, truly came into its own in the years following the Depression and World War II. After two decades of economic and international disruption, many women and men longed for the safe haven glorified in myths of the "good old days." They wanted what they perceived to be the perfect family, with Mom staying at home and Dad going to work. The prosperity of these years made this dream a possibility, at least for a time. In fact, the enormous increase in the variety and availability of consumer goods helped turn the nineteenth-century "true woman" into a shallower version of herself in the 1950s. The earlier woman had lived for the moral good of her husband and children; the 1950s wife and mother spent much of her time trying to maintain the symbols that marked her family as middle class.[8]

A deeply entrenched and comfortable image of middle-class prosperity became a valuable tool for both men and women activists as they worked to enlist the majority of American women in their campaign against communism. Glorifying the role of housework and the position of homemaker, anti-communists showed women that they could participate in politics without abandoning their traditional roles. At other times, activists recognized the valuable role housewives played in the economy and used that to their advantage. Whichever strategy they utilized, these men and women succeeded in more than simply drawing women to their cause. They also reinforced the current domestic ideal of femininity as the only viable option for women.

Although female activists all along the ideological spectrum utilized the expanded housewife imagery, it was especially vital for more conservative women. Because women on the Right theoretically supported status quo gender roles, advocating women's political participation contradicted their underlying principles, much as the activism of anti-suffragists had challenged their deeply held convictions. They could avoid appearing hypocritical, however, by explaining their behavior as a temporary breach of the norm required by the serious threat of communism. They reassured the men in their lives, and themselves, that everything would return to "normal" once the danger had passed.

Conservative anticommunist women followed this tradition and used it to their full advantage. Draping their work in maternalistic rhetoric and housewifely images, women activists reassured their male colleagues that they wanted nothing more than the end of communism; they posed no threat to the power structure. In many ways, in fact, they became storm troopers for patriarchal dominance. They did, however, expect to be taken seriously as concerned citizens; they assumed they had a right to participate in the struggle to save their homes and families from the communists. Far from submissive, hesitant "little women," conservative anticommunist women boldly jumped into the national debate on the issue of communism, all the while acting as though they were not challenging the existing gender structure.

Out of necessity, conservative anticommunist men accepted this version of reality. The fact that women were not challenging men's political dominance helped ease the minds of conservative male activists. Convinced of the virtue of the housewifely woman, men generally treated women activists with the tolerant respect accorded to mothers and "ladies." In turn, the women became adept at overlooking male condescension, paternalism, and sexism as they pursued advocacy of their cause. With no one's worldview threatened, men welcomed female participation—within limits—in the anticommunist movement.

To fight communism successfully, men needed women's involvement in at least three ways. First, they needed the women's vote. As a result, men frequently spoke to groups of women, encouraging them to be informed, to write letters, and to support strong anticommunist candidates. The men usually couched their speeches in very traditional ways; they spoke to the women as wives, household managers, and mothers. Second, male anticommunist crusaders recognized that within their "careers" as wives and mothers, women could provide valuable service to the cause. Women willingly did much of the educational work needed at the grassroots level to build support for the cause and for right-wing candidates. Third, male anticommunists used women, especially in their roles as housewives and mothers, to define both the evils of communism and the virtues of America. In fact, the image of an idealized family lay at the center of most anticommunist versions of the American way of life.

Although they lacked much formal power to battle communism either around the world or at home, female anticommunist zealots did possess certain tools that benefited both the cause and themselves. In short, they utilized their gender as an asset rather than a limitation in fighting against the Reds. As a result, women were involved in all levels of anticommunist activity. Coming from a variety of backgrounds, these overwhelmingly white, middle-class women did not let preconceived notions of femininity stop them from participating in a battle they felt was vitally important. They claimed the right to speak and write about the evils of foreign and domestic communism. Sometimes they spoke in general terms as Americans; other times they framed their arguments as women who could and should speak to and for their gender.

Gendered language and images pervaded discussions of communism's danger to the world and to the American way of life. From the testosterone-laden speeches of "Tailgunner" Joe McCarthy to the portrayals of Soviet women as heartless amazons, anticommunists utilized gendered symbols in making their arguments to the American people. Gendered subtexts allowed anticommunists to broaden their appeal by linking the fight against communism to concerns over the shifting roles of men and women in the postwar world. Americans who might not understand the intricacies of government machinations abroad or bureaucratic spy networks at home had no difficulty seeing a threat in the increasing number of women working, African Americans protesting, or homosexuals coming out of the closet. Additionally, emphasizing their femininity provided "cover" for anticommunist women who adopted masculine characteristics and language in their advocacy of crushing communism. Whereas this gendered language legitimized their participation in the crusade against communism, anticommunist women found it could also be used to undermine the value of their work for the cause.

Like the anticommunist movement itself, the women in this book are a diverse but not all-inclusive group. They are overwhelmingly white and middle class, as mentioned previously. There were a small number of conservative anticommunist African American women, but I chose not to include them because their focus tended to be less on anticommunism than on obtaining civil rights and fighting segregation. Additionally, although working-class women were concerned with communism, most lacked the time and extra income necessary to join an active crusade.

Within these parameters, the anticommunist women in this study include a variety of American women. Some were well-known and powerful; most were not. Some feared elements of the U.S. government almost as much as they did the Soviets. Others focused on threats closer to home to protect their children from outside influences. Most were genuinely concerned about the future of their country and their families. Some, however, were extremists who took their beliefs to irrational ends. I have included a few of the more zealous to show the variety of women's views and the responses of the community at large. Often, men and women used the obsessive behavior of a few women to undermine all women's political activity.

Whether they stood on the extreme Right of the ideological spectrum or leaned more toward moderation, anticommunist women shaped the anticommunist crusade. They brought anticommunism into the home, motivating women to expand their domestic duties to include ridding their houses of the Red menace along with dust and grime. In the process of enlightening less politically aware women, anticommunist activists created a space for themselves within the political arena. Particularly on the local level, women discovered their power to effect change through demonstrations, letter-writing campaigns, and newsletters. Other women tried to influence national domestic and foreign policy through research, speeches, and writing books. Anticommunist women utilized gendered language and imagery both to reinforce their right to participate in the crusade against communism and to emphasize the importance of their cause. In the end, these local campaigns and controversial books and images transformed the anticommunist movement in ways both contemporaries and historians have overlooked. Only by examining women's participation in the struggle against the Left can we begin to understand the depth of the influence anticommunism had on American society and politics. Conversely, without probing anticommunist activity, we cannot see the complexity of women's lives during those years.

CHAPTER ONE

THE COLD WAR WORLD

Even for men and women who did not actively participate in the anti-communist crusade, the Cold War changed their lives. The development of hostilities between the United States and the Soviet Union seemed to make the world a more dangerous place by creating the potential for armed conflict. In a nuclear age, that potential threatened even to include civilians in small towns and large cities in the American heartland. The outbreak of fighting in areas of Eastern Europe and especially in Asia confirmed the validity of those fears. At home, the discovery of a communist spy network frightened Americans who worried that the government might be overrun with infiltrators. The paranoia proved contagious; in their fear, citizens questioned anyone or anything that was "different," assuming the differences were a sign of communist sympathies.

On a more positive note, Cold War–driven defense spending fueled an economic prosperity that allowed many families to move into the middle class. Accompanied by increased consumer spending, the ever-growing defense budgets provided jobs and rising incomes for many Americans. This prosperity, combined with the effects of government initiatives such as the GI Bill and the Federal Housing Authority, pushed many families into middle-class status and allowed others to appear so through increased consumerism. The growth of suburbia developed alongside a new emphasis on family and conformity that resulted in part from Cold War anxieties.[1]

The Cold War, the rise of the middle class, and the renewed emphasis on domesticity had a particularly powerful impact on women. They were supposed to find their ultimate fulfillment as wives and mothers, staying at home and tending to home and family. Everyone, from preachers to teachers to government officials, believed that was what women wanted. Many women mouthed similar sentiments, even as the reality of their lives proved the "feminine mystique" was a myth. Although men and women continued to insist that domesticity should be every woman's ideal, women took jobs, joined clubs, and volunteered with organizations that took them away from home.[2]

The Cold War was actually much more complex than the black-and-white explanations American leaders gave their fellow citizens. Tension between Russia and the United States predated the creation of the Soviet Union in 1924. Nationalism on both sides, combined with American distrust of the autocratic and anti-Semitic Russian czars and Russian resentment of American arrogance and expansionist tendencies, created an underlying hostility between the two nations. The Bolshevik Revolution in 1917 added an ideological element to an already existing antagonism. While the onset of World War II forged a temporary alliance between the two countries in an effort to defeat fascism, the smoldering mistrust never completely disappeared. Even as the Soviets stood alone in their struggle in 1942, Franklin Delano Roosevelt had difficulty convincing both Congress and the American people to extend Lend-Lease aid to their new allies. Recognizing American ambivalence toward them and determined to protect their borders from future invasions, the Soviets reacted defensively as they liberated Eastern Europe from Nazi control by maintaining armies in the countries of that region. By the end of World War II, the allies were deeply suspicious of each other.[3]

In the five years following V-J Day, misunderstandings between the Soviet and U.S. governments hardened into belligerent defensiveness. Beginning from a position of suspicion, government leaders on each side saw the other's actions as threatening and dangerous. Officials in the Kremlin and the U.S. State Department refused to recognize their own part in the growing conflict. Soviet leaders ignored the call for free elections and crushed any opposition to their authority. When the Americans, British, and French began cooperating with one another in Germany, the Soviets suspected a Western plot to isolate them. Their response, closing off ground access to Berlin, only heightened the Western nations' concern that the Soviets planned to take over Europe. Each side assumed the other was out to destroy it and saw every action as a threat.

Meanwhile, Americans developed the containment policy. At heart, this policy divided the world into two, and only two, spheres: the free world (those on America's side) and the communist world (those on the Soviets' side). Nations had to be on one side or the other. Containment thus left little room for negotiation or compromise; you agreed with the good guys, or you were assumed to be one of the bad guys. One result of U.S. officials' acceptance of that bipolar vision of the world was their blindness to the existence of those who fell into gray areas; in other words, those who did not fit neatly into one category or another. For example, Yugoslavian president Josip Tito, technically a member of the communist bloc, stood up to Soviet premier Joseph Stalin and wanted to form a relationship with the United States; Chinese leader Mao Zedong practiced a variation of communism that troubled Stalin almost as much as it did the Americans; and various nations of the developing world, such as India, did not want to be drawn into the great power struggle. From the opposite perspective, Americans reacted incredulously to French president Charles de Gaulle's refusal blindly to accept U.S. dictates. In ignoring nations that did not fit the containment mold exactly, Americans missed opportunities to develop a realistic vision of the international situation. The Cold War world was much more complicated than the containment view allowed.[4]

Despite its complex reality, American political leaders described the Cold War to the U.S. public in very simplistic terms. FBI chief J. Edgar Hoover, who first expressed concern over the Bolsheviks in 1919, epitomized the standard anticommunist refrain. Bolshevik doctrines, he explained, "threaten the happiness of the community, the safety of every individual, and the continuance of every home and fireside." Ultimately, this system would "destroy the peace of the country and thrust it into a condition of anarchy and lawlessness and immorality that passes imagination."[5] The passage of time did nothing to change Hoover's views of the Bolsheviks-turned-Soviets. In fact, his continued study of the ideology and its practitioners deepened his hatred and distrust of the enemy. Fearing the Truman administration underestimated the seriousness of the threat from the Reds, Hoover testified before the House Un-American Activities Committee in 1947. Once again, he emphasized the sinister nature of communism. "It stands," he proclaimed, "for the destruction of our American form of government . . . American democracy . . . [and] free enterprise." Communism's goal, according to Hoover, was the "creation of a 'Soviet of the United States' and ultimate world revolution."[6]

Like many Americans, Hoover viewed the threat of communism in ideological terms. Rather than speak of tanks and totalitarian countries, Hoover tended toward religious language. "The real danger in communism," he explained, "lies in the fact that it is atheistic and seeks to replace the Supreme Being." Without God as the center, he stated, there would be no moral guidelines, and society would fall into chaos. Not only would Americans lose their everyday freedoms, but their families would be destroyed as well. "Children," Hoover explained, "would be placed in nurseries and special indoctrination schools." Women, relieved of child-care responsibilities, would go to work in factories and mines with the men.[7] This scenario contrasted sharply with the American ideal of a stay-at-home mom who served as the bulwark of the family. Obviously, Hoover believed the American system was superior.

For others, such as President Harry Truman, ideology took a back seat to questions of an international balance of power. Already bothered by the Soviets' refusal to allow free elections in Eastern Europe, Truman decided to take a firmer stand when asked to help anticommunist forces in Greece in their battle against the Red menace. Truman realized he needed to convince Congress and the American public to spend sufficient funds to halt communism in Greece and the surrounding area. He feared Congress and voters would be reluctant both to commit such a large sum and to re-engage in a worldwide struggle. After consulting with his advisers and congressional leaders, Truman decided he needed to frighten the public into agreement. The Truman Doctrine, as it became known, warned that if the

United States did not aid Greece and Turkey "in this fateful hour," the consequences would "be far reaching to the West as well as the East." With this speech, Truman implemented the containment policy and established a pattern anticommunists, particularly those in government, would continue to follow for decades. Combining frightening rhetoric about the potential threat to U.S. shores with a sense of American duty, government anticommunists legitimized the reality of the communist danger.[8]

Nongovernmental anticommunists echoed the concern. In 1948, James F. O'Neil, national commander of the American Legion, used vivid imagery to explain to his fellow Legionnaires that the "rape of Czechoslovakia" posed a threat even to Americans safe within their meeting halls. What happened in far-off places, he wrote, foreshadowed what could occur in the good old United States if Legionnaires did not open their eyes to the foreign agents in their midst.[9] Containment, it seemed, was not just a policy for diplomats.

President Truman, struggling to stay ahead of the public's concern, turned the problem over to his National Security Council (NSC). The NSC issued its report in April 1950, but NSC-68 did little to calm the growing fears. In fact, the report set a very somber tone. The situation Americans faced was "momentous, involving the fulfillment or destruction not only of this Republic but of civilization itself." According to the NSC, the Soviet Union desired "to bring the free world under its dominion by methods of the cold war." The report exposed the "risks" if the free world—that is, America—did not begin to build an adequate defense system. Using words and phrases meant to instill a sense of urgency, the report cautioned that a delay in decision making could prove fatal. Americans must accept "that the cold war is in fact a real war in which the survival of the free world is at stake."[10]

By the early 1950s, the Cold War battlefront had shifted from Europe to Asia. The success of Mao Zedong and his communist forces in pushing American-supported Jiang Jieshi into exile, combined with the creation of the People's Republic of China, shocked Americans. Suddenly, it appeared to many Americans as though communism was winning the struggle to control the globe. The situation worsened in June 1950 when communist North Korea invaded U.S. ally South Korea. The Cold War had turned hot. Despite nominal United Nations support, Americans paid for the war in Korea in both blood and dollars, as American GIs provided the bodies and U.S. taxpayers footed the bill for the conflict. Expecting an easy victory, Americans watched incredulously as the conflict settled into a stalemate. Only a limited victory seemed possible, and no one was sure exactly what it would entail. They did know, however, that it was not the same as winning the war. America, which had defeated both Japan and Germany in 1945, suddenly seemed incapable of defeating a small developing nation. Frustration over the situation exposed what for most Americans proved the bitter reality of the containment policy—it worked to maintain the status quo instead of vanquishing the enemy—and caused some Americans to push for increased defense spending; they could only rationalize that the Korean stalemate had resulted from a failure to prosecute the war to the fullest.[11]

Wisconsin senator Joseph McCarthy and numerous other political leaders continued to pursue this theme in the coming years. In his career-making speech in Wheeling, West Virginia, in 1950, McCarthy chillingly reported that the number of people living under communist rule had increased by 400 percent since 1945. He stated that this increase indicated "the swiftness of the tempo of Communist victories and American defeats in the cold war." Richard Nixon, senator and future vice president, cautioned Americans who wanted to stay out of the struggle that this was no longer an option: "If Europe [were] allowed to go Communist, it [would] mean that within five or ten years we will be faced with a war which we are likely to lose." FBI director Hoover also urged Americans not to relax their guard. Facing "formidable weapons," Americans could not afford the "luxury of waiting for communism to run its course like other oppressive dictatorships."[12] Instead, according to New Hampshire senator Styles Bridges, Americans had to assume a leadership role. The U.S. government should concentrate less on the people already lost to communism and more on the "millions of Asiatics waiting to be arrayed against Communism. They are waiting only on American leadership."[13] Without a willingness to press on with the struggle as well as continual vigilance, these leaders warned, Americans risked losing their way of life.

Other Americans disagreed with this way of thinking. Although they also found the Soviet system repugnant and feared its intentions, these Americans worried that the obsession with defeating communism everywhere might prove equally dangerous for Americans. Some, like President Dwight Eisenhower, warned that the ever-growing defense expenditures were weakening the budget and could permanently damage the economy. In his Farewell Address,

Ike encouraged Americans to refrain from thinking that "some spectacular and costly action could become the miraculous solution" to destroying their "ruthless" enemy.[14] Others, such as author, critic, and philosopher Lewis Mumford, thought the increasingly belligerent language ruined any chance to seek peaceful solutions to crises. They were concerned that the government would only consider military options to resolve conflicts.[15] Democratic presidential candidate in 1952 and 1956 Adlai Stevenson expressed concern that the actions of some of the more zealous anticommunists undermined "the bright image of America" held by peoples around the world.[16]

Meanwhile, the development of more overt conflict between the United States and the USSR invigorated existing anticommunist and antiradical factions across the country. Building on the anti-immigrant and anti-labor sentiments of the late nineteenth century, this early anticommunist movement came into its own during the Red Scare following World War I. Attorney General A. Mitchell Palmer, aided by his young and dedicated assistant, J. Edgar Hoover, succeeded in deporting a number of communists (most notably Emma Goldman and Alexander Berkman) before overplaying their hands in a series of highly publicized, ethically questionable, and ultimately unproductive raids on supposed communist cells. Palmer's loss of prestige did not lead to cancellation of the Investigative Bureau (later the Federal Bureau of Investigation [FBI]) he had created to look into subversive groups. The new head of the FBI, J. Edgar Hoover, took his responsibilities seriously and began compiling lists of individuals and organizations he found "subversive."[17]

Hoover was not alone. In fact, during the 1920s and 1930s, concern about the threat from the Left arose in different areas. Corporate leaders and some members of the middle class increasingly associated communism and socialism with the efforts of various labor groups to organize and protect laborers. The Catholic Church proclaimed its opposition to the communist regime in Russia, citing both Lenin's atheism and the treatment of priests and nuns under radical regimes. Disillusioned former leftists, such as J. B. Matthews, and virulent anti-Semites, such as Elizabeth Dilling, worked to build libraries of information and published books in their attempts to warn the American public of the continued threat communism posed.[18] The creation of the House Un-American Activities Committee in 1938 provided a perfect springboard from which to launch a crusade against the Red menace. Although initially formed to investigate German Americans' connections to the Nazi regime, the committee—under the influence of Matthews, who served as chief investigator, and Texan Martin Dies—soon turned its attention to communism.[19]

On the eve of World War II, an ill-defined, disorganized, and multifaceted anticommunist sentiment existed among Americans. Most Americans could not have defined the philosophy of communism, but they sensed that it was bad. They knew communists did not allow people to practice religion or own private property. Some feared the Soviet Union's power to spread anti-capitalist sentiment throughout Europe and the rest of the world. Many others conflated concerns about foreign communism with a dislike of the political policies of the Roosevelt administration. These people were not certain where the line ended separating true communism from the makework programs of the New Deal. In their view, encouraging the poor to expect help from the government, which would take money from the rich in the form of taxes, sounded radical enough to be communism. Still, the vagueness of their apprehensions meant most Americans willingly suppressed their anxieties about the Soviets during the period of the Grand Alliance.

Those underlying doubts came roaring back, however, after the exposure in 1945 and 1946 of Soviet spies in Canada, England, and even the United States. At that point, most Americans recognized the need to eliminate any legitimate threats to the government. The convictions of former State Department employee Alger Hiss (for perjury) and Julius and Ethel Rosenberg (for espionage) appeared to prove that a serious problem existed.[20] Building on these concerns about national security, politicians such as Senator Joseph McCarthy began to hunt for spies in every nook and cranny of the government. In their quest to ferret out any potential subversives, McCarthy and his ilk willingly accused people based on circumstantial evidence, hearsay, or other seemingly unrelated factors. Spy hunters, for example, declared open season on homosexuals. Similarly, anyone who appeared to support the growing Civil Rights Movement drew criticism from McCarthy and his associates. Even being friends with someone of a different race was suspicious behavior and raised concerns that one was a potential communist, or "fellow traveler."

The extreme nature of many of McCarthy's views caused concern among some anticommunist politicians and intellectuals, who feared that the obsession with spies blinded Americans to reality. They believed the danger from any remaining communists was slight compared with the damage being done to the American justice system.[21] For example, historian Arthur Schlesinger Jr. accepted that communism posed a threat but ridiculed the idea that a party of 70,000 or fewer members would "contemplate a violent revolution" in the United States.[22] Even President Truman, one of the original creators of containment, worried that some anticommunist measures went too far. In vetoing the Internal Security Act of 1950, he wrote that the proposed measure would discredit "as hypocrisy the efforts of the US on behalf of freedom." He warned that implementation of the bill could constitute the "greatest danger to freedom of speech, press and assembly, since the Alien and Sedition Laws of 1798."[23] McCarthyites charged that such an attitude indicated a "softness" on the part of the individual and marked that person as a "pinko"—a commie sympathizer at worst and a dupe at best. Historian Richard Gid Powers separated what he labeled "countersubversives," those who saw little difference between a Soviet communist and an American Democrat, and liberals, who worried about the Soviet Union's power but saw little threat in the American Communist Party.[24]

Increasingly, these differences in approach to anticommunism took on a partisan flavor. Both Republicans and Democrats—in fact, almost all Americans—professed to espouse some measure of anticommunism. Moreover, within the major political parties were those who disagreed on the amount of time and money that should be spent fighting communists abroad and searching out subversives at home. In general, however, Republicans pushed continually to increase defense spending and sought military solutions to problems abroad. At home, they were more vehement in their efforts to sniff out Reds. Democrats, who had originated the Cold War under Truman, also voted for large defense budgets but were more leery of an over-reliance on military solutions. In addition, they feared the quest for spies in government had run amok. Democrats argued that what they had begun as a legitimate security measure, Republicans had turned into a free-for-all.

More important than these slight variations in tone and degree, however, was the way anticommunism became a weapon to be used in partisan warfare. Mud slinging reached new lows as Republicans and Democrats smeared one another every shade of red and pink. Republicans proved particularly adept at this in their effort to regain control of the White House after their long exile under the Roosevelt-Truman presidencies. The GOP had grown impatient and frustrated after a twenty-year banishment; they wanted control of the Oval Office. Anticommunism was a way to get there. Joe McCarthy, Richard Nixon, Barry Goldwater, and numerous others successfully defeated their Democratic opponents by accusing them of being "soft on communism." Taking the charge a step further, some Republicans began equating "liberalism" with communism, thus making it even easier to undermine not just their opponents but also any programs they disliked. Reaching its peak in the early 1950s, Red baiting remained a useful partisan tool throughout the rest of the twentieth century.[25]

Even as the hysteria of the Red Scare climaxed in the early 1950s with the Army-McCarthy hearings, circumstances abroad and political developments at home provided Americans with the opportunity to reevaluate their Cold War thinking. The death of Stalin in 1953, followed by the eventual rise to power of Nikita Khrushchev and the increasingly visible and important role in geopolitics of developing nations in Asia and Africa, changed the players and settings of the Cold War drama without interfering with the basic plot. The standoff between the United States and the Soviet Union settled into a tense stalemate, with an occasional exchange of hostile words or displays of military prowess. Despite his campaign promises to get tough with the commies, Republican Dwight Eisenhower's victory in 1952 did not intensify the battle, liberate "captive nations," or take the Soviets to the brink of nuclear war. In fact, much to the regret of some of his supporters, Ike spent much of his time—especially after winning reelection in 1956—trying to thaw the ice blocking communication between Washington and the Kremlin. His willingness to meet with Khrushchev and his desire to end the arms race met with little ultimate success, as the containment view of the world still predominated. That mind-set continued into the early 1960s even as Eisenhower's Democratic successors, John F. Kennedy and Lyndon B. Johnson, heated up the conflict in places like Cuba and Vietnam. The thick layer of ice keeping the United States in the Cold War proved very difficult to thaw.[26]

The Cold War played a similarly influential role in Americans' economic lives. The prosperity of the postwar years was intimately connected to the evolving Cold War in a number of ways. At its most basic level, America's campaign against communism cost a tremendous amount of money. The containment policies required huge expenditures to arm and maintain a large standing army, fund the training of foreign troops, aid the development of evolving nations around the world, and continue research and development on everything from weapons to medicines to space exploration. By funneling all this money into defense expenditures, the federal government helped create thousands of new industries and jobs, many of them in the southern and southwestern states. New jobs combined with the educational benefits available through the GI Bill helped keep the unemployment rate consistently low throughout the 1950s and into the mid-1960s.[27]

The combination of shifting populations, returning veterans benefiting from the GI Bill, and increased employment affected various segments of the American population in different ways. For many African Americans, their new middle-class status was bittersweet, since it did not guarantee an end to segregation in schools or housing. New income and educational levels, however, did help fuel existing civil rights organizations such as the National Association for the Advancement of Colored People, which was challenging the old system through the courts, and the Montgomery Women's Political Caucus, which attacked segregation on the streets and buses. Building on half a century of work, the African American Civil Rights Movement of the postwar years would utilize every weapon at its disposal, including Cold War fears, to demand equality.[28]

Even as they fought for equality, many middle-class African Americans joined their white counterparts in fueling another key ingredient of the booming postwar economic stew—consumer spending. Released from the enforced frugality of the Depression and war years, Americans eagerly gobbled up consumer goods as fast as they could be produced. They bought houses and filled them with furniture and appliances, including new technological wonders such as televisions and transistor radios. In their new cars, they zoomed off on the new interstate highway system (defended as a military necessity as an escape route in case of an atomic blast but sponsored by automobile manufacturers and trucking and oil companies), pausing to eat at a new McDonald's and spending the night at a Holiday Inn on their way to Disneyland. The old adage "a penny saved" was replaced by the seductive tones of advertisers (and government officials) encouraging people to spend, spend, spend. Consumerism, the ads and politicos promised, would not only make you a happier and better person, it would also help keep the economy going and the Reds out.[29]

The most important purchase most people made was a new house in the suburbs springing up around most large and many smaller cities. Returning veterans and others with new families needed a place to live and longed for their own bit of land. The need for housing was particularly acute in the South and Southwest, where the population was exploding exponentially. Answering the call, home builders utilized mass production to create entire communities almost overnight. The federal government contributed by making easy loans available through the Veterans' Administration and the Federal Housing Authority. Children of immigrants and working-class men and women, whose parents' dreams of home ownership had never been realized, eagerly leaped at the chance to fulfill their parents' and their own fantasies and rushed to buy up these houses as soon as they became available.[30]

In part because of this rise in home ownership as well as the increase in the number of white-collar, managerial jobs, America seemed more and more like a middle-class nation. As people poured into the suburbs, buying new houses and cars and the accoutrements that went with them, Americans began to look middle class, even if their incomes did not always fit within that sociological range or their shirt collars were not white. Even many of those who remained solidly working class found themselves with incomes sufficient to join the ranks of suburbanites. Some unions, frightened by threats from McCarthyites, abandoned their leftist members and goals and traded worker loyalty for job security, higher wages, and benefits. As a result, plumbers and machinists shed their uniforms in the locker rooms at work and looked like every other father and husband returning to his castle at the end of a long workday.[31]

An essential element of this middle-class suburban existence was the family. For a variety of reasons—making up for lost time after the Depression and war years, anxiety over the Cold War, taking advantage of prosperity—more and more people were getting married and having more and more children. Prosperity allowed people to marry younger, which gave them time to have more children; concern over the future created a need for family comfort and security; and the housing boom created a safe and roomy environment for a family. In turn, the baby boom fueled consumer spending and necessitated the development of more housing units. Regardless of whether people consciously thought of it, and few probably did, this emphasis on family life also served as a counterpoint to the accepted view of the lonely, rigid existence under communism.[32] For many Americans, their ability to have a barbeque in the backyard surrounded by friends, neighbors, and kids proved they were living the American dream.

In this idyllic image of suburban family life, women played the key role. They were wives and mothers, cleaners and cooks in the man's castle, nurturers and chauffeurs for the children, the linchpin that kept everything running smoothly. Although they could not control their own economic existence (a woman needed a man's signature for a loan application, for example), women usually served as managers of the household budget and thus as the chief consumers. A woman was her husband's partner, albeit a junior one, in the quest to enhance his career, obtain the right house, and function as the perfect family. In other words, she was to have no existence apart from her family. Most important, perhaps, she was not supposed to want anything else.

At least that was the message delivered by political, cultural, and economic leaders. Presidential candidate Adlai Stevenson told a group of female college graduates that they could have no higher career aspiration than that of wife and mother. The new media, television, reinforced the image of woman as domestic goddess. Sitcoms of the era such as *Leave It to Beaver, Father Knows Best,* and *The Adventures of Ozzie and Harriet* emphasized women's important supporting role as wife and mother. The few single characters on the shows almost always spent their time searching for a husband or lamenting their "spinsterhood." During breaks in the shows, businessmen acknowledged women's role as consumers by aiming ads at them. Rarely did the commercials portray women as anything other than a housewife obsessed with cleanliness, a mother protective of her children, or a young beauty looking for love. From all sides, women constantly heard that they should be happy and fulfilled by their role as wife and mother.[33]

Commentators and historians in succeeding years uncritically accepted this view of postwar women as reality, establishing it as the norm for American women at the time. The most famous example was Betty Friedan's *The Feminine Mystique.* Based on questionnaires completed by Smith College graduates, the book exposed the vague unhappiness of women who felt constrained by the role of housewife-mother. For women who had felt alone in their discontent, the book was a godsend. It meant they were not crazy. Interestingly, although this best-seller indicted the era as oppressive for women, it also assumed that the image had been an unpleasant reality for most women. Friedan and later scholars focused on the predominant image and ignored contrary evidence.[34]

Most women, however, did not neatly fit the image Friedan and others accepted as real. Despite advertising's whitewash of happy, smiling women mopping floors, a closer examination of 1950s media reveals that women reacted in various ways to this emphasis on domesticity. Women's magazines discussed the difficulties women faced in trying to live up to an impossible ideal. Although the editors usually ended up encouraging women to look to the home for solutions to their frustration, many articles acknowledged that a problem existed. In their responses to these articles, many women asserted that they were neither "sheep following the rest of the herd" nor "poor little housewives." They rejected the idea that they were passive victims and claimed to be happy with their choices. Similarly, television shows presented conflicting images of women. Alongside *Ozzie and Harriet* was *Our Miss Brooks*, in which a single female teacher proved to be the smartest character.[35] Armed with this evidence, historians have begun to challenge the traditionally held view of the "feminine mystique." Studying the lives of women of color, as well as those of politically active and career women, scholars have begun to agree that many women of the era chose alternative lifestyles or consciously molded the image of housewife to suit their particular needs.[36]

For example, middle-class African American and Mexican American women were very much a part of the emerging Civil Rights Movement of the postwar years. In joining and helping to create various activist groups, women fulfilled traditional female functions of writing letters, stuffing envelopes, making coffee, and generally working in the background of such groups as the Southern Christian Leadership Conference and the Community Service Organization. They used their positions as wives and mothers to convince other women to register to vote or to sign petitions to protect their children. Women of color moved beyond these roles and took on leadership responsibilities in various organizations. For example, the highly organized Montgomery Women's Political Caucus (MWPC) was able to capitalize on Rosa Parks's arrest in 1955 and mobilize the black community in an effective boycott of the city's transportation and commercial services. In fact, the MWPC chose Parks's arrest as the catalyst because she was a respected woman in the community. Similarly, Dolores Huerta played such a key role in founding the Farm Workers' Association that she became the group's first vice president. Huerta might have been the most visible woman in the organization, but she was far from the only one. Thousands of women combined their duties as wives and mothers with their organizing activities. Protecting the future of their families was more important to them than obeying societal and cultural norms that would have kept them at home.[37] Although these women frequently dealt with sexism among the men in their communities, the overwhelming racism they faced necessitated that all volunteers be utilized.

Women in labor organizations fought both the biases of their male colleagues and the backlash against left-wing organizations. The unions' male leadership hesitated to include women because they feared the wrath of men who held traditional views of women's place in society. Moreover, male workers often believed the presence of females in the workplace lowered wages and prevented men from getting jobs. Women persisted, however. As they had in earlier years, female members demanded that union leaders protect women workers from unfair practices such as job segregation and wage discrimination. In addition, during the 1950s, as women still reeled from postwar layoffs, some women aggressively fought both union and corporate leadership to maintain employment and wage levels. As women moved increasingly into new areas of work, they took their positive view of labor organizing with them and insisted on having a voice in existing unions and in the creation of new locals where that proved necessary. Of course, women were more successful at arguing their cause in some labor organizations than in others. As the anticommunist crusade chilled support for labor organizing, unions sometimes had no choice but to turn to their female members for continued support, providing those women with new leadership opportunities.[38]

Despite prevailing domesticity and anticommunist rhetoric, women on the Left continued to voice strong support for political causes. Members of the National Woman's Party (NWP), the Communist Party USA (CPUSA), and groups such as Women Strike for Peace (WSP) faced ridicule, ostracism, and even the threat of federal investigation and prosecution. Interestingly, organizations lumped together as "left wing" by mainstream American culture frequently disagreed with one another and shared commonalities with the dominant society. For example, NWP members, although continuing to fight for the Equal Rights Amendment and actively pursuing a "feminist" agenda, distanced themselves from the CPUSA by forcing out communist members. The WSP followed a similarly anticommunist agenda. Both CPUSA and WSP female members frequently emphasized marriage and children, relating to more typical womanly occupations even as they challenged the dominant political powers. In other words, these women frequently looked like "normal" housewives, even as they participated in "abnormal" activities.[39]

But what about the "normal" housewife? Did the white, middle-class suburban woman—the model for the normal housewife—fit the image of the feminine mystique? Was she sitting at home, cooking, cleaning, parenting, and slowly going out of her mind? Certainly, some women appeared to live out this scenario. There were wives and mothers who claimed to be perfectly happy as homemakers, but there were obviously others who claimed to be happy when all the while they were drinking bourbon or popping pills.

Even for women who embraced the domestic ideal of the time, wife and mother were only two of their job titles. To help maintain the newly attained middle-class lifestyle, an increasing number of women worked outside the home. By 1960 there were 23.3 million women in the workforce, more than the number during the war years. Included in this figure were a large number of white married women who joined their African American, Mexican American, and immigrant sisters as wage laborers. Like other traditional working-class people, these women had jobs but not careers. Many saw their employment as a temporary measure to help pay for braces for the kids' teeth, a new car, or their children's education. Answering the "Help Wanted—Girl" ads in the newspapers, women usually found work in traditionally female occupations—teacher, nurse, sales clerk, secretary.[40] Moreover, this outside employment was undertaken in addition to, not instead of, her main responsibilities at home.

For those fortunate enough not to have to work, life frequently did not fit the "happy homemaker" pattern. In addition to caring for their families and homes, middle-class suburban women also participated in many community service and volunteer organizations. Groups ranging from the League of Women Voters to the PTA noted an increase in membership during these years. Especially for women whose children were in school or who were childless, such organized activity helped fill the time between household tasks. A particular beneficiary of this impetus was the General Federation of Women's Clubs, whose membership increased significantly during these years. This national organization allowed local chapters to choose their own agendas. Thus, women could shop around for a group that fit their personal likes and needs.[41]

The mainstream political parties also utilized women volunteers. During the 1950s, political organizers increasingly turned to suburban women for help with the day-to-day operations of party machinery. The booming economy meant men were employed full-time, leaving them with less time for party work and creating a need for new volunteers. Middle-class housewives had both the time and the desire to participate. In addition, male workers found that women excelled at the tasks necessary to maintain a party during and between elections. Women had excellent "people skills," making them perfect for what historian and activist Jo Freeman called the "grunt work of canvassing, telephoning and mailing." As a result, by the 1960s women had completely infiltrated both the Democratic and Republican parties at the lowest levels. Men claimed the spotlight, but women were running the operations.[42]

Obviously, despite the lingering image of the 1950s woman as a homebody with little concern about the "outside" world, many women involved themselves in some kind of political activity. Whether they worked for a mainstream political party, a civil rights organization, or a local women's group, these women frequently saw their actions as an extension of their responsibilities as mothers, wives, and citizens. They explained their involvement not just as a way to fill leisure time but also as a means to protect their children's future. Frequently, local issues served as the impetus for their movement outside the home. Once that initial issue was resolved, however, many were eager to remain active. As with earlier generations of American women, these "June Cleavers" discovered that family responsibilities and political activism were not mutually exclusive.

The Cold War world existed on two levels. The first seemed simple to understand. Soviets-communists-Reds were bad; Americans were good. Americans who understood this and who fought against everything that looked or sounded remotely communist were good; Americans who were willing to tolerate communists or leftists of any variety were bad. The American family during the Cold War era consisted of father, mother, and children, all living happily in their new suburban home and enjoying the fruits of father's hard labor. Mother flitted around the house cleaning and cooking or dabbling in gardening.

The second level was more complicated. The conflict between the United States and the Soviets proved difficult to fight and very expensive to maintain. Military engagements such as the Korean War lacked clear, decisive outcomes. There were a few Soviet spies, but most seemed to have disappeared by the time the FBI got around to looking for them. Many Americans enjoyed unprecedented prosperity, which led not only to an increased emphasis on material goods but also to the development of new forms of debt. While the economic boom sent some Americans scurrying to the suburbs, others used their newfound security to launch an aggressive Civil Rights Movement, attacking the Jim Crow system in the South and the racist attitudes of white Americans across the country. Women of all races and classes absorbed the message of the feminine mystique even as their lives seemed to deny its existence.

Accepting the simplistic version of the Cold War and manipulating the complexities of the evolving Cold War world to their advantage, a significant number of women who appeared to epitomize the feminine mystique joined the crusade against communism at home and abroad. These women took advantage of the free time afforded them by the economic prosperity of the time, as well as of pervasive anticommunist attitudes, to justify leaving the suburbs (at least metaphorically) to become politically active. Although their individual circumstances and motivations varied, they were united in their dedication to root out communism and protect the American way of life.

CHAPTER TWO

WHO WERE THESE WOMEN?

The Cold War world might have been confusing and frightening, but American women eagerly took it upon themselves to calm the worries and take up the struggle to protect their loved ones from whatever enemies threatened them. Particularly remarkable were the actions and commitment of white, conservative, anticommunist women. These were the women who, theoretically, believed in the domestic ideal and espoused a role for women limited to home and family. Ironically, this very dedication to home and children was what led them to political involvement. Following in the footsteps of earlier generations of conservative women activists and echoing the refrains of right-wing women around the world, American women saw no contradiction between their involvement outside the home and their continued support of domesticity. Although their individual backgrounds and life experiences differed, conservative female anticommunists shared a belief that the communist threat was so great that they must defy convention and work for its destruction. From their perspective the situation was simple—fight communism or risk your children's lives and the American way of life.

These women activists did not spring up in a vacuum, however. Their actions resulted not only from the realities of the Cold War world in which they lived but also from the convergence of two other developing movements. First, these women benefited from the work of a significant number of right-wing women who had come before them. Working against suffrage; fighting communists, immigrants, and radicals during and following World War I; and protesting the changes wrought by the New Deal, earlier generations of women had laid the foundations on which Cold War women operated. Second, just as these women were mounting their campaigns against communism, conservatives of various persuasions were beginning to work together to create a viable political right-wing movement. Both of these factors created an atmosphere in which anticommunist women could more easily conduct their activities.

Conservative anticommunist women of the 1950s and 1960s repeated the refrains made common by their mothers and grand-mothers, as well as their sisters in other countries. Emphasizing the importance of their role as wives and especially as mothers, women had fought against woman suffrage, immorality, urbanization, and all manner of liberal political reforms. Internationally, women had utilized similar rhetoric to explain their participation in fascist movements in Germany, Britain, and Chile. They sang the glories of mothers who stayed home and cared for their families even as they themselves left home to join the masculine world of politics. They rationalized that they were not contradicting themselves because their political activities were actually an extension of the maternal instincts to care for and protect their young. Frequently, they added that since women were, by their very nature, more moral than men, it was women's responsibility to do whatever was necessary to preserve the home and family.[1]

The connections between Cold War anticommunist women and their earlier sisters were not limited to similar rationalizations of their actions. Most significant, conservative women played a role, ignored by many scholars until recently, in the evolution of women's political culture. Obviously, women suffragists, progressive women, and feminists pushed for women to be able to take part in the political process

in a formal way. Their female opponents have usually been represented as the antagonists in this drama, the players who held back
progress. Such analysis overlooks the reality that conservative women
were, as historian Jane Jerome Camhi put it, "variations on a trend
toward activism among women." Both suffragists and anti-suffragists
shared many characteristics in terms of background and actions; they
differed, however, in the solutions they proposed to deal with existing
problems. Suffragists argued that women's direct participation in the
political system would allow them to help alleviate the suffering of the
poor and eliminate corruption in government; anti-suffragists warned
that granting women the right to vote would undermine the patriarchal order and create more instability and corruption.[2] Consequently,
just as liberal feminists built on the foundations laid by suffragists
and progressives, conservative anticommunists took advantage of the
examples of their anti-suffragist sisters.

Anticommunist women also benefited from the birth of a more
organized and stable conservative movement. For years, men and
women who believed in classical liberal economics as well as those
who preached a traditionalist morality had claimed to be "conservative." The inherent contradiction between a group that supported
limited government and people who wanted government to impose
a moral standard kept the two groups separate and "conservatives"
politically divided and weak. Anticommunism gave them common
cause. Classical liberals despised the idea of a planned economy, while
traditionalists feared the atheism inherent in communist ideology. In
the face of an overwhelmingly dangerous enemy, conservatives of
both varieties began to work together to defeat communism as well
as any policies or politicians they perceived were leading them down
a leftward path.[3] One result of this development was the creation of
a number of conservative organizations and publications. These peri-
odicals provided interested anticommunist women with a forum in
which to discuss and promote their ideas.

These three situations—the Cold War, the historical pattern of
conservative female activism, and the emergence of a viable conservative movement—provided a comfortable setting in which anticommunist women could assert themselves. These circumstances still do
not explain why some women became caught up in anticommunist
activity while others did not. Were these women housewives-turned-
activists or career agitators who happened to have families? Were they
forced into the political arena by their fear of communism, or did they

use anticommunism as a convenient opening for their political ambitions? The answer was obviously different for different women. Some activists, especially those who made something of a career of anticommunism, were ambitious women who used their belief in anticommunism as a lever to open opportunities that might not otherwise have existed. For other women, fear of communism led them to participate in political activity they might otherwise have avoided. Whether they remained active over a long period or became involved only in response to specific short-term fears probably depended on individual personalities and circumstances. Even if they went "back home," their limited participation indicated the profound impact anticommunism had on society at the time.

An examination of earlier conservative women provides insight into potential motivations. Similar to the situation of the anti-suffragists and anti–New Deal activists of the 1930s, Cold War women found themselves in a transitional phase for their gender. Just as earlier women struggled to understand what their new voting power might mean for them, women emerging from World War II wondered how to reconcile their sometimes new middle-class status with the reality of their lives. All the propaganda told them that women stayed home and devoted themselves to their families, yet they saw the numbers of women who held jobs and participated in activities outside the home. In trying to understand exactly where women fit into the scheme of things, women found the anticommunist cause comforting. They could explore the potential of doing something more than housework while justifying it as an extension of their duty to family.[4] Like their predecessors, their conservative cause provided them with a safe way of confronting other, more complicated issues in their environment. Just as the anti-suffragists saw their movement as a way of holding back the onslaught of modernization, urbanization, and immigration, Cold War women could attack communism rather than face the more difficult issues of racism, poverty, and the threat of nuclear annihilation. The simplicity of the dichotomy between communist and noncommunist seemed easier to confront than the reality of whether a black family should be allowed to move into their neighborhood. Blaming communists for everything removed the gray areas of modern life. Conspiracy theories are so popular because they offer simple solutions to complex problems.

Who were these conservative anticommunist women? We can begin with a few generalities. Most, though not all, were middle class, married, white, reasonably intelligent, and well educated. Although politically active women were spread throughout the country, significant pockets of activists formed in the Southwest, which was growing tremendously during the postwar years. Many of these new arrivals had relocated from areas such as the Midwest or the South, where there was a long tradition of conservatism. As might be expected, these women's husbands were part of a growing army of upwardly mobile white-collar workers, small businessmen, and professionals (doctors, lawyers, engineers) who enjoyed the benefits of an expansive economy. By and large, these men were also conservative—some active participants with their wives, others not. Many of the women had children, but most of the particularly active women either had older kids or no children. A very few had experimented with left-wing movements before "seeing the light" and moving to the other side. Few had outside jobs; most did conservative work as a hobby—although that word is misleading because it implies that they took their political activity lightly, which they did not. In fact, some were fairly ambitious and found anticommunism a useful path to political office. For others, activism grew out of anger over a particular incident and dissipated once that situation had been resolved. For others, the anticommunist crusade remained a lifelong vocation.[5]

Identifying these women is easier than discovering their individual motivations for becoming activist anticommunists. Why did these women become anticommunists and political activists? Although the answer varied for each woman, understanding some of the commonalities provides a more complete analysis of their situation.

The reason women embraced the anticommunist cause appears deceptively simple. After all, almost all Americans embraced some form of anticommunism. Considering the political speeches, media reports, and religious proclamations constantly bombarding the American public with messages about the evils of communism, it would have been more peculiar if these women had rejected the concept. The women in this study, however, went beyond mere acceptance of the evils of communism; they saw it as a serious and immediate threat to their country and their way of life. They did not just pay lip service to the necessity of wiping out communists abroad; they tended to link the Red threat to domestic issues, equating communism with any form of liberalism or socialism and decrying federal government regulation in any form and on any level. For some of these women, any economic or political policy, any cultural practice, any social norm that diverged from what they considered "the American way" could be perceived as communistic. Their anticommunism, then, often could not be separated from their conservatism. In fact, the two perspectives proved mutually reinforcing. The more conservative—either economically or morally—the woman, the greater her sense that communism threatened all she held dear. The more she feared communists, the more she wanted her government to do all it could to safeguard her way of life and the less willing she was to tolerate anything that provided an opening for communism. She missed the inherent contradiction between her philosophies: she demanded a limited government that actively worked to protect her from all forms of communism. She was willing to accept government intervention as long as it was connected to fighting communism.

The reason so many women embraced this conservative mindset has been the subject of recent study by a number of scholars. In analyzing right-wing American women, scholars such as Kim Nielsen, June Melby Benowitz, and Catherine Rymph have emphasized the centrality of gender to discussions of conservative ideologies and movements.[6] Men frequently utilized contemporary assumptions about feminine and masculine traits to characterize their cause and their opponents. Moreover, protecting the status quo often meant maintaining existing gender relationships. For women, who remained excluded from exercising formal power even after they won suffrage, safeguarding their informal power became extremely important. Although, as historian Nielsen put it, women accepted "the rightness of patriarchy," they did not "believe that it implied invisibility on the part of women." In fact, they assumed they had a responsibility to defend the traditional system.[7] Often, particularly early in the twentieth century, they appropriated the perception that woman were morally superior to men to legitimize their involvement in political affairs. This connection between morality and political activism eventually fell out of favor with progressive women but remained, as Rymph argues, a tradition with Republican women and others on the Right. If men would not protect the existing order, these women asserted their right to do so. They felt the need to defend whatever avenues they could find to gain power. Additionally, because women remained outsiders to a large extent even after they gained suffrage, they had less need to compromise their principles for the sake of political expediency. They frequently felt they had nothing to lose by sticking to their ideals.[8]

With these justifications supporting their beliefs, some women found concrete reasons to shift from having anticommunist sympathies to crusading for the cause. The motivators for each woman were as varied as the women themselves. Some came from families with traditions of political activism; others acted under the influence and encouragement of parents or husbands. Religious convictions drove some, while others reacted to a traumatic experience by getting involved with the fight against communism. Sometimes women joined a club in search of something to do and found themselves drawn into the political fray.

For women who fought on a local level, the driving force behind their involvement was more readily apparent. They believed there was a concrete threat to their children, families, and community. They felt they had to take action. As will be demonstrated in later chapters, women in communities across the country responded to perceived dangers from school officials and national and local politicians. Usually, the leaders of the anticommunist crusades had been politically active prior to whatever incident inspired the participation of a larger segment of the population. The bulk of women who temporarily laid aside their regular duties to attend meetings and demonstrations or write letters apparently returned to their normal lives. Historians have begun to discover similar examples all over the country. Like their more liberal sisters, conservative anticommunist women rose to meet a challenge to what they perceived to be a direct threat to their well-being.[9]

The easiest way for women to get involved in a local crusade was to join a national organization with local affiliates. These groups had the advantage of a set infrastructure, experienced leaders, and an established reputation. Participation in such an enterprise educated women in various modes of political activity. The General Federation of Women's Clubs and the Minute Women of America are two examples that represent the spectrum of anticommunist fervor.

The more moderate of the two organizations was the General Federation of Women's Clubs (GFWC), founded in 1890. Since the early nineteenth century, a wide variety of clubs had served the educational, intellectual, and social needs of middle- and upper-class women. By the end of the century, however, a number of club leaders recognized that without more organization, each individual club would be "working on in its own rut . . . and well satisfied with small things." These women founded the GFWC in hopes of creating "a rallying center" for "consultation and comparison of methods," as well as a "common fellowship and central bond of union."[10] Created during the Progressive era, the GFWC served as a means for women to become involved in the reform movements discussed by politicians and journalists. For women with political interests, clubs camouflaged female challenges to the masculine world of policy, government, and law. Men tended to underestimate the potential power of clubwomen and thus let the organizations do as they wished. Women activists took advantage of this benign neglect to push various causes and find new recruits among fellow club members.[11] For women with no aspirations beyond being wives and mothers, clubs offered a way to expand their concept of "home" and broaden their activities. Raising funds for libraries or scholarships or protecting poor children gave such women an outlet that did not undermine their vision of who they were or what constituted acceptable behavior.[12]

Although the activities of individual clubs varied, membership in the organizations was fairly uniform. Most of the women were white, middle-class suburbanites whose husbands supported their families very comfortably. There were branches of the GFWC in rural areas, but their numbers were much smaller than those among their urban sisters. Citing the existence of the National Council of Negro Women, members of the GFWC saw no need to break the color line and integrate their clubs. In addition to race, class also distinguished the GFWC from other women's affiliations, such as some religious and labor groups. GFWC members, particularly the leadership, tended to have more in common with women active in the Business and Professional Women's Organization or the American Association of University Women.[13] Although the latter groups tended to consist of "career" women as opposed to housewives, similar educational and class backgrounds linked the groups.

As might be expected, most women's clubs engaged in community service projects that were not specifically political. For example, in 1948 the presidents of the New Hampshire clubs listed their accomplishments for Doloris Bridges, wife of New Hampshire senator Styles Bridges. They had planted trees, prepared hot school lunches, and raised money for scholarships, ball fields, and libraries. For many, their most political actions involved previewing movies coming to town or pressuring the town council about a variety of issues.[14] Building on their long tradition of reform, many women's clubs focused on community service projects or social service activities. Individual women within these groups might become heavily involved in direct political action, but the clubs generally did not endorse or encourage partisan activity. During some club meetings, however, before the tea and cakes and after the reporting of the minutes, clubwomen listened to speeches that challenged them to become more politically aware and involved. As the Cold War climate chilled in the years following World War II, clubwomen joined the rest of America in becoming increasingly concerned about the communist threat at home and abroad. For many clubwomen the severity of the danger overshadowed their reform and service goals.

As a result, by the 1950s most clubwomen regarded involvement in what they called "public affairs" as one of their main functions. Proud of what they had accomplished in the fields of education and service, members expanded their goals to include "making their home towns better places in which to live and to rear their families." Clubwomen approached this goal from several angles. First, they emphasized education—not just for their children but also for themselves. National leaders encouraged local chapters to host study clubs—what they called "the married woman's university"—publish book lists, and invite political speakers to their meetings. They dedicated significant portions of their monthly newsletters to informational and editorial pieces on national and international political activity. Whether written by club members or guest editorialists, these pieces frequently reiterated the common view that communism threatened "not only our ideology of government, which provides freedom and economic security for our people," but also "our religious way of life which Democracy has as its basic concept."[15] Second, they created a special department to deal with international affairs as well as one to deal with "Americanism." National club leaders challenged these divisions to organize the study clubs, bring in pertinent guest speakers, and help members sort through the information on the dangers of communism they received.

Although the GFWC abhorred communism and worried about the threat of socialism at home, the leadership, at least, rejected some of the more rabid views of other anticommunist organizations. For example, they seemed not to participate in the McCarthy-style witch hunts or share the "anything Russian is evil" mind-set exhibited by many of their contemporaries. In an interesting continuation of the legacy of progressive women such as Jane Addams, they repeatedly encouraged their members to learn about other cultures; they also offered support to the United Nations and especially for the United Nations Educational, Scientific, and Cultural Organization's (UNESCO's) educational efforts. The fact that rank-and-file members accepted their leaders' moderate anticommunism was indicated by the latters' continual reelection to office. Obviously, any member who felt her club was too liberal would simply leave and find an organization more suited to her political leanings.[16]

Women who wanted a more conservative organization might have opted for groups such as the Minute Women of America. Founded in 1949 by Suzanne Stevenson, the Minute Women of the USA quickly spread across the country. By 1952, Stevenson bragged that her original Connecticut-based group had grown to include chapters in twenty-seven states. The platform of the national committee was very general. Promising "to preserve, protect and promote the Constitution of the United States . . . and the freedom it guarantees to individual citizens," Minute Women worked to "protect our country from Communism, Socialism, Fascism or collectivism in any form." In response to what they perceived to be a malicious newspaper article, the Minute Women explained in their newsletter that their group constituted a "[c]rusade and not an organization." New members paid a small fee and pledged only "to vote in every election." Inspired by Stevenson and the Connecticut group, members of local chapters operated autonomously. This allowed women to focus on whatever problems seemed to threaten their particular neighborhood. To protect the organization, Minute Women were forbidden to "take action as a pressure group. They [were supposed to] act only as individuals."[17]

Even following these rules, however, Minute Women sometimes proved a formidable force. An article in their newsletter calling for letters to congressmen, the president, local school board members, or religious leaders could generate thousands of pieces of mail seemingly overnight. Moreover, because many Minute Women were housewives with school-age or older children, they had the time to attend meetings, ask questions, and research the backgrounds of individuals or books they found problematic. Rapid dissemination of information through a national network allowed concerned members to attend meetings or write protest letters armed with information.[18] The Minute Women appeared to act as individuals rather than as an organization, but the results of their actions indicated the power of their cooperation and coordination.

In contrast, women active in the mainstream political parties wore their affiliation on their sleeves for everyone to see. In fact, in the postwar years, women worked very hard to increase their power and influence within both major parties. Although at first Democratic women seemed to make greater strides in gaining power within their organization, the Republicans began to catch up during the postwar period. For conservative, anticommunist women who felt much more at home with the GOP than with the New Deal Democrats, this was a godsend. With strong female leadership, women Republicans increased their presence at all levels of the GOP.[19]

Similar to the party as a whole, however, female Republicans argued among themselves about the future of their party, the threat of communism in the nation, and the best ways for women to be active politically. Building on disagreements existing from the earliest days following suffrage, Republican women struggled to define their relationship with the men in their party. Women working in the Women's Division of the GOP tended to be single career women who argued that the best way for women to gain influence and power within the party was to cooperate with the existing division of authority. They hoped this strategy would lead men to recognize that women deserved to be equal partners in party matters. To this end, they encouraged the largely middle-class, married members of the Republican women's clubs to support whatever candidates the national or state parties nominated. Club members usually cooperated, willingly doing the party's grunt work, knocking on doors, making phone calls, and mailing fliers.

The situation changed during Eisenhower's first term in office. Women's Division leaders maintained their stance, but the clubwomen had become restive. According to one observer, the increasingly conservative women were frustrated with Eisenhower's moderate brand of Republicanism. Many first became involved in political campaigns during the heady McCarthy days, and as one right-wing witness explained, they had "lost all their spirit of fight" in the face of Eisenhower's Modern Republicanism. The observer's husband met with the Rock Creek Republican Women's Club and got "a real bang out of" the fact that they had settled for Eisenhower and Nixon as speakers when they really wanted to hear Barry Goldwater.[20] In contrast to the professional career women of the Women's Division, the clubwomen did not seek formal power. Instead, they accepted that male party leaders would make key policy decisions; the clubwomen assumed, however, that they could decide whether to support those policies. When they did, they expected the male leaders to appreciate their contributions. When they disagreed with the party leadership, they felt it was their duty was to point out what they perceived to be errors. They did not depend on the party for a salary or for fulfillment of their ambitions. Like other conservative women, then, they felt free to follow principle rather than compromise.[21]

Mainstream political parties were not the only organizations confronted by memberships who began to find existing structures and perspectives too moderate and confining. When conservative Phyllis Schlafly took over as State National Defense chair of the DAR in Illinois in 1957, for example, she used her position to expand her "little nucleus of conservatives" by encouraging other members of the organization to read the "right kind" of literature.[22] Another group, All American Conferences to Combat Communism, served as a platform for groups not specifically tied to anticommunism, such as Business and Professional Women (BPW), to voice their position on the Red menace. Producing an issue of *Freedom's Facts* allowed the BPW women to establish their right-wing credentials and warn their membership of the specific threat communists posed to women's groups.[23] Even the American Association of University Women (AAUW) faced difficulties from members who questioned the motives of their leaders. One disgruntled member went so far as to resign from the organization and publicly accused the national AAUW office of "aid[ing] the Communist conspiracy."[24]

In addition, countless smaller groups formed across the country to focus on particular problems that concerned their members. Because these organizations tended to be local and were often temporary, their histories can be only partially reconstructed. Sometimes the existence of such a collection of women became apparent through others discussing them. For example, anticommunist activist Alfred Kohlberg wrote to Senator Joe McCarthy about "some ladies . . . who have been greatly stirred up lately" and asked McCarthy to address them. "Under the sponsorship of the Defenders of the Constitution, Inc.," this group had already begun distributing McCarthy's speeches at their meetings.[25]

The plethora of women-sponsored and women-run newsletters provides another area for examining women's motivations and beliefs at the grassroots level. Sometimes the sheets published the official views of a specific organization; often they appeared to represent the opinion of a single woman who felt compelled to share her views with others. The fact that many of the papers were published for at least one year indicates a serious commitment to their production. For example, *Alerted Americans*, operated by Helen Corson, was first published in 1955 and still existed in 1964. The publications ranged from handwritten, typed, or mimeographed sheets to professionally printed newspapers. They were produced in all sections of the country and were read by unknown numbers of people. Although some of the newsletters were financed by their sponsoring organizations, many editors of smaller papers accepted advertisements or lamented that they operated on a shoestring budget. Some, such as *The Farmer's Voice* and *Alerted Americans*, depended on subscriptions and contributions for their operating expenses. Florence Fowler Lyons, who produced a series of "Reports on UNESCO," explained to fellow activist Elizabeth Brown that she was operating on "the very edge of total economic collapse."[26]

Among the newsletters was the previously mentioned *Freedom Facts*, published by the All American Conferences to Combat Communism, headquartered in Washington, D.C. This publication served as a platform from which various organizations (such as the BPW) could expose the evils of communism. In Pennsylvania, Helen Corson sold subscriptions to her *Alerted Americans* newsletter and had a mailing list of around 1,100 in 1958. In Florida, Bette Logan edited *The Spirit* as an outgrowth of Woman's Right to Know, Inc., an organization of unknown size or influence. The Midwest contributed both *The Farmer's Voice*, the work of Christiana Uhl of Wooster, Ohio, and periodic pamphlets from the American Woman's Party of Detroit, Michigan. Mrs. M. Conan of Phoenix, Arizona, drew her own cartoons and sent out numerous copies of single-page news sheets titled *What Do You Think?* Meanwhile, *New Mexico Women Speak*, the work of Mrs. James Thorsen and Mrs. Reese P. Fullerton, encouraged readers to send "letters setting forth the happenings" in their areas and to buy new subscriptions.[27]

Some of these women included explanations for their efforts. Christiana Uhl, who sent out *The Farmer's Voice* in the mid- to late 1950s, explained her motivation for creating a newsletter. Although she thought of it as a "hobby," she also saw it as a "reason to study and learn. It is an attempt to share my discoveries with you. It gives background facts you can use in understanding the community, the state, the nations and our world." In typical 1950s female fashion, she presented her political crusade as a harmless "hobby" that threatened no one. Others were less demure. The editors of *New Mexico Women Speak* proclaimed their "intent and purpose" to be "to defend and protect the CONSTITUTION OF THE UNITED STATES." Worried that people in New Mexico would "continue to be uninformed about, and apathetic to[,] the extent and progress of Communist infiltration into our government and life," they took it upon themselves to try to "WAKE UP" their state and country. Likewise, *The Spirit* took a strong stand on its purpose. In fact, the editors put their raison d'être on the last page of every issue. "We believe," the editors wrote, "the American woman cherishes her Independence and her Liberty. We believe she will insist on preserving for her children the heritage of a FREE AMERICA."[28]

Similarly, some anticommunist women worked to influence national policy. Like local activists, these women came from diverse backgrounds and met with varying degrees of success. Additionally, although they proudly claimed to be "anticommunist," the intensity of their fear of communism differed, sometimes significantly. They also shared a certain anonymity despite their sometimes recognizable names.

Anticommunist women active on the national level have been neglected by scholars for several overlapping reasons.[29] First, many were married to famous (or infamous, depending on one's perspective) men who cast a large shadow. Many people, including historians, have assumed that as good wives, they were merely supporting their husbands' careers. From such a perspective, there would appear to be nothing to study. Moreover, the wives themselves frequently encouraged this impression by frequently referring to their spouses or refusing to take credit for their own actions, ideas, and writings. Second, with few exceptions, women active on a national level willingly stayed in the background and let the men do the talking and take the credit for their work. Some women wanted to run for political office and wield the power that went with political positions; however, most conservative women chose to influence events from behind the scenes. As mere wives of "important men," women often left less detailed and less organized collections of papers for historians to examine. Either they or later archivists did not see the need to retain their letters and speeches. Finally, since most of these women were responsible for running households and raising children, they did not have the time or perhaps the inclination to keep a journal explaining their motivations and beliefs. Like many historical actors, their lives must be reconstructed backward from speeches, letters, newspaper articles, and the words of others. For this reason, the availability of source material guided my selection of the important female figures of national stature who appear in my study.[30]

The backgrounds of various women active on the national level indicate the variety of experiences that could have led them to espouse conservative anticommunism as well as the range of fervor with which they approached the cause. Unfortunately, because few of these women left introspective diaries, we have no definitive proof of what led them to embrace anticommunist activity. Instead, we can only surmise their reasoning based on what we can determine about their lives. Even that can be challenging, however, since women activists frequently undervalued their own importance. An examination of a few case studies will reveal the possibilities as well as the limitations of a historical investigation into the activities of prominent anticommunist women.

Of all my examples, Margaret Chase Smith left the fullest records, held the most power, and was the most moderate in her beliefs. Ironically, she also represents a more average American than many of the others. Coming from a simple background, nothing in her early life seems significant enough to have caused her particularly to fear communism. Instead, like most Americans, Smith learned to see communism as a serious threat in the years after World War II, based on information coming out of Washington. Perhaps because there was no dominant psychological or political motivation behind her anticommunism, she tended to be more temperate in her views than many other prominent anticommunist women.

Born in Skowhegan, Maine, to a working-class family with deep roots in the community, Margaret Chase appeared destined for an ordinary life. But early on there were hints that something more lay beneath the surface. She played a key role in her high school basketball team winning a state championship, in the process discovering her addiction not just to victory but also to the thrill of competition. The only experience that rivaled the thrill of that victory was her senior trip to Washington, D.C. Chase left Maine for the first time and realized that there was an exciting world to conquer. This realization increased her frustration as she tried her hand at teaching right after high school. Bored, lonely, and away from family and friends, she soon moved back to Skowhegan and away from the classroom. Instead of remaining a teacher, Chase became a businesswoman. Working her way up through various organizations, including the telephone company, a newspaper, and a mill, Chase pushed herself to meet the challenges presented by her male bosses.[31]

Like many single working women in the 1920s, Chase enjoyed a wide network of female acquaintances, some social and others professional. Through these social clubs, such as Sorosis, and more serious organizations, such as the BPW, Chase learned that she was a good leader and that she enjoyed both the responsibility and the challenges leadership offered. Her years with the BPW, including one term as state president, reintroduced two themes from her high school years: the thrill of challenge and the chance to travel beyond Maine. Chase learned two crucial skills from her club activities as well: how to defy convention without threatening those who were traditional-minded and how to recognize the potential political power these organizations had. Moreover, her years in these organizations taught her some political skills and helped her make a statewide name for herself.[32]

Her private life revealed a proper young lady who managed to challenge convention without permanently damaging her reputation. While still in her teens and working as a switchboard operator, she began a relationship with Clyde Smith, one of the wealthiest and best-connected men in town. From the beginning, rumors surrounded the relationship. Clyde was divorced, twenty-one years older than Margaret, and a former state representative and ex-sheriff. Margaret was still in high school when she and her parents began taking rides with Clyde in his car, a novelty in Skowhegan. Over the next several years their relationship continued amid rumors of Clyde seeing other women and the couple's impropriety. In 1930, when Margaret was thirty-three, the couple married. She continued working for six months and then quit to become a full-time homemaker. Margaret's respect for housewives perhaps originated during the early years of her marriage as she struggled to learn to cook and clean and care for a husband.[33]

Smith did not remain a housewife, however. Her husband's political ambitions provided her with the opportunity to continue her earlier lessons in the art of politics. As he ran for various state offices she traveled with him, learning the ins and outs of campaigning. When he won election to the House of Representatives, she became his office manager. As her husband's health declined, she assumed more and more of his duties. When he died, she successfully ran for his seat in Congress, a position she held until 1948 when she won election to the U.S. Senate. As a senator, Smith used her influence to stand firm against communist encroachment abroad without losing sight of concerns about civil liberties at home.[34]

If Smith represents everywoman USA, who had a healthy yet controlled concern about communism, Jean Kerr McCarthy represents the everywoman whose fears turned her into a zealot. Unfortunately, McCarthy left many fewer papers to help us understand the source of the intensity of her views. Although her anticommunism seemed to predate her introduction to Joe McCarthy, his influence and the success of his political campaign against communists cannot be discounted as factors in her continuing obsession.

Born in 1924, Jean Fraser Kerr was the only child of Scottish immigrants who came to the United States in the early twentieth century. Her father was a builder who ran a successful business in the Washington, D.C., area. From all indications, Kerr had a normal, happy childhood. After high school, she worked for three years in an advertising agency before leaving for college. After entering George Washington University (GWU) in 1944, she joined a sorority and participated in various extracurricular activities. Both her good looks and her intelligence set her apart from her peers. While at GWU and, later, at Northwestern University, Kerr won various beauty queen awards. In 1946 her essay "The Promotion of Peace among the Nations of the World" won GWU's Alexander Wilbourne Weddell Award. Her classmates described her as "bright" but aloof. A little older than the average university student, she kept to herself. Although her sorority sisters thought she was "a good catch," she seldom dated. Her intense interest in politics led her to work part-time for the Senate War Investigating Committee and then for Republican senator Albert W. Hawkes of New Jersey.[35] In 1947, while still a student, Kerr stopped by Wisconsin senator Joseph McCarthy's office to visit a friend. According to various stories, he tried not only to hire her but also to date her. She declined both invitations until after her graduation in 1948, when she joined his staff as a research assistant.[36] She also began an on-again/off-again relationship with McCarthy that culminated in their marriage in 1954.[37]

Kerr's responsibilities in McCarthy's office quickly expanded beyond just research. Joe particularly valued Jean's writing skills. She worked on several booklets he published, including a compilation of his most repeated charges titled *McCarthyism, the Fight for America*.[38] Although she insisted that McCarthy's preoccupation with the communist threat had nothing to do with her, her interest in anticommunism certainly reinforced Joe's attitudes. Always interested in politics, Jean was fascinated by the Hiss case and eagerly shared her opinions with others. Her knowledge of and dedication to the cause cannot be overlooked as a factor in influencing the senator when he began to search for a new issue in the fall of 1949. Kerr did not push McCarthy into the anticommunist crusade—he did not take up the cause until almost a year after she started working for him—but her strong opinions helped keep him aware of the topic. The more he worked for the cause, the more power she gained in his office. Although Joe's oldest friends doubted that she forced him into anything he did not want to do, they nevertheless acknowledge that her presence contributed to the ease with which he moved into the field.[39]

Like Jean McCarthy, many activist women had husbands who reinforced their anticommunist inclinations. In some cases, women with latent political ambitions married men who provided them with an entrée to the world of politics and encouraged their participation. These women must have had some buried interests or ambition, however, since not all wives of powerful men eagerly and enthusiastically jumped on the anticommunist bandwagon.

Both Elizabeth Churchill Brown and Doloris Thauwald Bridges owed their presence on the national political stage to their husbands. Born in Nashville, Tennessee, in 1908, Elizabeth Churchill lived in the privileged world of high society. On her father's side, she was descended from pioneer New England families; her mother's ancestors included both English nobility and prominent families of colonial Virginia. Her grandfather had been a surgeon major in the Confederate Army. Sometime during her youth the family moved to New York, where the young Elizabeth enrolled in Rye Seminary before attending the Spence School in New York and Oldfields School in Maryland.[40] With her education completed in 1926, Churchill spent her time attending balls, visiting friends, and eventually getting a job. During many summers she and her mother traveled to Newport, Rhode Island, to escape the heat before returning to the city. During the winter months, numerous social activities—balls, parties, teas—consumed her time. Even as the country settled into the Depression during the 1930s and unemployment reached epic proportions, Churchill found a job as society editor for the *New York Evening Journal*. Interestingly, throughout this period one popular theme for fashionable parties was Imperial Russia. Touting the grandeur of Tsarist Russia, these fetes exposed the breadth of the division between the partygoers' lives and those of the majority of Americans.[41] In addition, the emphasis on pre-communist Russia displayed upper-class Americans' displeasure with the Soviet Union.

In 1939, Elizabeth Churchill married Thomas Stonborough, a descendant of the founder of the Austro-Hungarian steel industry. Stonborough had a doctorate from the University of Vienna and worked for a firm on the New York Stock Exchange. The young couple continued to participate in the social scene, including attending dances sponsored by Republican organizations. In 1941, however, Stonborough rented an apartment by himself in New York. The following year, Elizabeth Stonborough took a job as the Washington, D.C., representative for *Town and Country* magazine. At some point during this time, the couple divorced. Reassuming her maiden name, Churchill never publicly mentioned her first marriage.[42]

Years later, in her prologue to her book about Joe McCarthy, she summarized her life. Interestingly, she began not with her childhood or her first marriage, which she completely ignored, but with her introduction to political life in Washington. She did not acknowledge the significant role her upper-class background played in her willingness to fling herself into the conservative anticommunist world.

In her autobiographical prologue, the young, naive Elizabeth "Liz" Churchill, actually a thirty-three-year-old divorcée, said she decided to move to Washington, D.C., because it "was a city of trees and flowers." The fact that it pulsed with political activity did not hurt. The new arrival became a Washington correspondent for, in her words, "the hoity-toity Town and Country [sic] magazine." "The shenanigans of high officials and the social didos of their wives" provided her with plenty to write about and introduced her to life in the nation's capital. During this time, she later claimed, "the meaning of the political intrigues by politicians and statesmen in high places and power entirely escaped me."[43] Interestingly, Brown's autobiography evidenced not only her willingness to edit her life story but also her skillful manipulation of gendered language and imagery to suit her purpose. She could sound as cold and calculating as any schoolmaster or play an ignorant, flighty little woman with equal ease.

Her life changed when she met the man who would become her second husband, Constantine "Connie" Brown. Like Liz, Connie, as his friends called him, was a journalist, although he had much more experience than she did. He had parlayed a small inheritance into a

European education, earning a Ph.D. from the University of Berlin. His reports from behind enemy lines during World War I caught the attention of American editors, and he became a celebrated foreign correspondent. Eventually, he returned to the States and ended up writing a syndicated column on political and international events. Well respected by people of all ideological stripes, Connie was, in Liz's words, "intimately acquainted . . . with the . . . unrehearsed and spontaneous drama" unfolding in Washington. Liz was enthralled, and they were married in 1949.[44] She found numerous opportunities to explore her "new" interest in politics as she served as her husband's secretary, editor, and agent. In addition, she continued her own writing career, with numerous articles and several book projects.

Another politically ambitious, although much less successful, woman spent her early years halfway across the country. Born in St. Paul, Minnesota, in 1916, Doloris Thauwald probably grew up in relative comfort as the daughter of a doctor.[45] She attended the University of Minnesota during the Depression years and graduated in 1935. Thauwald then joined the growing number of single women confronting a depressed job market. The economic turmoil of the 1930s created both crisis and opportunity for women seeking employment. On the one hand, employers tended to give jobs to men who needed, in the accepted view of the day, to support their families. On the other hand, desperate times forced many women into the role of breadwinner and in some ways encouraged acceptance of working women. Moreover, gender segregation in the workplace meant employers and male workers were reluctant to take women's jobs.[46] Women like Doloris thus continued the trend toward increased numbers of women in wage labor. Perhaps through her father's influence, she went to work in Midway Hospital in St. Paul for three years before going to Washington.

As tensions mounted in Europe and Asia, job opportunities abounded in the nation's capital, and Thauwald joined the swell of applicants. American entry into World War II had dramatically increased the need for women workers, as the government expanded its bureaucracy to prepare to fight the enemies. When the Pentagon opened in 1942, officials needed 35,000 office workers; many of the jobs were clerical, acceptable work even for young ladies. Pay was relatively good, especially compared with salaries back in the Midwest. Then there was the prestige of working for the government and living in glamorous, if terribly overcrowded, Washington, D.C.[47]

According to an interview conducted years later, Thauwald was not certain she wanted to remain in Washington, so she took only short-term jobs, working for numerous agencies—including the Internal Revenue Department, the Communications Commission, the Department of Agriculture, and the Maritime Commission—before settling in as an administrative assistant in the World Trade Division of the State Department.[48]

Despite her success as an independent woman, Thauwald willingly moved into a more traditional role when the opportunity presented itself. At a dinner party she met New Hampshire senator Styles Bridges, an increasingly powerful man and a very eligible bachelor in Washington. Thauwald approached her relationship with the senator seriously; before the wedding she "oriented herself" to New Hampshire politics and people. Although some Senate wives chose to remain behind-the-scenes, immersed in private life, Doloris recognized that marriage to Styles provided the possibility of an active political life. She leaped at the chance.[49]

Although the newlywed Doloris moved into the postwar domestic realm, her interest in politics triumphed over her interest in housework. Styles clearly expected Doloris to play a role in his political as well as his private life, which explains her trip to New Hampshire to meet both his family and his constituents. Soon after their marriage he gave her books on poultry and dairying, key industries among his constituents. Drawing on her previous job experience, he turned to her for help with navigating Washington bureaucracy when his aides were not around. He encouraged her to read about the issues of the day.[50] Soon, she felt ready to share her knowledge with other people. Very early in her marriage a college club asked her to give a speech. With her husband's encouragement, she accepted the invitation. She decided that she would "talk about what [her] husband was doing" and set out to do research. She ended up with a "13-page, 45-minute speech" that "went over very well." As she became more comfortable, she stopped writing speeches beforehand and just spoke from notes. Still, she worked hard to "check [her] facts and figures and be absolutely accurate."[51]

In fact, speaking before groups in New Hampshire became one of her favorite and most important duties. Organizing her time efficiently, she was careful not to interfere with her husband's schedule or disrupt his routine. She also made it a practice only to speak to women's groups. Feeling it was "overdoing it talking to both [men and women]," she explained to one club president that she found mixed audiences a "little disconcerting."[52] The reasons for this apparently self-imposed rule remain murky. By all accounts, Doloris Bridges exuded charm and vitality. Various audiences responded well to her speeches and applauded her style. Her letters do not indicate that she suffered from stage fright. Moreover, other evidence suggests that Bridges was no retiring wallflower. She once left an important reception because she felt she had been snubbed by the woman in charge. Another time she led the fight to return Pentagon funding to a charitable agency. Obviously willing to speak with men when it was necessary for her cause or when it seemed appropriate, Bridges must have felt it was not her place to speak before mixed groups. Perhaps she recognized that a growing audience of women needed politically knowledgeable women as role models.[53]

Some women's motivation for political activism stemmed from personal experience. Phyllis Stewart, for example, credited her Roman Catholic background and staunchly Republican parents with creating a solidly conservative foundation upon which she could build. Although they suffered during the Depression after her father lost his job, the Stewarts remained adamantly opposed to the New Deal. Her family did not actively participate in politics, but conversations around the dinner table surely shaped young Phyllis's views on government. After obtaining a Catholic school education, she enrolled in Washington University for her undergraduate degree before heading to Radcliffe for a master's degree in political science. She hoped to land a government job but ended up at the American Enterprise Association, a conservative think tank. Her experiences there focused her opinions and intensified her tendencies toward right-wing thinking. With her newly honed conservative ideals, Stewart moved back to St. Louis. She set the pattern for the rest of her life by sharing her ideas with others through speeches, newsletters, and, eventually, political activism. After she married fellow conservative Fred Schlafly in 1949, she moved to Illinois and continued her activities there.[54] She first tried to work through existing institutions, including the Republican Party. In fact, Schlafly played a crucial role in the previously mentioned disagreement among women in the GOP. That fight built in intensity throughout the 1950s and culminated in Schlafly's attempt to become chair of the National Federation of Republican Women's Clubs in the mid-1960s. Her defeat convinced many conservative women, including Schlafly, that they would have to move outside the party and create their own organizations to continue their anticommunist work.[55]

Like Schlafly, Freda Utley was driven to fight communism. Her motivation, however, the most clearly articulated and understandable of that of any of the women discussed here, came from her personal experience with communism. In many ways, Utley's life mirrored that of a number of male activists. Born in Manchester, England, in 1898, she explained in her autobiography that she "came to communism . . . by a happy childhood, a socialist father, and a Continental education." She attended boarding schools in Switzerland and England, absorbing her parents' left-wing, internationalist values during holidays and summer vacations. When her family's fortune disappeared, she found a job but continued her involvement with liberal and socialist groups. Utley also found the time and the money to attend the London School of Economics, earning a master's degree. She joined the British Communist Party in 1928; married Arcadi Berdichevsky, a Russian intellectual; traveled with him to Japan and China; and eventually moved with him to the Soviet Union.[56] Despite the warnings of friends and relatives, Utley believed socialism could achieve great things in Moscow.

Her years in the USSR, however, transformed her from a devout communist into a dedicated anticommunist. Witnessing firsthand the corruption of party officials, the starving masses of workers and farmers, and the abandonment of Marxist ideals by government officials, Utley became increasingly disillusioned with the party. Still, she and her husband continued to try to make a life for themselves and their young son in Moscow. Utley believed her foreignness (these were Popular Front days, and the Soviets wanted to cultivate the British), her poor Russian-language skills (which, she explained, "saved me from the necessity of making speeches at meetings"), and her established credentials as an author protected her, even as Stalin's purges wiped out hundreds of her co-workers.[57] Her husband had no such protections. In 1936, with no apparent warning, the police arrested him as a Trotskyite and sent him to a gulag. She never heard from him again. Only years later would she learn that he had been executed in 1938.[58]

Frustrated, angry, and fearing for her child's safety, Utley went back to England with her son. To support her small family, she worked for the *Manchester Guardian* as a foreign correspondent in Japan and later in China. In 1939 she moved to the United States, where she continued her writing.[59] Throughout the 1940s and 1950s Utley wrote three books analyzing the West's failures in China; one examining pre– and post–World War II Germany; another warning that the Middle East was the communists' next target; and finally her autobiography, tracing her shift from socialism to communism to vehement anticommunism.[60] She continued to work as a freelance writer, a researcher, and a guest speaker.

Despite the prolific output from her typewriter, her accepted scholarly credentials, and her proven research abilities, Utley spent most of these years living on the edge of bankruptcy. She blamed the unpopularity of her views for her financial troubles. As she explained in her later memoirs, she was a communist before it was popular to be one, and she turned anticommunist as the British and Americans were allying themselves with the Soviets. By the time other Americans began to share her fears of communism, she had been shouting at them for almost a decade. Moreover, because she had started out as an idealist who believed in socialism and communism on a philosophical level, she had little patience with zealots who "confused the quest for social justice with Communist treason."[61] Nevertheless, like Margaret Chase Smith, Utley did not let her hatred of the Soviets blind her to the dangers of rabid anticommunism.

Using the lives of these women activists as examples, a number of comparisons can be made. First, with the exception of Brown and Utley, all of the women came from middle-class or even working-class backgrounds. The Depression hurt the families of Schlafly and Smith, but Bridges, McCarthy, and Brown seem to have felt few of its effects. Even Schlafly and Smith, however, did not seem to have experienced true financial hardship. Utley suffered later in her life as she struggled to support her son as a single mother. The fathers of most of these women were small businessmen or white-collar workers. Smith's father, a sometimes barber, earned the most sporadic income. As a result, Smith's mother worked at various odd jobs to help support the family. The Depression forced Schlafly's mother into similar circumstances.

The women were all well educated; all of them, except Smith, attended college. Two, Schlafly and Utley, had graduate degrees. Most expressed interest in political issues while in school. Schlafly and Utley had degrees in political science, while McCarthy's was in history. Despite her lack of higher education, Smith saw herself as a student of life and quickly absorbed whatever information came her way. She gained much of her political knowledge while helping her husband run his campaigns and, later, his congressional office.

With the notable exception of Utley, whose parents were avowedly left wing, all of these women were raised in families and communities with traditionally conservative values. Specific information about the political leanings of Brown's parents is elusive, but their upper-class lifestyle, interest in Tsarist Russia, and comfortable bank account all fit the image of a traditional Republican couple. Brown's marriage to a conservative European businessman and their involvement with the local Republican Party suggest the same. Similarly, there is scant evidence concerning Jean McCarthy's parents except their immigration records and release papers from the Royal Air Force following her father's service during World War I. Although their immigrant background might have made them likely to vote Democratic, the father's successful business may have pushed them into the Republican ranks. The same need to protect business interests that may have motivated Mr. Kerr's conservatism might also have influenced Bridges's doctor father to adopt right-wing views. Smith, on the surface, appears the exception to this rule. Her family struggled the most economically and remained blue collar. For her, the key factor might have been the traditionally Republican nature of her home state of Maine, as well as her mother and grandfather's Catholicism. An emphasis on religion certainly played a role in Schlafly's conservatism. Unlike Smith, Schlafly remained active in religious affairs and intertwined her political and spiritual beliefs throughout her lifetime.

Although Utley presents a contrast to the other women, her transition to conservatism was in many ways equally normal. Like fellow former leftist anticommunists Whittaker Chambers and Elizabeth Bentley, Utley first joined the Left out of idealism and conviction, only to become disillusioned, bitter, and angry. She experienced Soviet communism firsthand and decided that it was not what she had expected. Even before her husband was arrested and sent away, she had turned against the party. Her reversal was complete by 1950 when, as a naturalized American citizen, she testified against Owen Lattimore before the House Un-American Activities Committee.[62]

All the women had complicated relationships with the men in their lives. McCarthy, Bridges, and Brown were married to powerful, important men who gave them access to national audiences and introduced them to national political figures. Evidence indicates that all three were politically knowledgeable and ambitious even before they met their husbands. Although they deferred to their husbands, they all played crucial roles in maintaining their spouses' power and position. Conversely, Utley and Smith were widows whose husbands had played a role in their political education. Although neither remarried, both still depended on the advice (in the case of Smith) and financial help (in the case of Utley) of different men. Schlafly's husband was also a conservative activist, although he never became as famous as his wife. He encouraged and worked with her on numerous occasions.

Finally, all of these women were, in one way or another, politically ambitious. Smith was the most successful, winning election to the House of Representatives and then the Senate. Both Bridges and Schlafly campaigned for office but did not win. When Joe McCarthy died, some urged Jean to take over his Senate seat. She refused, citing her new baby as the reason. She steadfastly clung to her position as McCarthy's widow, however, and continued to try to control his legacy and image. Brown and Utley used their writings and speeches to educate men and women about the evils of communism.

Despite their different backgrounds and circumstances, anticommunism enabled all these women to involve themselves in their nation's political life. Although one could classify almost all of them as career women, they portrayed themselves, at some point, as wives and mothers fighting for an important cause. In their view, they were housewives with political interests, despite having careers as well as families. Utley and Smith, the two who seemed to violate convention the most, rarely admitted at the time that any challenges they faced resulted from their gender. Instead, Utley blamed her political views, which she argued were always out of sync with the rest of society, and Smith cited the fact that she was the only female senator rather than the fact that she was a woman. Smith seemed to think that if she had been one a few, rather than the sole, female senators, the men would have treated her no differently than they treated one another. These women's conservatism would not allow them to admit that they wanted more than society allowed. Anticommunist activity permitted them to become public figures without disturbing their own or anyone else's worldview. In addition, compared to women working for more liberal causes, such as civil rights for minorities or the Equal Rights Amendment, these women seemed "safe" to conventional-minded Americans. The Cold War, then, did more than just terrify some women; it provided them with a respectable way out of the house.

Their backgrounds also prepared them to speak knowledgeably about the political and diplomatic ramifications of the Cold War. Their education, access to powerful national figures, and experiences created the potential for them to contribute to the ongoing debate about the communist threat. Their ambition compelled them not to remain silent. Only their gender kept them from being recognized as valuable additions to the movement.

CHAPTER THREE

"WOMEN BEWARE"

THE FEMININE VIEW OF FOREIGN COMMUNISM

Even though women in post–World War II America were largely concerned with family and domestic responsibilities, they were soon forced to recognize the importance of events throughout the world. Soviet domination of Eastern European nations seemed unbreakable, while Mao's victory over the U.S.-backed Nationalists raised new worries about the security of Asia. Moreover, the Soviets' successful detonation of an atomic bomb raised the stakes to terrifying levels. Confused and frustrated, Americans wondered how their government, which had so competently dispatched the Japanese and Germans simultaneously, seemed so incapable of stopping the rapid spread of communism all over the globe. Anticommunist women thus had little choice but to address issues of American foreign policy in an effort to defend the United States against the spread of communism.

In turning their attention to foreign policy, anticommunist women utilized all the weapons in their arsenal to mount a counterattack. Their newsletters alerted their less-aware compatriots of the threats events in other countries posed for America and stressed the necessity for the U.S. government to form an effective foreign policy to counter these dangers. As guest speakers at luncheons for women's clubs as well as in letters to prominent people, anticommunist women lectured about the seriousness of the situation Americans faced, challenged their audiences to join the struggle, and pressured political leaders to take a stronger stand against the Red menace. A number of women wrote books explaining the background of the current crisis in an attempt to deepen the public's sense of outrage and broaden their understanding of the state of the world.

These women's efforts helped shape the anticommunist discourse as it related to the conduct of American foreign policy. Excluded from positions of power within the foreign policy establishment, the women nevertheless affected a portion of the public's understanding of the international situation. Many Americans did not have access to detailed information about worldwide events. Busy mothers and housewives in particular got their news from catching snippets of radio broadcasts, skimming newspapers, or gossiping with their neighbors. At a club luncheon, however, they listened to speakers addressing foreign policy; they might also peruse a newsletter or glance at a book suggested by their bridge partners. With this information, they made decisions about which politicians to support and which causes deserved donations. With a few notable exceptions, such as Margaret Chase Smith and Phyllis Schlafly, anticommunist women lacked direct access to real political power or a national audience; still, through their everyday efforts, they played a significant role in describing the Cold War for the American people.

Anticommunist women who wanted to influence the U.S. government's decisions concerning events around the world faced an impenetrable foreign policy establishment. Labeled the "Imperial Brotherhood" by historian Robert Dean, the men who dominated the State Department during much of the twentieth century shared class as well as gender characteristics. They attended the same prep schools and Ivy League universities, joined the same clubs, and worked for many of the same law firms or corporations. The version of masculinity preached and accepted by this elite emphasized conformity to the established order, obedience to those in authority, loyalty to one's class, and knowledge of that class's superiority. Applauding athletic ability, physical strength, and aggressive spirit on the playing field, these men carried the same values into their adult relationships and careers. Dean's research and the earlier work of Richard Barnet indicate that these men formed a foreign policy elite that controlled many offices in the State Department and made most key decisions concerning foreign affairs. Their worldview excluded women except as victims, wives, or mothers.[1]

Denied access to formal power, anticommunist women found alternate methods of influencing the national debate over foreign policy. Senator Margaret Chase Smith, the woman who held the highest political office among the anticommunist women, fought long and hard and finally had to obtain considerable support from well-placed male senators before she won a position on the Armed Services Committee.[2] In the meantime, she joined numerous other female activists in giving speeches on foreign affairs. Other women used newsletters or books as a platform to try to encourage Americans to join their crusade against communism and to force government policy makers to stand tough against the Soviets and the Chinese. Some women utilized their positions as wives of powerful men to play a role in international relations. The correspondence between Elizabeth Churchill Brown, wife of journalist Constantine Brown, and Francesca Rhee, wife of Syngman Rhee, president of South Korea, provides an interesting example. Mrs. Brown and Mrs. Rhee frequently commented on world events and served as conduits of information for and about their husbands. At one point, for example, Rhee "wish[ed] a newspaperman" would question President Eisenhower about a certain policy in hopes of getting Ike to change his stance on the issue. She did not want Brown's husband to do so, perhaps because of their known association, but she thought the question needed to be asked.[3] Like countless women across the country, Liz Brown took any opportunities that presented themselves to educate the public.

Liz was hardly alone. Anticommunists spent much of their time presenting their version of the complicated foreign policy situation in which the United States found itself. Since few Americans, male or female, thoroughly understood what was going on in Europe or Asia, most knowledgeable anticommunists attempted to explain the key issues in simple terms. The American public might lack the knowledge, ability, or desire to discern the intricacies of the Yalta Agreement, for example, but they immediately comprehended the accusation that President Franklin Delano Roosevelt "surrendered to Russian imperialism" and gave Eastern Europe to the Soviets.[4] Since conservatives already thought of FDR as the Antichrist because of the New Deal's social welfare legislation, they readily accepted anticommunists' version of Roosevelt's failures. Similarly, the anticommunist argument had appeal for Americans with religious or ethnic ties to the peoples of Eastern Europe who had watched in frustrated anger as the Iron Curtain cut them off from their compatriots. In a widely distributed report prepared for fellow Roman Catholics, John F. Cronin explained that the Soviets were bent on world domination and intended to take over all of Europe before moving on to Asia and Africa. The U.S. government, he concluded, was aiding the communists by adopting a "do-nothing policy" that gave the Soviets a free hand.[5] Again, conservative anticommunists found a receptive audience as they blamed Roosevelt and then Harry Truman for being too soft in responding to Soviet aggression.

Anticommunists were further outraged by the U.S. government's response to the situation in Asia. In fact, for some anticommunists, particularly those with more conservative leanings, their concerns about Asia—especially China—far outweighed their fears about Europe. Known as the China Lobby, these men fought to keep the situation in Asia before the American public. *Time* publisher Henry Luce, the son of a missionary to China, along with successful importer Alfred Kohlberg and California senator William Knowland, whose constant refrain won him the title "senator from Formosa," used their influence to build support for Nationalist China generally and for Jiang Jieshi personally. These men had the financial means, as well as the access to political power and a national audience through various publications, to keep pressuring Congress and the White House to fight the communists. They constantly reiterated the same message: Truman had "lost" China through incompetence at best and through deliberate action by communists working in the State Department at worst.[6]

The outbreak of war in Korea added fuel to the anticommunist conspiracy fires. According to the anticommunist theory, Truman's wimpy stance toward Mao and Red China had encouraged the North Koreans to attack the South. Right-wing columnist George Sokolsky argued, "[I]f our far eastern policy was not betrayed, why are we fighting in Korea?"[7] Truman's eventual firing of conservative hero General Douglas MacArthur further infuriated those on the Right by providing them with proof that Truman did not want to defeat communism. MacArthur, after all, agreed with them. In his famous (and career-ending) letter to House Minority Leader Joe Martin, MacArthur summed up the conservative viewpoint: "[H]ere [in Asia] we fight Europe's war with arms while diplomats still fight with words. . . . [T]here is no substitute for victory."[8] (The general echoed the anticommunist view that all communists, whether Chinese or Korean, still took their orders from Moscow. Hence, the real war should be fought in Europe.) Anticommunists across the country lambasted Truman for firing the general. Indiana senator William Jenner demanded Truman's impeachment for turning the country over to a "secret coterie" of communists, while a *Chicago Tribune* editorial advised that the nation was being "led by a fool surrounded by knaves."[9] Meanwhile, the fighting in Korea continued, frustrating a public that could not understand why a military machine that had crushed both Germany and Japan could not defeat North Korea. Anticommunists, especially Republican ones, blamed the situation on the Democratic administration's lack of will and understanding.

Consequently, many anticommunists initially hailed the Republican Eisenhower's election, assuming that he would take a stronger stand against the communist threat. His military background, political instincts, and active campaign against communists in the State Department greatly calmed the growing hysteria. Moreover, Eisenhower's ending of the Korean conflict and his skillful handling of crises throughout the world reassured the general public that the Cold War had become manageable.[10] Conservative anticommunists were less impressed. Eisenhower's campaign promise to liberate the captive nations of Eastern Europe and his appointment of John Foster Dulles as secretary of state heartened the Right momentarily. However, when Ike failed to come to the aid of Hungarians challenging Soviet domination in 1956, conservatives unleashed their anger at and frustration with his policies. His willingness to open a dialogue with Moscow sent some over the edge. Robert Welch, founder of the John Birch Society, went so far as to accuse the president of being a conscious agent of the communists.[11]

Other conflicts emerged between the president and conservative anticommunists. One major issue that exploded during Ike's tenure involved the relationship between the U.S. government and the United Nations. From its inception, the United Nations had given some conservative anticommunists a queasy feeling. Old isolationists such as Ohio senator Robert Taft feared the United Nations would force Americans into foreign wars.[12] Over the years others, such as writers James Burnham and George Sokolsky, found that elements of UN policy made them uneasy. Appalled that the United States belonged to an organization in which the Soviets had so much influence, many worried that they were being led into "one world" government. For example, during his term as president of the American Bar Association, Frank Holman gave numerous speeches warning that the United States was at risk of becoming "a puppet state in a world-wide hegemony."[13] Of particular concern were the United Nations Educational, Social and Cultural Organization (UNESCO) and the UN Declaration on Human Rights, both of which contained what the Right perceived to be socialistic elements.[14] In 1951, anticommunists across the country joined conservative Republicans in Congress in supporting the Bricker Amendment, a Senate resolution attempting to ensure that the United Nations could not make laws binding on U.S. citizens. Eisenhower vehemently opposed what he saw as an unconstitutional infringement on his presidential powers. The amendment was introduced in various forms throughout the mid-1950s. Conservative senators came close but never achieved the necessary votes to pass it.[15]

Anticommunist women were very much a part of these arguments. Sometimes they sounded eerily like their male counterparts, shocking the public with their militancy. In other instances, however, women used their gender to add a unique perspective to the ongoing debate. Fear of communism compelled these women out of their homes and into the public arena to try to educate others about the seriousness of the situation. They were determined to convince Americans that communism could be stopped only if the people forced the government to take a firm stand. Driven by their concerns, they worked to frighten, challenge, or cajole other women to join the crusade. In so doing, they affected the language and imagery of the larger debate not only by feminizing anticommunism by bringing it into the home but also through their willingness to adopt a masculine stridency.

Crowning anticommunism with the mantle of patriotic motherhood proved a powerful lure for legitimizing women's participation in politics. Instead of using maternalism to argue for pacifism as Women Strike for Peace had done, however, anticommunist women used motherhood to legitimize their more aggressive stance.[16] Their biological makeup, some activists explained, provided women with knowledge men did not possess but that could—and should—influence governments. Because of their special insights, activists believed, women would not make the same mistakes men did when dealing with their enemies. Women would willingly do whatever was necessary to protect their offspring, whether the threat came from a foreign nation or ideology or an insidious influence within their own communities. They would even guard against women who did not carry out their maternal responsibilities as they should. Motherhood, like housewifery (discussed more fully in Chapter 4), legitimized women's political involvement in any endeavor that protected their offspring.

In 1948, Congresswoman Frances Bolton explained the connection between motherhood and politics to participants at the Women's Patriotic Conference on National Defense. This meeting, which had been held annually since the late 1920s, brought together representatives from various organizations including the Marine Corps League Auxiliary, Women of the Army and Navy Legion of Valor, Ladies Auxiliary of the Veterans of Foreign Wars, Daughters of the United States Army, National Women's Relief Corps Auxiliary to the Grand Army of the Republic, and American Gold Mothers. Rejecting the idea that women represented a "poor downtrodden minority," Bolton challenged women to play an active role in the defense of their country. "National defense," she explained, consisted of more than the traditionally masculine "soldiers, trained reserves, guns, navies, planes and bombs." Women might lack knowledge of these aspects of defense, but they had a "peculiar preparation" for involvement. Women knew, she stated, "that all birth is out of darkness through pain." The birthing experience showed that women had the kind of "creative courage" necessary to go "down into the dark valley" and save the world. "This deep understanding of the meaning of suffering" gave women license to move into the male world of politics.[17]

Other anticommunist activists built on this image of mothers' innate abilities to encourage female participation in their cause. Editors of *New Mexico Women Speak* agreed with Bolton that women had "a practical understanding of the worth of the family and the community." As a result, more women had become involved in politics. They feared, however, that this was not enough. The editors felt there was a "great necessity for alarming the women of New Mexico of the dangers that beset them as individuals . . . [as well as] their state . . . and their country."[18] Leaders of the American Woman's Party agreed that "woman power is mother power." Since, in their view, there was "no nobler human power" and "no power more just" than a mother's influence, women had a duty to act.[19]

Their emphasis on a mother's instinctual need to protect her offspring did not mean right-wing anticommunists were pacifists. Like earlier generations of conservative women, anticommunists during the 1950s and 1960s accepted the necessity of some wars to destroy great evils, such as communism and fascism. Moreover, conservative women tended to blame the communists for tricking gullible U.S. political leaders into military conflicts that drained American resources and morale. Once the United States was involved in a war, however, these women expected the government to do everything it could to protect their sons by fighting "to win." As the victors in World War II, Americans should, anticommunists believed, be able to defeat easily anyone who challenged them. When victory proved more elusive, anticommunist women assumed communists must be undermining the war effort.[20]

Generally, however, female anticommunists focused on many of the same issues and used many of the same images utilized by their male colleagues to describe the communist threat. Like anticommunist men, women who spoke out against communism tended to use dramatic phrases designed to shock and frighten their audiences. They obviously perceived communism as the most serious danger existing at the time and felt compelled to ensure that their listeners or readers understood this fact. Moreover, they hoped their words would persuade others to join their crusade against the Red menace.

In contrast to the public perception that women were only interested in home and family, these women crusaders spoke and wrote knowingly about foreign policy issues and expected their frequently all-female audiences to be interested in and capable of understanding the information. They used the recent past to discuss the state of affairs in Europe and Asia. They showed little hesitation in accusing U.S. government officials of making mistakes in dealing with both allies and enemies. Like their male counterparts, they assumed that their research and intelligence gave them every right to question U.S. government foreign policy decisions. They willingly waded into the fray without limiting their analysis to "womanly" topics.

Women, like many male anticommunists, focused on the atheistic basis of communism as the root of its problems. J. Edgar Hoover, for instance, said communists had no compass to guide their actions since they lacked any foundation in Judeo-Christian values. The absence of core beliefs allowed communists to do whatever they deemed necessary to achieve their goals. One of those goals, anticommunists feared, was to eliminate religion wherever it existed. Arizonan Mrs. M. Conan's concern over the communist threat drove her to send out her own newsletter to spread the word about those "demon-possessed persons." She believed Soviet communists wanted to "control the world for Satan," since they "hate God and all forms of religion." Founded on "hatred and injustice," the USSR, she claimed, had caused much of the suffering in postwar Europe. She included visual representations of her beliefs in her newsletter as well. One cartoon showed Stalin, his hands bloody, threatening Uncle Sam.[21]

Others focused on more earthly, but no less immoral, aspects of communism. Doloris Bridges, wife of the New Hampshire senator and an outspoken anticommunist crusader, for example, constantly reiterated communists' wickedness in her speeches before women's organizations. In one instance she lambasted the Soviet regime as a government of "pathological liars" that had proven over the years that its members could not be trusted. More shockingly, that same leadership, particularly Soviet premier Nikita Khrushchev, "close[d] his eyes to murder all around him." Senator Margaret Chase Smith also blamed the Soviet and Chinese governments, rather than the people of those countries, for the situation. She emphasized that those leaders made false promises to their constituents; communists, she explained, guaranteed "the Chinese coolee [sic], the Hungarian peasant, the starving Rumanian" land reform and an improved lifestyle if they adopted communism. These desperate people, she implied, foolishly believed their conquerors. She did not want Americans to fall for the same tricks.[22]

Many anticommunist women shared the fear that the American people did not recognize the severity of the crisis and so would not step up to fight. Smith found it amazing that people criticized her for journeying to Moscow so she could see for herself how the Russians lived. She was "very glad" she had made the trip, since now she could tell Americans from firsthand experience "how lucky" they were not to be in Russia. In letters to her numerous correspondents, Elizabeth Churchill Brown described the American people as "amorphous" and worried that they would sleep through a communist takeover. While the rank and file clung to their false sense of security, she wrote, "the weak-kneed, the pinkoes and one-worlders" pressured the White House to get along with the Soviets. Without an effective counterbalance, she worried that the "tides of evil" would overtake the free world.[23] Helen Corson, another newsletter writer, put it more bluntly: "The only way to lick this hidden menace is for all free, God-loving people to unite in a strong opposition to them." Corson cautioned her readers that the Reds would stir up trouble between the groups arrayed against communists. Without unity, she wrote, the free world would be doomed.[24]

These anticommunist women wanted Americans to lead the unity effort and take control of the worldwide anticommunist movement. The problem, they explained, was not just a lack of initiative on the part of the U.S. government. They also worried about Europeans who refused to follow American guidance and so risked being seduced by communism. Former ambassador to Italy and Congresswoman Clare Boothe Luce wrote General A. C. Wedemeyer in 1947 saying it was time for Americans to make up their minds whether to assume "the complete leadership of the democratic world or turn Europe and Asia over to the Soviets." The devastation resulting from World War II made Europeans vulnerable to communist propaganda. Even though Mrs. Conan wrote in her newsletter that "much of Europe's suffering [was] due to Russian plundering," she fretted that the weak and starving people might succumb to Soviet seduction. Doloris Bridges, back from a 1947 tour of Europe, told her clubwoman audience about the malnutrition and hopelessness she had seen. She recommended that a "sensible, self-supporting program" be designed to prevent the growth of radicalism and to keep Europe from becoming a drag on the U.S. economy. Years later, she still worried about U.S. aid to Europe and its effect on the budget at home. She did not want American dollars "sent down the drain all over the world" by pouring funds into countries harboring communists or adopting socialist policies. Journalist Brown agreed. Her concern was less the U.S. economy and more the willingness of aid recipients to go their own way. Frequently warning her correspondents and readers about the treachery of America's European allies, she predicted that a "neutralist Europe" would work to thaw the Cold War by encouraging talks between Americans and the Soviets.[25]

In addition to blaming American allies for communist victories around the world, many of the women found fault with various aspects of U.S. foreign policy. Margaret Chase Smith blamed Americans' preoccupation with themselves for their having lost the propaganda war around the world. "We can't get far," she scolded the women of the Rumford Rotary-Lions club, "by telling the poverty stricken people of how wonderful life in America is with cars, homes, television sets, refrigerators, washing machines." Instead, she advocated teaching these people how the American system would "actually and specifically . . . bring such things to them in their own country." With her Yankee practicality and frugality, Smith assumed that plans to bring about a change in living conditions would attract more converts than philosophical tracts preaching the wonders of capitalism and democracy.[26]

Others saw the problem in broader terms. Since the earliest days of the Cold War, some anticommunists had worried that government officials did not truly understand the problem they faced. According to these individuals, although American leaders said they were fighting the communists, the truth contradicted them. For example, the Women Investors Research Institute (WIRI) warned that American foreign policy "ignore[d] the very heart of Stalin's program to conquer the world." WIRI members looked to history to understand current Soviet actions. Stalin's strategy, they declared, was a "combination of 10th century Russian plans to conquer Eastern Europe and Genghis Khan's plan to rule the world." Ironically, their perspective mirrored that of the men they were chastising. Like many of those working within the foreign policy establishment, this group of women saw the struggle between the United States and the USSR as a geopolitical/balance-of-power fight rather than an ideological one.[27] In fact, despite their maternalist rhetoric, these women thought about the struggle in very masculine terms; rather than advocate compromise, they pushed the competitive angle. They wanted more, not fewer, guns.

Despite this area of agreement, however, some anticommunist women felt the State Department and, in fact, the entire federal government were implicated in the communist victories, particularly in Asia. Echoing the sentiments of the China Lobby, the Minute Women printed a letter in their Houston chapter newsletter from Dr. Marguerite Atterbury, a missionary in China. In the letter, Atterbury described conditions in China before and after the communist victory. With nothing but praise for Jiang Jieshi and his government, Atterbury lamented the current limitations to his power. She blamed the United States for allowing the communists to "push Free China around" by continuing to accept "the fiction that the Nationalist Government was a culprit in the loss of the Mainland." In her view, the Americans maintained a false story to cover the mistakes they had made in their Asian policy. Other Minute Women took a darker view of the situation. In a 1951 statement in response to Truman's firing of General Douglas MacArthur, the Minute Women argued that Secretary of State Dean Acheson and British prime minister Clement Atlee had conspired to give Eastern Europe and China to Stalin. MacArthur, in their estimation, had been trying to stop this move, which was why he had to be removed from the scene.[28]

Elizabeth Churchill Brown looked higher than the State Department for responsibility for America's failure to stop communist encroachment around the world. She blamed President Dwight Eisenhower for not providing decisive leadership against the Soviets and the Chinese. She lamented that what she labeled his "confusion" had spread throughout the White House, the Pentagon, and the National Security Council—turning his foreign policy into a mishmash of ideas and actions. Some of Ike's confusion, she wrote, stemmed from his reliance on his brother Milton Eisenhower, who Brown saw as a bad influence on the president. Milton Eisenhower encouraged his brother to talk to the Soviets and had even gone to Moscow to arrange for the Soviet premier to visit the United States.[29] Many anticommunists saw this as the ultimate in hypocrisy and stupidity. How could the government claim to be fighting the Soviets with everything it had and allow its leader to pay a diplomatic visit? In fact, the trip set off a wave of protests and demonstrations against the Eisenhower administration, including one featuring William F. Buckley Jr., publisher of the *National Review*, that filled Carnegie Hall almost to capacity.[30]

Some anticommunist women found things to praise about the Eisenhower administration. Doloris Bridges, according to a news account of one of her talks, "commended the administration for moving forces into Lebanon and the standing up in defense of Formosa [Taiwan]." In particular, Bridges applauded Ike's actions in supporting Quemoy and Matsu, two islands claimed by Nationalist Chinese and attacked by the People's Republic of China. Without such a reaction, much of Asia would eventually "go behind the Bamboo Curtain." Rather than lay all the mistakes on the president's shoulders, Bridges looked accusingly at Congress and its role in not supporting the president in his efforts to fight communism at home and abroad.[31]

Another favorite target of anticommunists was the United Nations. Criticism generally fell into two categories, although both were related to the same larger issue—surrendering control to a non-American authority. One theory expounded by Conan in her newsletter argued that the United Nations was "only a cloak for Communism, the most horrible form of slavery ever hatched out of the mind of Satan." Communism's influence at the United Nations resulted from Soviet control of the votes of its satellite peoples. According to Florence Dean Post, vice chair of the Minute Women of the USA, the Soviets represented over 800 million people, while the United States had only 160 million. In addition, she asserted, the Russians could usually count on the votes of "undefined nations." This meant, she explained, that the United States would be outvoted at almost every turn. Compounding the problem for both Post and Katharine Reynolds of the Daughters of the American Revolution (DAR) was their belief that the United Nations was harboring communist spies. Sometimes these undercover agents were described as foreign workers who used their diplomatic status to send information and technology back to the mother country. More shocking for these women, however, were the Americans at the United Nations who did not represent the interests of the United States but instead were working with America's enemies. According to groups like the DAR and the Minute Women, some Americans working at the United Nations had failed security screenings by the federal government or had "taken the fifth" at congressional hearings. Still, the United Nations hired them. No wonder the institution could not be trusted, they maintained.[32]

The other concern many anticommunists voiced about the United Nations was what they perceived to be a tendency toward world government. Unwilling to relinquish American control over U.S. territory and citizens, these women feared UN leaders planned to undermine federal and state constitutions in the name of international peace. Anticommunists who espoused this belief feared the "one-worlders" would "seek a gradual approach to world government through the United Nations." Mrs. James Lucas, executive secretary of the DAR, explained in testimony before the Senate Judiciary Committee that the DAR's position was that "our national sovereignty is essential to the freedom of the American people and the preservation of our constitutional Republic." She went on to "expose the fallacies inherent in the world-government idea." Chief among these flaws, in her opinion, was the idea that the peoples of the world had so much in common that they could unite as one. She found this absurd. She also worried that a world government would be allowed to tax the American people as well as create its own army and set up an international court system. Many of the Minute Women joined Lucas and the DAR in their views, and the New York chapter reprinted Lucas's statement in its newsletter.[33]

Florence Fowler Lyons was another concerned opponent of world government. She set her sights on UNESCO as the main culprit in trying to bring about world government. In particular, she focused on UNESCO's educational efforts, fearing the group was spreading one-world propaganda to innocent children without their parents realizing what was happening. Lyons spent years examining UNESCO's activities and reports so she could expose anything with which she found fault.[34]

Although Lyons and most other newsletter writers had a limited readership, making it difficult to ascertain the true extent of their influence on the broader anticommunist movement, the plethora of publications and the longevity of some of them indicate that these women were, at the least, getting their opinions out to the public. Even if they did not change the view of one person, which seems unlikely considering that some of the newsletters required subscriptions, their writings added to the overall debate on the issues. These activists explained the issues of the day in their own words, in language their readers would understand. For women who did not have the time or the inclination to read through a newspaper or watch the news, these brief newsletters might have been their only source of information on these topics.

A few women succeeded in helping shape anticommunist dialogue on a national level. Freda Utley, Elizabeth Churchill Brown, and Phyllis Schlafly are three examples of such writers and activists. Although they shared the same basic message—that American political leaders had allowed communism to gain strength throughout the world—the three women came from divergent backgrounds, wrote under different circumstances, and met with varying levels of acceptance. Utley, a highly educated, cosmopolitan former communist, used her own experiences in the Soviet Union as the foundation to try to convince the American public to heed the dangers of communism. As a former society columnist and a journalist's wife, Brown struggled to be taken seriously as a political writer. Through her obstinate refusal to be silenced and her willingness to almost force people to read her book, she succeeded in making her opinions known. Schlafly gained more commercial success, perhaps because she was the most politically astute of the three women, perhaps because she benefited from a resurgence of conservatism.

Freda Utley was one of the few women who belonged to a small group of former communist intellectuals who helped shape the evolution of modern conservatism. Along with men such as Whittaker Chambers, Max Eastman, and William Henry Chamberlin, Utley provided firsthand knowledge of the reality of communism. These former leftists did more than tell tales of good and evil; they laid an intellectual framework to justify the emerging anticommunism of the Right. Their work imbued a political and partisan movement with philosophical overtones, tying anticommunism to a conservative ideology and helping to unite sometimes dissenting factions on the Right.[35] After all, economic conservatives, traditionalists, and right-wing politicians all feared communism's effect on their world. Focusing on the Red menace gave them common ground to overlook differences and concentrate on their enemies at home and abroad.[36]

Although the writings of each of these former communist intellectuals had a specific focus, they all tended to agree on the general outline of what they portrayed as America's disastrous foreign policy. In their minds, Europe's fate had been predetermined before World War II ended. FDR and a communist clique in the State Department, with the help of General George Marshall, organized their military strategy to allow the Soviets to gain control of Eastern Europe. They argued that the insistence on the unconditional surrender of Germany, the naive view of Stalin's actions, and tolerance of the Soviet presence in Poland were proof of the conspiracy.[37] Unfortunately, as they saw it, Roosevelt's death had not ended the troubles. Truman had continued the same plan. His containment policy only made things worse.

For her part, Utley concentrated on Asia. Prior to 1941 she had written several books and articles on the conflict between Japan and China, encouraging American policy makers to take a tough stand and expose what she called Japan's "feet of clay."[38] American policy during and especially after the war further frustrated and angered Utley. As early as 1946, she warned publisher Clair Boothe Luce that "illusions about the Chinese Communist are largely responsible for our absurd policy in China." In her book *The China Story*, published in 1951 with Mao Zedong's successful seizure of power still fresh in Americans' minds and in the midst of the Korean conflict, Utley argued that China had been delivered to the Communists "with what amounted to the blessing of the United States Administration." A combination of "ignorance, refusal to face facts, romanticism . . . political immaturity or a misguided humanitarianism, and the influence of

Communist sympathizers and the careerists who staked their reputations on a pro-Soviet policy" resulted in the United States selling out its ally, Jiang Jieshi, and abandoning the people of Asia to communism.[39] Even after the communists forced Jiang and the Nationalists to Formosa, Americans continued, according to Utley, to "nurture illusions about Communism." Their naïveté led to the conflict in Korea and was ultimately leading, she warned, to a potential "third world war."[40]

Utley released *The China Story* at an opportune time. The domestic Red Scare was in full swing, the war in Korea appeared mired in stalemate, and Truman's dismissal of MacArthur had aroused fierce debate. The timing of the publication, combined with her reputation as an experienced journalist with solid academic credentials and her experience as a former communist, helped legitimize both the book and its message.[41] Utley's appearance the year before the book was published during the Senate's investigation of Owen Lattimore added to her reputation. In reviewing the book for the *New York Times*, Richard L. Walker, a history professor at Yale, pointed out these facts. Although troubled by her "bitterness" and willingness "to view events and personalities in black and white colors," he encouraged his readers to take up the volume, absorb her "useful information," and engage in the national debate. The *Times* continued its support later that year by listing the book among the 110 volumes chosen as recommended "vacation" reading.[42]

Utley continued her work throughout the decade even as the public became less obsessed with the communist menace. Her later books resulted from extensive reading as well as research conducted during personal visits to the Soviet Union, China, and the Middle East. She feared that Americans had not learned from their earlier mistakes and would allow communism to take advantage of crises around the world. In her Preface to *Will the Middle East Go West*, she explained that although she "did not presume to know all of the answers," she did "hope" the "tentative suggestions" she made in the course of the book would "help to build a wise United States policy, serving the interests of both America and the free world." She feared that Americans would foolishly let the Middle East slip under Soviet control, as they had with Europe when they ignored her earlier warnings. Almost ten years earlier she had expressed a similar sentiment at the end of her book on Germany. She was "convinced" that "once the American people are made aware of the facts [concerning the treatment of postwar Germany] which have for so long been withheld from them," facts she exposed in her book, they would "impel a radical change in United States policy."[43]

Determined to expose the errors she found in U.S. foreign policy, Utley dedicated herself to anticommunist work. In addition to her books, she wrote speeches for Joe McCarthy and worked briefly for the Office of Strategic Services and later for the McCarren Subcommittee on Investigations.[44] She recognized that in doing so, she was giving up the "material interests" she could have gained from her "brains, knowledge and literary ability."[45] Convinced of her high intelligence and powerful analytical skills, she believed wholeheartedly in her cause and never questioned her right to engage in a traditionally male preserve. Moreover, her books were written for both the male and female public, although she particularly hoped to influence the men in power. No evidence indicates that Utley in any way considered her gender a limiting factor in her work. She appeared to assume that she could engage the male foreign policy establishment as an equal and even influence the decisions that emerged from this elite group.

In contrast, Elizabeth Churchill Brown approached the situation from a completely different set of circumstances, and her work directly addressed gender issues. Two factors in particular worked against Brown's efforts to publish the same basic message Utley preached: the changed status of the Cold War both at home and abroad, and Brown's personal background. Because of these difficulties, Brown found herself in need of a tool to pry open a space for herself in the anticommunist world. She used her gender as a crowbar.

Brown began work on her book on U.S. foreign policy in 1954 just as the Cold War entered a new phase. The Republican Dwight Eisenhower was elected president in 1952, Joseph Stalin died in 1953, and the war in Korea was over. After the tensions of the early 1950s, the American public gladly put itself and its foreign policy in Ike's hands. There were crises, certainly. But when the Soviets demolished the Hungarian rebels or the Chinese bombed the Nationalist-held islands of Quemoy and Matsu, public alarm was momentary. There were too many other things to distract them: the booming economy, the plethora of consumer goods, rising racial tensions. The Cold War became something Americans learned to live with.[46]

Additionally, the mid-1950s witnessed the birth of modern conservatism. Fueled by lingering resentment over twelve years of New Deal politics, conservatives, especially within the Republican Party, pushed for greater access to political power. Anticommunism helped those economic conservatives find common ground with tradition-alists who feared all the social and cultural changes of the postwar years. Seeing the opportunity to bring these groups together, William F. Buckley Jr. and others such as writer/philosophers Willi Schlamm and Frank Meyer created a new publication, the *National Review,* to give voice to all varieties of what they considered legitimate conser-vatism. They wanted to rid conservatism of its more lunatic elements to justify the Right's demands for national power. In particular, they moved away from anti-Semitism and conspiracy theories.[47]

Caught up in her own anticommunist work, Brown did not recog-nize that the public's attitudes had changed anymore than she could see how her personal situation limited her potential as an author. As noted in Chapter 2, Brown's journalistic training had been limited to the society pages. Only her marriage to journalist Constantine Brown brought her into contact with the movers and shakers in Washington, DC. She lacked not only Utley's academic credentials but the former communist's experiences as well. Brown might have been well trav-eled, but she had not lived through Stalin's purges or been in Asia during the war. Even critics who might disagree with Utley's conclu-sions could not overlook the reality of her firsthand knowledge. Brown started with no such advantage.

In many ways, she had more in common with the newsletter editors than she did with Utley. Like them, she was a housewife who engaged in political work between household chores. She took her commitment to anticommunism as seriously as they did. Similar to women like Florence Fowler Lyons, she put in many hours doing research from government reports, published memoirs, and congres-sional hearings. As discussed in more depth in Chapter 4, she devoted much time and effort to encouraging other women to get involved in the fight against communism.

In 1954, Brown tried to combine her research with her desire to increase women's participation in the movement. She sent conserva-tive publisher Henry Regnery a manuscript proposal for what she thought would be a unique and important contribution to anticom-munist literature. As she explained in her letter, in her view, intelli-gent women interested in important issues had no time to learn about them because of household responsibilities. Cooking, cleaning, and caring for their families were important, but these jobs left little time to expand their knowledge of the threat of communism. They had "time only for the headlines," not for editorials or detailed analyses. Assuming that most of the women she was writing to were mothers, she recognized that their foremost concern was that their sons might be called upon to fight and die in another war. They wanted to know what was going on in the world but dreaded men's condescending attitude if they asked too many questions. In Brown's view, women needed to discuss these issues with other women who would treat them with respect.[48]

Brown promised to tell other women "the truth" about politics because she was one of them. Explaining that she had not paid attention to politics until she started reading her new husband's newspaper columns, she put herself on the same level as her readers. She might live in Washington, DC, and be married to a famous journalist, but inside, she told them, she was as ignorant of events as they were. For example, she had questions concerning the U.S. government's actions during and after World War II. Despite the men who "maligned" her curiosity and encouraged her to let "the menfolks take care of running the world," she sought answers. Even then, she refused to play the men's game. Since she was not a "military strategist" but a woman, she "look[ed] at things like women do." She asked "questions no intelligent man would ask." Although her husband thought her suspicions about the Roosevelt administration resulted from her "being emotional, 'just like a woman,'" she persisted in pursuing them.[49]

Brown carried this attitude into *The Enemy at His Back*, published in 1955. The first paragraph of her Introduction set the tone for the book: "This book is the result of a woman's curiosity. It is not the work of a student of history nor even the work of a student. Neither is it written for students but rather for ordinary people like myself who would like to know 'who killed Cock Robin?'"[50] She then proceeded to lay out her argument in a straightforward manner that would have been easy for anyone for follow. Rather than rely on academic or diplomatic jargon, Brown quoted herself, wondering, "Why do we have to kiss [the Soviets] on the mouth?" Her colloquial language and inclusion of personal narrative echoed the style of the newsletters of various women's groups.[51]

Her argument, however, followed much the same line as Utley's. In the book, she examined the actions and words of key American leaders involved in decision making in the Pacific theater during and after World War II. She concluded that General George Marshall and President Franklin Roosevelt had deliberately prolonged the war against Japan because it suited Soviet purposes. Without actually calling them communist agents, she questioned their reliance on advisers of doubtful loyalty. According to her analysis, these same advisers rushed America into demobilization, leaving the rest of the world defenseless against encroaching communist forces. She also concluded that these same men had prevented General MacArthur from winning the war in Korea by unduly restraining his actions. The American people, in her view, had been betrayed.[52]

Brown's book and her interactions with various editors exposed much about her way of dealing with her position as an anticommunist woman. On the one hand, she accepted certain stereotypes about women: they were "different" from men, they were housewives, their connections to world affairs were related to their family interest. On the other hand, she used those assumptions to justify her book: she could talk to other women in ways men could not. She also turned her assumptions against men: she could see things men could not because she looked at the situation from a different angle. Flashes of defiance appeared in her cutting remarks about "menfolks" running the world. Most important, she insisted, her book told the "story that ought to be told to other women" and was not a fluffy, watered-down version of world affairs. It was a hard-core indictment of American policy makers. Despite her emphasis on writing a book for women, her conclusions were very similar to those of most right-wing men.

Further, Brown did not approach publication as a retiring "lady." She had been working on the manuscript for over a year, corresponding with Henry Regnery, who was both a personal friend of the family and one of the nation's leading conservative publishers. By early 1955 she had sent Regnery the manuscript. After three and a half months, he returned it with a polite refusal. He did not think her book would "lend itself to" distribution in bookstores. He thought she should turn the manuscript into a series of pamphlets that would be useful to the new organizations "springing up around the country." As a businessman, Regnery based his decisions on the need to make a profit; obviously, he did not believe Brown's book would be a commercial success.[53]

Since the book did go on to sell a reasonable number of copies, Regnery's stated reason for not publishing it seems disingenuous. In particular, his suggestion that she publish the material in pamphlet form rather than reorganize it (which her next publisher required) indicated that Regnery saw Brown as the wife of an author rather than an author herself. Regnery proposed that an organization such as the Minute Women might provide a market for such a pamphlet series.

Brown did not let Regnery's decision discourage her. She sent the book to Devin Garrity at Devin-Adair, who made favorable comments and helpful suggestions. By August 1955 she had not only a publisher but also a distributor. Interestingly, Liz did not blame Regnery for his actions even though she told him he had been "mean" to her. His cruel rejection of her manuscript, she explained to him and to another friend, was not his fault. She did not think anyone at Regnery's press had actually read her manuscript. Consistently conspiratorial, she believed "Henry has some one in his outfit who does him no good." Like the political leaders in her book, Regnery was the victim of bad advisers who could not spot valuable material (i.e., her manuscript) when they read it.[54]

The Enemy at His Back received good, if not outstanding, reviews from the conservative press, and Liz earned congratulations from fellow right-wingers. The *New York Herald Tribune*'s reviewer thought she had done a "creditable" job of proving her point. One Chicago paper's reviewer thought she had raised interesting and important questions that needed answering. Arizona senator Barry Goldwater had a favorable review of the book read into the *Congressional Record*.[55]

Even after she had finished the book and found a publisher, Brown remained very much involved in its distribution and publicity. She took control of the situation after publication to make certain reviewers and influential people received copies of the book. She personally sent copies to 100 "very wealthy men," expecting them to send her the purchase price, and then she had to scramble to receive payment from them. Checking to see if reviewers received their copies consumed much of her time and that of her assistant. Her efforts in this regard showed how knowledgeable she was about political influence and publishing; she knew the book would be worthless if not properly reviewed and publicized. More revealing, however, was her complete faith that the book would receive favorable reviews. Unlike many writers, she appeared to have no doubts as to the value and importance of her work.[56]

Unquestionably, however, Brown had to work much harder than Utley to promote her views. By the mid-1950s, the story Brown told was familiar to the conservative faithful. She did not provide her readers with any new material, even though her language might have held more appeal to a female readership. As previously mentioned, much of the American public had become less obsessed with the topics she discussed. The *New York Times* did not review Brown's book. In fact, it was only reviewed in conservative publications. In contrast, Utley's later book repeated a similar message but focused on the Middle East, a new player in the Cold War game, and was reviewed by the *Times*.[57]

Dedicated anticommunists like Brown became even more frustrated as the public's attitude continued to mellow. Communism had not ceased to be an enemy ideology for most Americans, but they had learned to live with that enemy as long as there was no immediate threat. Concerns about Fidel Castro in Cuba and of nuclear fallout forced the abstract image of Soviet or Chinese soldiers invading American soil to the background. Politicians continued to call up the Red menace in campaign speeches and Red-baited their opponents if they thought it would help their campaigns, but the frequency and intensity of those accusations had changed.[58] Voters and the public in general seemed more worried about race riots and right-wing extremism than about the communist threat.

Elizabeth Churchill Brown found this nonchalance about communism absurd and dangerous. She predicted to her publisher friend Henry Regnery in October 1963 that "within the next two or three years, the ring will be visibly closing around us. . . . Our military will be disaffected, demoralized, and torn within themselves. We'll be disarmed and old Uncle Nikita will be calling the shots." A month later, after President John F. Kennedy was assassinated, Brown again saw the Soviets' hand at work. According to her rather convoluted logic, Castro had ordered Lee Harvey Oswald to kill JFK, and Soviets had then killed Oswald to protect the conspiracy. Now, she explained to Francesca Rhee, the culprits feared that if Americans learned that communists were behind the murder, everyone would become anticommunist, which would undermine peaceful coexistence and world peace. She believed some "infiltrated red in the ranks of conservatives" might do something drastic to distract America from the truth.[59] Brown's zealousness better suited the nation's paranoid mood of the McCarthy era of the early 1950s. By the early to mid-1960s the nation, while still anticommunist, was less convinced of the reality of conspiracies against American freedoms.

Brown was not alone in her frustration with the American public or in her continuing efforts to fight communism. In fact, by the early

1960s, even as Americans returned the Democrats to the White House, a grassroots movement was gathering momentum to move the country to the right. Utilizing Republican women's clubs and other local organizations, a small band of conservative Republicans was plotting to win the GOP presidential nomination for one of its own: Arizona senator Barry Goldwater. More moderate Republicans underestimated the determination, ability, and numbers of right-wingers and so were caught off guard. Their last-minute efforts to deprive Goldwater of the nomination backfired, and the Right had its candidate.[60]

Playing a key supporting role in Goldwater's early campaign was longtime activist Phyllis Schlafly. A dedicated anticommunist, Schlafly liked Goldwater's demand for a stronger defense against the Soviets and for less socialism at home. She had voiced similar complaints throughout the 1950s, during her unsuccessful campaign for Congress in 1952 and in her work with the DAR and the Federation of Republican Women's Clubs. Like Brown and Utley, she refused to give up on her mission to educate the American public about the dangerous state of the world. She saw Goldwater's 1964 campaign as an opportunity to reinvigorate the fight against communism. Schlafly signed on.[61]

She did much more than ring doorbells, however. As historian Donald Critchlow pointed out in his recent biography, Schlafly had always believed in the importance of translating "the ideas of intellectuals and anticommunist authors" for grassroots consumption. One of her continuing projects over the years was developing "A Reading List for Americans," which included congressional reports as well as intellectual tomes and popular nonfiction, such as Whitaker Chambers's *Witness*.[62] Consequently, when Schlafly joined the Goldwater campaign, she decided that she could be most useful by writing a book that would explain to the public the obstacles conservatives had faced within their own party.[63]

The result was *A Choice Not an Echo*, which she wrote and privately published in 1964. The book focused on exposing "the kingmakers" who, she claimed, ran the GOP and prevented conservatives from having any input. These men had been undermining the party and America for much of the twentieth century. She devoted one of her longest chapters to an analysis of U.S. foreign policy. Entitled "Who's Looney Now?" the chapter listed "Defeats around the World," including Vietnam—which was, she wrote, "slipping fast into Communist clutches"—as well as "Communist Agents in the State Department and the CIA." She pulled few punches, named names, and accused President Lyndon Johnson and his aides of ignoring America's anticommunist friends and "lavish[ing] millions of dollars . . . and every possible hospitality" on pro-communists.[64]

Written in a colloquial, simple style reminiscent of Brown's book and the various newsletters, *A Choice Not an Echo* became a sensation. Schlafly had chosen to publish the book privately to speed up production and allow her to control distribution. Using her own mailing lists, compiled over the years from her associations with various right-wing organizations, Schlafly promoted the book widely. She offered bulk discounts and sold close to 2 million copies in the first six months of publication. By November, she had sold 3.5 million copies.[65] According to a *New York Times* review, the book was "in such demand that copies could not be obtained in many places along the East Coast."[66] The book was particularly important during the California primary. The margin separating Goldwater from his main rival, New York governor Nelson Rockefeller, was extremely narrow. Targeting districts where Rockefeller was strong, Goldwater workers distributed hundreds of copies of *Choice*. When Goldwater won the primary, his staff gave Schlafly's book much of the credit.[67]

Later that same year, Schlafly repeated the pattern with a book written with Retired Rear Admiral Chester Ward. *The Gravediggers* brought Utley and Brown's message up to the present day. According to Schlafly and Ward, Roosevelt and his aides had set the dangerous precedent of handing the Soviets everything they needed to conquer the world. Their successors had continued in the same vein. Khrushchev, the authors explained, promised to "bury" the West, and "American gravediggers" were shoveling the dirt. Echoing her predecessors, Schlafly did not claim these Americans were communists. Instead, they were "card-carrying liberals."[68] She accused the Johnson administration of undermining America's defense by encouraging disarmament and leaving America vulnerable. She also went after Hollywood for producing movies such as *On the Beach* and *Fail-Safe* that presented falsehoods as facts, serving only to frighten the public.[69]

Although Schlafly mentioned communism's impact on the family, she did not directly address women in her books. Rather, like Utley, she appeared to assume that women would be as interested and as knowledgeable as men but would not need or want "special handling." Again, like Utley, she did not refer directly to her gender, further proof that anticommunist women did not allow their gender to inhibit their right to participate in the foreign policy dialogue of the era.

None of the activists could entirely escape the prejudices of their times, however. Despite the obvious knowledge of international events exhibited by these anticommunist women, the vast majority of the public still believed foreign affairs and anticommunism were primarily issues for male consideration. Talk of missile strength, combat strategies, and weaponry seemed to fit more naturally into a man's sphere. For women, it was an uphill battle to be accepted in such a world. Freda Utley, who had written extensively about Russia and China, complained to editor Clare Boothe Luce that she had more difficulty getting her material published than John Hershey, a better-known male author who wrote about similar subjects.[70] During Schlafly's 1952 congressional campaign, her opponent suggested she go back home and take care of her children.[71] Brown, of course, recognized that women might need some remedial education on foreign policy, but she did not let that fact deter her efforts to publish her book.

The world might still accept the stereotype that foreign policy was a man's game, but women anticommunists knew better. Female anticommunists during this period focused on many of the same issues and used many of the same images utilized by their male colleagues to describe the communist threat. Like anticommunist men, women who spoke out against communism tended to use dramatic phrases designed to shock and frighten their audiences.

Women activists played a significant role in defining the relationship of U.S. foreign policy to the threat of communism. At least two such women took it upon themselves to translate foreign affairs issues for all Americans, male and female alike. Freda Utley was convinced that as a former communist, her experiences abroad, especially in Russia and China, qualified her to write authoritatively about the dangers these communist states posed to the United States. Phyllis Schlafly, less cosmopolitan than Utley but supremely confident of her ability to write in a style that could reach the masses, published with the goal of informing her fellow citizens about U.S. foreign policy and the necessity of putting Goldwater in the White House. Most women, however, undertook the task of alerting other women—their neighbors and friends—through newsletters, speeches, and books about the nature of the communist threat overseas and the effect it would have on their lives at home.

Liz Brown stands out from this large group of anticommunist women because of her conviction that she could write in a manner that would allow busy American housewives and mothers to learn about the implications of U.S. foreign policy in the battle against communism. Nevertheless, other women, although perhaps lacking Liz's connections in the world of publishing, undertook the same role in their clubs and organizations or by writing newsletters and pamphlets. No matter the method of communication utilized or the level of fame achieved, all of these women were convinced that American foreign policy must be designed to halt the Red menace and that only by arousing the housewives and mothers of America could such a policy be developed.

The work of these women, in effect, transformed the male preserve of foreign affairs into an arena in which both sexes were expected to participate. Anticommunist women did not view their actions as unprecedented or irregular. Their hatred of communism blinded them to the larger implications of their actions, namely that they were stepping out of the role of the little homemaker into the rough-and-tumble arena of foreign policy debate. Concerned that not all Americans, especially women, seemed to understand the seriousness of the situation in foreign affairs, they were committed to sounding the alert and educating the population. By undertaking this task, they were fulfilling their patriotic duty to help defend the United States from its communist enemies worldwide; at the same time they were helping to transform an element of the female population into ideologically motivated political activists.

CHAPTER FOUR

WOMEN ARISE

THE RED THREAT ON THE DOMESTIC SCENE

Not content just to talk about the evils of communism, conservative anticommunist women across the country participated in various efforts to rid America of the evil forces that lurked within the nation's borders. Some women acted in ways that defied conventional limits regarding female behavior. Others took a more traditional route. They joined clubs; they wrote letters, newsletters, books, and articles; they gave speeches and organized demonstrations. They even ran for public office. They seemed not to think twice about whether women should participate in the anticommunist crusade. In fact, the opposite appeared to be the case. Underlying the activities of most of these women was an urgent sense of responsibility. Joining the fight against communism seemed one more duty of good wives and mothers. If, in the process of combating this enemy, they ended up expanding their overall political participation, that was a consequence most of them had not consciously anticipated or, for the most part, desired. They were just fulfilling what one Texas clubwoman called woman's "special mission." Women, she explained, were called "to do battle, continuously and evermore, with any power or influence which threatens the unity and perpetuity of this first of society's institutions—the family in its home."[1]

Many right-wing anticommunist women translated their concern about the communist threat into worry about practical issues. Rather than focus exclusively on spies within the government leaking military secrets to the Russians, conservative women frequently concentrated on the impact communist agents had on community organizations such as school boards, libraries, and health care facilities. In addition, many women served as their families' money managers and thus fretted about the Red influence on the economy as it related to their household budgets. In contrast, male anticommunists tended to look at the big picture, especially in regard to economic matters, rather than focus on bread-and-butter issues.

Actually, anticommunists in general tended to focus so intently on the menace of communism that they ignored the changing realities around them. Economic turmoil immediately after World War II, followed by unprecedented prosperity intermixed with periods of recession, confused people who had experienced the Great Depression. The plethora of consumer goods available enticed more women, eager to purchase those goods, into the workforce at the same time "everyone" assumed women were content to stay at home. Prosperity also fueled a rising Civil Rights Movement. Even the government seemed to acknowledge that changes needed to be made in this area of domestic policy. The 1954 Supreme Court verdict in *Brown v. Board of Education, Topeka, Kansas* introduced a potential new level of federal involvement in local affairs. Similarly, President Dwight Eisenhower's failure to "undo" the New Deal meant the government would continue to grow.[2] Conservative to begin with, anticommunists would have disliked increased federal intervention and challenges to the social structure under any circumstances. The continued emphasis on the communist threat provided anticommunists with a simplistic way to understand the transformation of the world around them. Anything they disliked or found frightening could be blamed on the communist presence.

As discussed in Chapter 1, the American public became aware of the supposed danger of communism in the United States from a variety of sources and events. Former communists, such as Whittaker Chambers and Elizabeth Bentley, who had found Jesus or grown disillusioned with the cause identified their previous associates and exposed the existence of a spy network within the United States. Responding to these allegations, members of the House and Senate held open hearings and called hundreds of witnesses. The resulting trials of Julius and Ethel Rosenberg, Alger Hiss, and the Hollywood Ten seemed to confirm that a real problem existed. Further legitimizing this fear, President Harry Truman created a Loyalty Review Panel to check the backgrounds of all government employees. His attempt to wrest control of the spy issue from his political enemies seriously backfired, as Republicans used his own committee to prove the depth of the problem.[3]

Republicans succeeded in using the issue of domestic subversion as a springboard to political power. Wisconsin senator Joe McCarthy proved particularly adept at attacking Democrats and anyone else who opposed him, smearing them with the Red label. By the time Eisenhower won control of the White House, McCarthy had become a household name, and McCarthyism had come to symbolize a disregard for civil liberties in the quest to root out communism. Ike, who intensely disliked McCarthy and his methods, even allowed John Foster Dulles, his secretary of state, to purge overseas libraries of "un-American" material. Eisenhower also, however, worked behind the scenes to undermine McCarthy and the more extreme forms of anticommunism.[4]

By the mid-1950s, the intensity of the Red Scare had begun to dissipate. The end of the Korean War, the death of Stalin, the election of a Republican president, and the televised Army-McCarthy hearings combined to weaken the anticommunist hysteria of the early 1950s. The cause did not disappear entirely, however. Politicians continued to find it useful to imply that their opponents were "pink around the edges" well into the 1960s.

While government officials concentrated on communism's political ramifications, many anticommunist crusaders were more concerned about its impact on their organizations, institutions, and way of life. In particular, true believers worried that Reds had already infiltrated community groups, influenced education, and undermined the free enterprise system.[5] In his best-selling book *Masters of Deceit*, J. Edgar Hoover encouraged Americans to be vigilant in searching out communists in everyday life. "Concealed communists are found in all fields," he explained. Because "they are difficult to identify," he warned, they "can operate freely" anywhere. He included frightening scenarios of a professor lecturing to his class or study group, all the while "subtly engender[ing them] with communist doctrine."[6] Businessmen took the opportunity to caution the American public about accepting unionism at face value. Seizing the moment, businesses launched an extensive propaganda campaign to teach employees and the community at large about the value of capitalism. For example, in the early 1950s the American Economic Foundation and the National Association of Manufacturers launched a major campaign in public schools. Modifying programs originally designed for employees, the groups taught high schoolers "How Our Business System Operates" and "How We Live in America." In this way, businesses emphasized the connection between economic and political freedom.[7]

These educational programs were necessary, according to anticommunists, because Americans just did not seem to "get it." Frustrated by what they perceived as the public's ignorance of the continuing dangers of communism, they spent much time and effort trying to counteract the apathy. In Wisconsin, for example, anticommunists staged a much-publicized mock communist takeover of a town to show what would happen without proper vigilance. On both national and local levels, people organized parades, marches, and informational "schools" to rally public support for their cause. Anticommunists promoted vigilance by investigating local officials, church leaders, and librarians. They believed that even the slightest leftist tint could eventually bleed over until it had turned the whole community Red.[8]

For women anticommunists, domestic subversion posed a special challenge. Since they were supposed to worry about threats to the home and family, women assumed they should be involved in the hunt for spies and fellow travelers. Female anticommunists particularly saw threats to the local community as deserving their attention. Most male anticommunists agreed as long as women continued to frame their concerns in a feminine way. Men assumed that women anticommunists would be happy and satisfied doing the mundane and necessary work of fighting their domestic enemies. Most activists assumed a man would serve as a spokesperson and even the leader of a mixed-gender group.

Women did not hesitate, however, to voice their sometimes very strong opinions on the subject. Mrs. M. Conan, an inveterate newsletter writer, put the matter bluntly. "America," she wrote in 1947, "is overrun with Russian spies." She warned that while the president had knowingly appointed men with "Communistic leanings to most responsible positions," his secretary of the treasury was handing currency plates to the Soviets. Democrats remained the focus of many anticommunist women who believed Republicans tended to be more aware of the sneaky nature of communists and their fellow travelers. Doloris Bridges resented Democrats who, she said, claimed to be anticommunists while they harbored all sorts of radical leftists. She cautioned her audiences not to be deceived by the mere appearance of anticommunism; communists, she implied, were not above infiltrating a good American anticommunist group and trying to destroy it from within. Slightly less than two years later, in another newsletter, a different, unnamed author went a step further. She warned that the entire two-party system had been undermined. Republicans, she stated, had become "dominated by the same evil forces" as the Democrats.[9]

Anticommunist women continued to voice concerns about communism throughout the 1950s even as others lost interest in the cause. Trying to shame men into action, members of the American Woman's Party announced that "women have been forced to take the lead, in self-defense, after waiting for some group of men to act" against the Red threat within America. Their phrasing both reinforced the existing stereotype that men should be in charge and justified their breaking those limits. If the men would not take care of the situation, the women had no choice but to take over the fight. Similarly, *New Mexico Women Speak*, a privately published newsletter, warned that "AMERICA IS DOOMED UNLESS AMERICAN PEOPLE WAKE UP!" The editors admitted that discussing communism had come to "be regarded as a sort of treason to a peace-loving community." Nevertheless, they believed it was imperative for all citizens to arm themselves with knowledge of the reality of the situation. Doloris Bridges took the issue a step further, stating that "subversive activities" had "engendered" the "growing lack of respect for those in authority." "Diminishing the stature of Congress" as well as respect for American political institutions, she informed the Keene Woman's Club in 1956, was a "favorite tool of the subversives." If Americans did not prove vigilant, she implied, communists could easily undermine the American way of life.[10]

Many of these women feared it was already too late: communism-socialism had gained the foothold it needed to destroy America. The

Minute Women certainly believed this was true. They stated in one newsletter that Americans had "advanced so far down the road to Socialism" that they did not see how we could "reverse our course." Finding the American practice of sending foreign aid to anticommunist crusaders abroad while letting communism "take root in our own country" hypocritical and foolish, the women warned that "the future looks dark." Florence Dean Post, in a review of fellow anticommunist Jo Hindman's book *Terrible 1313*, echoed those sentiments. Tracing the pattern back to the Wilson administration, Hindman warned that Americans had already been pushed far down the road toward collectivism. Hindman postulated that communists had sneakily fought to undermine political institutions from the federal level down through local governments.[11]

Who was to blame for this mess? Hindman divided responsibility evenly among all branches of the government. Executives of the American Woman's Party accused politicians in general of "blundering into socialism." Doloris Bridges criticized both the Supreme Court and Congress for playing a role in weakening the fight against communism at home. She acknowledged that Americans had learned to accept increased government regulation because of the "threat of totalitarian Communism." In a commencement address to students at New England College, she warned that unless Americans "plan[ned] skillfully," they would "plan freedom into the ash can." Helen Payson Corson, a dedicated writer of letters to the editor and political information officer of Eastern Montgomery County [Pennsylvania] Republican Women, also found fault with congressional leaders who failed to see the danger in incremental losses of freedom. She argued that everyone had to protect their rights.[12] These activist women challenged the American public, particularly women, to get involved and elect "persons of honesty and high integrity" to office. They believed this was the only way to keep creeping socialism at bay.[13]

In fact, one of the most consistent refrains among anticommunist women (besides "communism is evil") was their encouragement of women to join their crusade. All women, anticommunists emphasized, needed to take action immediately; it was their responsibility to get involved. The Minute Women claimed that "it" (communist takeover) could "happen here" if Americans were too "smug." The current level of resistance, they admonished, was "too little and many times too late." "Wake up, women of America" they warned before offering the hope that "there may still be time, but none to spare!"

Doloris Bridges echoed this concern as she told her female audiences that they should "be constantly on guard" lest they allow themselves to be duped by enemies abroad or at home. Warning that there was "a constant subversive movement in this country," Bridges encouraged the women she spoke with to "keep informed" about world events. Members of the American Woman's Party (AWP), generally more vitriolic, repeated the mantra. Without immediate intervention by right-minded women, Americans risked "blundering into socialism." Refusing to "give up what we prize the most," members of AWP invited all women to join them in the quest to protect the "freedom, liberty and independence of these United States."[14]

Some female anticommunists blamed men for the danger in which Americans found themselves. As mentioned, AWP writers explained that women had taken the lead because they were tired of waiting for men to act. "The blunders of politicians," they wrote, had led to the current state of affairs, adding that "stupidity is no excuse." The AWP asked men to "work with us" if they wanted their rights "as free men" returned to them. In frustration, Elizabeth Churchill Brown sometimes agreed with the AWP. As she struggled to fight communist influences throughout the United States, she was astounded by how "INEFICIENT [sic] some of the business men's groups are." She wrote one of her favorite correspondents that "many of the rich men are so utterly stupid when it comes to politics and the Communist conspiracy." Brown spread her scorn around. A few years later, she wrote the same woman complaining about "our armed forces men" who were not "junta minded" enough for her.[15]

Although the AWP and others implied that women must take up the slack from delinquent men, other female anticommunists argued that women had a duty to join the crusade against communism no matter what the circumstances. Congresswoman Bolton explained that "just being a woman [was] a responsibility" that necessitated involvement in the larger society. The editors of *New Mexico Women Speak* chided all women, who, they claimed, had "more time on their hands today than ever before," for squandering this opportunity. "Are you doing something constructive for America?" they wondered. (Obviously, they assumed their readers were middle-class housewives rather than poor or working women who did not have the luxury of excess time.) Margaret Chase Smith told members of the American Woman's Association that women were vitally important to the body politic. Unfortunately, she added, three major barriers discouraged women from being politically active: "(1) underestimation and lack of realization of their latent power, (2) indifference to public life because of their admirable, understandable and traditional roles of homemakers, and (3) the opposition of men to women in public offices." Women had to overcome these obstacles to protect the American way of life. During this dangerous time, women as well as men needed to be vigilant in protecting their beloved communities from destruction.[16]

Taking their cue from earlier generations of activists, anticommunists found that one way to overcome the barriers Smith listed was to incorporate women's role as homemaker into their call to participation. Earlier in the century, Jane Addams and other Progressive-era women reformers had argued that the male world of politics needed skills and talents only women possessed: an innate sense of morality combined with the ability to "clean things up." These women used their knowledge of domestic chores to improve the living conditions of their neighbors around settlement houses and cloaked their challenges to government officials in feminine promises of "sweeping away corruption." Both the abstract and the concrete housekeeping provided women with a nonthreatening route to political activism.[17]

Postwar anticommunists utilized both the metaphorical and the real image of housework as a way to draw women into their movement. Turning housework into a political act showed women that they could participate in the fight against communism without leaving their homes and families. For example, in an article written for *Ladies Home Journal*, Margaret Chase Smith asked women if they were "willing to get out [their] political broom and sweep clean?" Another activist, Leona Scannell, suggested that women lend a "hand to clean up this mess." The Federal Civil Defense Administration (FCDA) encouraged women to dust their homes as a way to protect their families from the dangers of fallout.[18] In all three instances, the boring, everyday chores of keeping house became invested with a greater significance. Sweeping, dusting, and general cleaning were transformed into political activities that would safeguard families from more than germs. Anticommunists used metaphors they knew women would understand and to which women could relate. At the same time, they implied subtle comparisons with the image of communist women who supposedly did not keep clean houses or do their own housework. Perhaps most important, the activists encouraged women to participate in their political activity, all the while reinforcing the stereotype of woman as housewife.

The best example of this glorification of housework can be seen in the actions of the FCDA. Created after World War II by the Truman administration, the FCDA was determined to turn the family into the frontline of defense against the communist menace. Many of the plans the FCDA made revolved around the housewife. She was the protector of the home; she was the one who stocked the pantry; she kept the house free of dirt, germs, and clutter; most important, she was the emotional center of the family, the spiritual leader. She would prove vital in helping individuals, the family, and the community survive a nuclear attack. To that end, FCDA officials worked hard to promote what historian Laura McEnaney called "atomic housewifery" through pamphlets, lectures, and magazine articles. According to this message, cleaning clutter would prepare the home for immediate evacuation, while dusting would free the home of possible radiation. Stocking the pantry and creating pleasant menus ensured that family members would thrive even if they had to live in a bomb shelter for a few days.[19]

Recognizing that he needed the cooperation of women, the president appointed a woman, Katherine Howard, to head the FCDA's women's division and enlisted the aid of the General Federation of Women's Clubs (GFWC). Government officials got more than they bargained for, however, as FCDA planners tried to turn theory into reality. Clubwomen, having read the propaganda and heard the speeches of Howard and others, assumed that they should be involved in planning the next stages of development of a civil defense plan. When FCDA administrators appeared to ignore them, club presidents organized their memberships into letter-writing brigades, putting enough pressure on the administration to force a meeting. The FCDA and its parent organization, the National Security Resources Board, appointed a woman to serve as a liaison to the clubs and called a general information meeting to inform them of their actions and plans. According to McEnaney, this was not what the clubwomen wanted, and they demanded more input into FCDA policies. When that did not happen, they met on their own to devise their own recommendations. They refused, in McEnaney's words, to allow "themselves and their contributions [to be] marginalized."[20]

Similarly, anticommunist leaders emphasized the importance of the housewives' economic role, both as a means of fighting socialistic influences and as an indication of their power within their homes. Everyone, the anticommunists seemed to assume, knew the housewife's most important role was managing the household budget.

Her abilities could make or break a family. Senator Smith, among numerous others, applauded this skill and challenged the government to follow the housewife's example. In her *Ladies Home Journal* article, Smith explained that "it would be wonderful if the budget of the Government could more nearly resemble the housewife's strict household budget." Her comment put complicated economic matters in terms almost every woman could understand.[21] Smith also implied that even a simple housewife had the requisite knowledge to protest action taken by the government.

Similarly, activists used women's role as mothers to draw them into political participation. Just as those on the Left brought their children to peace rallies or exploited a grieving mother's pain to build support for their cause, anticommunists played on the guilt and sympathy of mothers to entice women into their movement.[22] Anticommunists argued that mothers were the foundation of a strong America. Several organizations created pamphlets purporting to speak for the children. One, produced by "Democrat and Republican Women United for MacArthur for President," featured a somber mother cradling her child under the words "Our Country Needs Its Mother." Another took this tactic further. The Maryland Chapter of the Minute Women of the U.S.A. sponsored a pamphlet titled "What Kind of Country Are You Leaving Us?" Written in the voice of a child, the text chastised readers for not doing more to preserve America. "We are smart enough," the imaginary children chided, "to see what you are doing to the country in which we must grow up and support our family." The pamphlet ended by asking, "aren't you ashamed!" The obvious solution was to get involved in the fight.[23]

Anticommunist activists proudly boasted of mothers who had already taken the plunge. New York state representative Katharine St. George applauded the wives and mothers working to fight "the enemies at home and abroad." At the same time, she encouraged them to continue to "explain to those in your immediate circles" the severity of the situation. "You are the ones," she challenged them, "who can do so much to influence" your families and friends to stand up for America in its time of trouble.[24]

Further reinforcing mothers' centrality to the cause, activists linked mothers' "failures" to the weakening of the community and the spread of communism. In particular, they looked to working mothers as a group vulnerable to the Red influence. The Minute Women editorialized that "of course, they [communists and fellow travelers] want us [women] to go to work so they can take over the indoctrination of our children—making them into one-worlders and zombies." Even if children were not fully converted to communism, the absence of their working mothers would weaken society by encouraging juvenile delinquency. Frances Bolton saw the problem as much more insidious. Working mothers constituted only part of the problem. She felt there was too much emphasis on material goods and getting everything done quickly. Women had gotten away from the old ways, such as breastfeeding, and this had led to feeblemindedness and other forms of mental illness—weaknesses that made people vulnerable to communist influence.[25]

Mothers who lacked knowledge of the evils of communism were a particular concern for activists. They represented at least two problem areas. First, as Doloris Bridges put it, "how much respect would children have for an uninformed, inactive mother?" In the battle for children's souls, the mother must lead the charge. If she failed to earn the respect of her own offspring, how could she hope to protect them from the dangers lurking behind communist propaganda? Second, women uneducated in the ways of communism were susceptible to Red lies. Especially during periods of hostility, mothers without facts might fall for a communist ploy as exemplified by the poem "To the Mothers of America." According to the conservative newsletter *Freedom Facts*, the poem, published during the Korean conflict by the "communist press," played on maternal fears with lines such as "O from whose living breast he fed, Look! Your only son is dead!" Obviously, according to anticommunists, the communists hoped the mothers of America would be so upset that they would demand an immediate cease-fire, allowing the forces of evil to win. Anticommunists hoped that by exposing the subliminal message behind the sentiment, they could protect American women from falling victim to the ploy.[26]

In their use of the images of housewife and mother, activists worked to convince women that they had not just the duty but also the necessary skills to participate in the crusade against communism. A woman who thought of herself as "only a housewife" might be reluctant to join the struggle, arguing that she lacked the time or the ability to do anything of value. Anticommunists would counter that she possessed two powerful weapons that required little time away from her family. The first was her pen. As earlier generations of conservative women activists had found, letter writing gave women committed to remaining in the domestic sphere a means of contributing their ideas and support to various causes. Women's organizations hammered home the importance of this tool. In a 1953 newsletter, the Minute Women leadership scolded any member who was not "writing at least two letters a week for the principles you believe in." They had little tolerance for "citizens who believe in our form of government and want to keep it, but expect someone else to speak out for them." Another women's newsletter echoed the sentiments: "MRS. AMERICA . . . WHAT IS YOUR OPINION? Write, wire, Your Voice in Congress MUST BE HEARD!"[27]

Elizabeth Churchill Brown was one activist who not only practiced letter writing but worked to convince other women of its value. Liz Brown wrote to everyone, from local and national politicians to world leaders to housewives, seeking advice on how to become active in the anticommunist cause. Recognizing that she risked "being labeled as a 'letter writing mama,' " she forged ahead anyway, offering her mostly unsolicited advice and opinions on national and international issues.[28] She wrote the publisher of Scripps-Howard Newspapers a "disagreeable" (her term) letter to ask him if it was his papers' policy "to ridicule anyone attempting to expose the Communist conspiracy and defend their country." She used her typewriter to lecture numerous congressmen and senators on their shortcomings in regard to the anticommunist cause. For example, she chastised John Marshall Butler for his actions following the 1950 Maryland campaign. Throughout 1963 and 1964, as Barry Goldwater prepared to run as the Republican presidential nominee, Liz wrote him at least six times, giving him advice on how to approach his campaign. Goldwater answered her letters personally, despite the fact that she told him not to take the time to write while he was in the midst of the campaign.[29]

Although Goldwater answered Brown's letters, he never followed any of her suggestions or even acknowledged their validity. Other correspondents ignored her no matter how many times she wrote. No doubt, Brown irritated many people with her letters, but most, after all, were politicians who had to keep their constituents happy. But their attitude toward her was different than the one they displayed toward other constituents. Butler did not have to see her; he could have ignored her or written a standard reply. Goldwater did not have to answer her mail personally. Obviously, these men felt they owed her some level of respect. Whatever the reason, many of Brown's correspondents tolerated and humored her in a paternalistic manner. What was most apparent, however, was the limited amount of influence she and her letters actually had on their political decisions and actions.[30]

In her article "Women's Place Is Under the Dome," which appeared in *Human Events* in 1958, Liz urged women to educate themselves about the " 'great game of politics' which must be played in the Capital," to learn about the issues before Congress, and, most important, to write letters. Supremely confident that letters could affect policy makers, Liz encouraged women to organize their groups around this enterprise. By asking their representatives for information and sending back their own views, the women's club members and legislators' offices would learn about one another. Eventually, the "members of Congress will come to have a real respect for the work and the opinions of the club as a whole, to say nothing of its influence back home." She prodded women to push their involvement further by personally lobbying legislators to vote the conservative line. Challenging them, Liz announced that it was "up to the women of America" to defeat the "men in the Kremlin." "*Now*" [italics hers], she demanded, was "the time for all good women to come to the aid of their country."[31]

The women of the country seemed to respond. So many readers wrote to *Human Events* offering to subsidize distribution of the article to women's organizations that the editors published a public notice about the costs and the efforts. Editor Frank Hanighen had orders for 6,000 reprints the first week; less than a month later, the number had climbed to 21,000. Other organizations and news journals took notice and asked Liz to do similar or follow-up features. Liz gloried in her success. She accepted speaking engagements and started thinking about founding her own group to channel the energy she had unleashed. Most important from her perspective, she believed all this support was "a good sign" for the future of the conservative movement because, as she wrote a friend, "I truly believe that on them [women] rests the hope of the world."[32]

The second weapon women could wield without much effort was their vote. Voting correctly, activists argued, was the most obvious and easiest way for women to work against communism. Margaret Chase Smith informed readers of *Ladies Home Journal* that "failing to vote" was "un-American" because it indicated a "refusal to fight for and protect the American way of life, the American home and the American family." Both the GFWC and the Minute Women emphasized the importance of voting. Following the 1952 elections, Minute Women president Dorothy Frankton wrote her constituents, praising them for what they had accomplished during the campaign. She cautioned them, however, not to rest on their laurels. Having elected men whom they believed understood the dangers of communism, Minute Women now needed to "redouble" their efforts to make sure the new officials did their jobs. "Alert, patriotic women can be a determining force in the future of America if they will but take the time to make their wishes known," she wrote. The vitriolic American Woman's Party stated the notion more bluntly: "Men have ruled for 2000 years and will surely now give the American women a chance. . . . We will do well to let this just and kind power have full sway in this crucial hour when it is so desperately needed."[33]

Leaders of women's organizations were not the only ones to recognize the potential power of the female electorate. During the 1950s and 1960s, journalists, politicians, and activists frequently pointed out that women constituted a large voting bloc that could potentially control the outcome of an election. One ad claimed that "from 1948 to 1956, the number of women who exercised their right to vote increased by almost 40%." In 1960, a *Time* author stated that women formed "the largest single element in the American electorate." In 1966, while running for Congress, Doloris Bridges pointed out that 52 percent of all eligible voters were women. Female politicians and leaders often used such statistics to show women that they could make a difference. To encourage clubwomen, housewives, and mothers to exercise their franchise, activists pulled out the numbers to prove their point.[34] They also took their voting responsibilities very seriously. Texas women, for example, garnered praise from their governor for their "untiring efforts" in helping turn out a record number of Texas voters in the 1952 election.[35]

In addition to voting, women also felt more welcomed by the political parties. As discussed in Chapter 2, shifting economic and demographic circumstances following World War II created a large number of middle-class housewives with time on their hands.[36] The Republican Party especially benefited from this female infiltration. According to historian Jo Freeman, "[P]artisan differences in class, education, and religion created a much bigger pool of women available to the Republican party than to the Democrats." The traditionally working-class nature of the Democratic Party meant there were fewer Democratic women with the leisure time, educational background, and cultural impetus to volunteer for the party. As a result of their larger numbers, Republican women tended to be more organized and therefore more successful at getting other Republican women to the polls. This helped the party on election day and continually replenished the supply of new volunteers.[37]

The crusade against communism both helped to sustain and benefited from this pool of Republican women. Although most Americans professed to be anticommunists, the most zealous opponents of leftist ideas called the GOP their home. Moreover, because the danger from communism seemed so great, everyone, including those previously excused from political activities, was now expected to join the fray. This meant women could and should participate more fully in all aspects of party functions, since, to Republicans' way of thinking, that would guarantee more soldiers for the fight. Activist anticommunist women thus found themselves appreciated and encouraged by their Republican colleagues. In addition, women dedicated to the crusade against communism welcomed the abilities and experience of Republican women volunteers who did not need to be educated about their right to participate in the political system. The relationship between the Republican Party and activist anticommunist women proved to be something of a vicious circle, with one spurring the other on to further action.

The increasing number of women involved in the political system encouraged female activists to believe it was time for women to take the ultimate step and run for office themselves. Representative Frances Bolton, one of only seven women who held a national office, told the audience at the Women's Patriotic Conference on National Defense that women around the world were beginning to force their way into government. "Where," she wondered, "are you all?" "Very much embarrassed" to learn about the greater number of female representatives in various European governments, Bolton challenged American women to "take the responsibility of tomorrow's world." Bolton's colleague, Margaret Chase Smith, agreed that women needed to get involved, but she advised taking things slowly. She cautioned that women's progress into the political realm required "unlimited courage and patient perseverance" on the part of female challengers. "It is true of any work or profession outside the home," she explained, "that woman must be at least twice as good as a man in actual performance to get anywhere."[38] She believed women were up to the challenge, but she wanted them to know what they were up against.

Smith understood firsthand the challenges confronting women trying to break into national politics. Following her husband's death in 1940, she decided to run for his congressional seat. In fact, because of the timing, Margaret ended up having to run in three elections in her first year in office. First, she had to win a special election to fill her husband's vacant term; a month later she had to run in the Republican primary for election to her own term; two months after that she faced her Democratic opponent in the general election.[39] Eight years later, increasingly frustrated with her inability to advance in the House power structure, Smith took the unprecedented step of running for the Senate. No woman had ever won election to the Senate in her own right without first having been appointed to succeed her husband. Nevertheless, Smith became the first woman to win election in 1948.[40]

During her Senate years, as the Cold War raged around the world, Smith struggled to establish herself as a moderate but firm anticommunist. She could not, however, escape the prevailing gender stereotypes. In 1950, when Smith issued her Declaration of Conscience, she insisted that it attacked McCarthy's tactics and not the principle of anticommunism. Her explanations fell on deaf ears. The speech earned her the enmity of more rabid right-wingers and allowed her political enemies to use her gender against her. For example, Elizabeth Churchill Brown, using conventional male rhetoric, wrote an article in *The American Mercury* that mocked Smith's supposed tendency to have her "feelings hurt" too easily. As one of her biographers pointed out, Smith's colleagues even attributed their inability to pigeonhole her ideologically to her gender. Everyone knew it was a woman's prerogative to change her mind, after all. Following her own principles rather than the party line, Smith frustrated old-line conservatives with her willingness to support social welfare programs, while her dedication to large defense budgets worried liberals.[41]

Smith was not the only woman candidate who struggled against gender stereotypes during the Cold War. Styles Bridges's death in 1961 presented his wife, Doloris, with a unique opportunity. Doloris clearly wanted, and to a certain extent expected, New Hampshire governor Wesley Powell to appoint her to fill Styles's vacant seat.[42] When Powell appointed someone else, she decided to run against the new appointee in the upcoming election.[43] Bridges spent much of her time convincing people with contradictory notions that she deserved the job because she had the right experience and that they should vote for her because she was Styles's widow. Combining her own employment in government service with her years with Styles, Doloris claimed to have twenty-five years' experience in Washington. Moreover, as Bridges's wife, Doloris carried "his respected name, which opens doors to those who can help our State and Nation." Many people acknowledged that Doloris "had been the Senator's closest confidante during most of his Washington career," making her claims that she knew what he would or would not have done seem justified. Reporters pointed out that she was "considered politically astute."[44]

She was astute enough to associate herself continually with her husband's name, record, and philosophy. In fact, Doloris's platform closely resembled many of Styles's views. Echoing Styles's assertion that the fight against communism constituted a "third world war," Doloris warned her constituents that America faced "the greatest challenge in its history—a fight with godless communism." In dramatic tones, Doloris again attacked John F. Kennedy's anticommunist stance. "This is your money, not his private fortune," she told audiences, complaining that the United Nations was doling the money out to countries that had "consistently voted against us." Moreover, the money was also going—"hold your breath, girls," she warned—"to Cuba!"[45]

Bridges's gender also proved problematic for some of her constituents and colleagues. Although many people seemed to agree in principle with one supporter who believed the "women of New Hampshire" constituted the "solid backbone of the Republican Party," they frequently had a difficult time adjusting to the reality of a woman running for office. They could not seem to get away from traditional stereotypes about women. Some newspaper editorials conceded that Bridges was "the most attractive of the candidates" but found her qualifications for the Senate "grossly" inadequate. Other reporters could not escape the image of women candidates strictly as wives. Columnist Drew Pearson's article "The Influence of Women in U.S. Politics" characterized the women he mentioned as spoilers who threatened the power of several influential politicians. Marriage, he seemed to conclude, is the only way "women [should] influence politics and presidents."[46]

Newspaper publisher William Loeb, Bridges's most fervent backer, seemed also to have a difficult time dealing with her gender. Early in the campaign he wrote to Margaret Chase Smith asking for advice. He explained to the senator that he had never had "the occasion to help a woman candidate for the Senate." Smith did help in a limited way. She met privately with Bridges and offered "suggestions and advice" for dealing with her situation. Loeb, however, could not forget that Bridges was a woman, commenting at various times that she should "trim her claws" or "keep her chemise on," comments he obviously would not have made about a man. He also worried about her appearance, advising her to be "a little more dowdy" so as not to appear threatening to other women or sexually enticing to men. Declaring that the shorter skirts women were wearing were "ugly," he warned Bridges that they were too distracting to men, who would think of her as "Legs Bridges," something that "certainly wouldn't help the campaign!" Still, he recognized that Bridges's feminine charms could be an asset, especially when she spoke to important men who "liked women."[47]

When Doloris did not win her election, she did not give up on politics. Instead, she went on the offensive, demanding a recount of votes and charging her opponent with improper election practices.[48] In 1966 she again ran for the Republican nomination to the Senate. Interestingly, in stark contrast to her 1962 campaign, this time she consciously used her gender. At a time when many middle- and upper-class white women were beginning to consider themselves oppressed, Bridges cited oppression of women in attacking her enemies. In the same year a group of liberal women created the National Organization for Women, Doloris attacked Lyndon Johnson's Democratic administration for its "callous disregard for women." Her willingness to shift with the times did not accomplish her goal. She still lost the nomination.[49]

What is perhaps most interesting about these anticommunist women was not that they faced considerable problems running for office during the Cold War but that they kept trying. Although they recognized that they faced an uphill battle, they believed in their abilities and their right to do what they felt needed to be done. Phyllis Schlafly, another unsuccessful office seeker, explained it well in a letter to publisher Henry Regnery: "I apologize for the long delay, but I am sure you understand that I was busy trying to save the Republican Party." These women felt compelled to enter political races to save their party and their country from what they perceived to be imminent danger. They understood the odds but willingly faced them anyway.[50]

Whereas some women such as Smith, Bridges, and Schlafly braved the national political scene, practical issues inspired others to get involved. In particular, economic concerns motivated many. Mrs. Warren J. Le Vangin wrote to the editors of *Newsweek* in response to an article on Margaret Chase Smith, commending them for presenting her "intelligent and common-sensed opinion." Smith was "an ex-house-wife," who understood how frustrated women were with paying "more for items (from potatoes to sheets) than these items are worth."[51] From landlords to farmers to housewives, women across America complained about the state of the economy. The Minute Women listed the desire for "economy and efficiency in government" as one of their basic principles.[52] Many Republican women spoke in general of the need for fair taxes (or no taxes), protection of free enterprise, and limitations on the rights of unions. They saw a direct connection between what they perceived to be increased socialism in government and poor performance in the economy. Thus, any economic problems they experienced could be blamed on communist forces.

Rather than discuss the economy in general, many newsletters and speechwriters focused on specific examples appropriate to their audiences. Mrs. M. Conan declared President Truman "most inhuman" for his willingness to continue rent control. Giving the normal pattern of criticism an unusual twist, Conan portrayed landlords affected by Truman's policies as orphans and widows.[53] Later in the year, her attention shifted to even more sinister plots. Since, she explained, the Soviets were "preparing for war," Americans needed to stop "stripping" the country by destroying food and to increase production to stockpile food in preparation for the coming invasion. She had particularly harsh words for the "grower-hogs" who "would rather destroy their stuff than sell for lower prices." Obviously, in her worldview, farmers were not part of the victimized class of landowners.[54]

Interestingly, government intervention in local and family matters also bothered successful chicken farmer Christiana Uhl, producer of *The Farmer's Voice,* a newsletter she ran as a "hobby." Determined to discover what was "happening to our FREEDOMS which God gave us," Uhl used her newsletter to discuss agricultural legislation, taxes, profit margins, and the price of farm products. She was particularly concerned about the increased regulation farmers faced. She saw this as part of a larger problem involving government waste of taxpayers' money. In fact, she frequently published stories designed to show the evils of government taxation. In November 1958, she reported the actions of women in response to the government's seizure of a farmer's tractors for his failure to comply with government policy. The women "held up a bed sheet with lettering done with lip stick reading 'This is Communism in Action.' " Justifying the women's protest, she explained that "Social Security and the Wheat law are both Marxist laws which do not belong in a Christian Civilization."[55]

In another story, Uhl implied that government agencies were under the influence of foreign powers and specifically threatened women. Titling the story "Six Men Try to Scare Women," Uhl described Social Security officials, "some apparently foreigners," who had threatened to jail an Amish farmer for failure to pay a sixty-seven-dollar debt. According to the account, the "snarling" men "became angry and milled around the house most of the day" until they "way-laid" the farmer and grabbed his horse. These stories frightened readers by purporting to show evidence that communism had made inroads into the U.S. government. The incidents described showed readers that the threat from communism-socialism was not just an abstract ideological-political question for intellectuals and politicians; it was a danger to their very livelihood.[56]

More than just farmers needed to be afraid, according to these anticommunist women. Doloris Bridges told a newspaper reporter that housewives were struggling to make ends meet. "Respectable, proud, working Americans" could not afford the "fantastic food prices," she explained; meat had become a luxury in which they could not indulge. Why was this happening? The U.S. government, according to Bridges, had become more concerned about the welfare of the rest of the world than with that of its own citizens. She argued that dedicated Americans deserved to be "the first consideration." Helen Corson also indicted the government for the economic problems Americans faced. She broadened the scope of the danger, however, by showing upper-middle-class professionals how they were affected. In a speech to the Conshohocken Rotary Club, she blamed inflation and taxes for taking money out of the pockets of hardworking Americans. "Extravagances and waste in Federal Government" intensified the situation. Both women implied that the real culprit in the economic difficulties regular Americans faced was the leftward swing of government policy. A return to "true American principles," always vaguely defined, would solve the problems.[57]

Warnings about the economic situation continued through the 1960s. Doloris Bridges, in her 1966 Senate campaign, explained that "the government may not have to worry about balancing its budget, but housewives do. . . . They know bread and butter costs are getting out of hand."[58] Taking advantage of the periods of recession and inflation that undermined the overall prosperity of those years, anticommunist women hammered away at their audiences' worries, always connecting the problems with leftist policies. This proved an effective strategy for a number of reasons. Speaking to people who had experienced the Great Depression, the women found an audience easily incited by threats of an impending economic crisis. In addition, the focus on monetary issues made their arguments appealing to women across the socioeconomic spectrum. Both working-class and suburban women worried about the stability of their living situations; middle-class women wanted to "keep up with the Joneses," and working-class women desired middle-class status. Poor women, who desperately needed economic assistance, were beyond the scope of the anticommunists' concern. In addition, many of the activists were fiscal conservatives who disliked the New Deal and resented Eisenhower's continuation of its policies throughout the 1950s.

Finally, speaking of issues such as grocery shopping and household budgeting made the anticommunists' argument more accessible, especially to female audiences. Women who might otherwise not have cared about communism or creeping socialism paid attention to discussions of their economic future. A worldwide international conspiracy probably interested them less than their own struggle to maintain a household. If someone had an explanation for why this seemed so much harder than it had been for earlier generations, some women felt they should listen. The home was their domain.

The trick for politicians was to turn that worry and frustration into action. Smith, Bridges, and members of the American Woman's Party expected and hoped women would put their practical wisdom to use for the good of the country. As Smith repeatedly told audiences, "[T]here has been too little of the *home* in the Government and too much *government* in the home" (italics hers). The way to fix the problem was for women to become more actively involved in politics. The leaders of the American Woman's Party agreed. Men, they wrote into their platform, would "profit by woman's acceptance of her political responsibilities."[59] Again, the argument worked two ways. Inciting women to political action based on their experience with household budgeting did more than gather votes for those politicians; it also reinforced the idea that women could and should get involved in politics without abdicating their positions as wives and mothers. Everyone, it seemed, would be well served.

Businessmen of America, who also recognized the power women held over the purse strings, vigorously supported this plan. In the

1950s world, men earned the money and women spent it. Since many purchases revolved around the family and the home, most men and women saw this consumer role as an extension of housewifely duties. An advertisement for S&H Green Stamps explained that "[l]ike every other American woman [your wife] is constantly on the alert for any idea, product or service that will improve her family's well-being." The ad further stated that a woman's "interest in good government [was] a reflection of her concern for her family." Being a good consumer, then, meant that women made their families' lives more comfortable while also protecting them from the evils of the world. J. Warren Kinsman, a manager for DuPont, bluntly told his female audience that they were "managers of destiny . . . perfectly positioned to fight socialism." They could do this by teaching their children "the values of individualism and of personal freedom." They could teach these lessons even as they shopped. Once again, the housewife's importance as both home manager and political activist was intertwined.[60]

In addition to fears about communist influence on the economy, anticommunist women were particularly worried that the U.S. public education system provided an opening for communism to seize hold of the United States. They believed young children's minds were vulnerable to communist lies and manipulation. Youngsters must be protected from anything or anyone who might confuse them and make them question the American way of life. Many conservatives feared the schools' growing influence on their children. They looked nostalgically back to the days of "the little red schoolhouse" without seeing the limitations of that era. Ignoring the class and racial biases of those "golden days" (most of which continued to exist), they talked of the importance of parental control over their children. They feared that a publicly funded and controlled education system would indoctrinate their children with "progressive" ideas, which parents did not like. Conservatives feared sex education would be in and school prayer would be out. Communists and progressives, anticommunists warned, could use classroom time to undermine American principles by turning children into little socialist automatons.[61]

As a result, anticommunists attacked public education from numerous angles. Starting at the top, some anticommunists scrutinized school board members to ascertain their loyalty to U.S. principles. In cities such as Houston, Texas, school board elections turned into bitter battles over "creeping socialism," since the board made crucial financial decisions that determined the tenor of the entire school system. In

1952, the election of four school board members almost eclipsed the presidential election in generating voter interest. Although complicated by other factors such as the division of power within the school administration and pressure from local business leaders who wanted to retain their influence over the board, Red Scare issues dominated the campaign. Conservatives accused liberals of allowing "progressive educational" ideas into the schools and contaminating Houston children with anti-American rhetoric. They also worried that liberals welcomed federal monies, and thus federal interference, in what conservatives believed should be local educational policy. Liberals pointed out the dangers of blind loyalty and overzealous patriotism, all the while trying to defend their reputations and protect the school's curriculum from too much censorship. In the end, the people of Houston elected two conservatives and two liberals to the vacant seats. As historian Don Carleton explained in his book on the subject, the results indicated that Houston's grassroots population seemed less affected by the Red Scare than did the power elite who manipulated it to their benefit.[62]

The following year tensions escalated as anticommunists, with the Minute Women in the lead, succeeded in ousting Deputy School Superintendent George Ebey. Ebey proved the perfect target for anticommunists in Houston. A graduate of Columbia University's Teachers' College, Ebey was, in anticommunists' view, therefore connected to the "progressive education" taught there. A New Deal Democrat, he had supported Roosevelt throughout the 1930s. A believer in racial equality, he had insisted that the California chapter of the American Veterans' Committee, which he chaired, sponsor a "racial and religious cooperation week" and lobby for an end to discrimination in public housing. Ebey's background set off countless alarm bells among anticommunist Houstonians, including the Minute Women. He appeared to represent everything they hated in the postwar world, everything they believed threatened their way of life. He would teach, they feared, liberal, communistic ideas to their children and force good white children to go to school with black youngsters. Furthermore, he was an outsider, from New York and California of all places, who would not understand the Texas way of doing things. From their perspective, he had to be eliminated.

Working with other right-wing forces in Houston, the Minute Women investigated Ebey's career before he moved to Texas and scrutinized his every action once he settled in the Lone Star State. Not surprisingly, since they were willing to accept innuendo and hearsay as truth, they found what they were looking for. Ebey did believe in racial integration in the schools (although he never promoted that idea in Houston), he did try to introduce new ideas into the school system, and he had been a New Deal Democrat. The Minute Women grabbed their pens and mounted an intensive letter-writing campaign to newspaper editors, legislators, and, especially, school board members. When the board met to vote on Ebey's contract renewal, the Minute Women were there en masse ready to clap or boo as warranted. Under intense pressure, the board decided not to renew Ebey's contract. With considerable help from the Minute Women, Red Scare forces succeeded in running an able administrator out of town.[63]

Even as the Red Scare ebbed and Americans appeared less consumed by threats of the communist menace, conservative anticommunist men and women continued their crusade. For example, in 1961 a group of anticommunists in southern California organized a recall election of a school board trustee they found objectionable. The trouble had begun when the man in question invited a member of the American Civil Liberties Union (ACLU) to speak in his backyard. Recognizing that the ACLU did not condone the activities of many anticommunist investigations, including McCarthy's, anticommunists saw this as evidence of the trustee's own leftist ideas. Organizing a grassroots campaign, they succeeded in forcing his ouster. Women again played an essential role in this effort. They held informational meetings in their homes, went door to door with petitions, and prepared numerous handbills to distribute. Although their names did not appear in newspapers as spokespersons, their participation proved crucial.[64]

Other anticommunists turned their attention to the teachers and librarians who influenced what children heard and read. Teachers found themselves under intense scrutiny as parents and community members worried that educators might use their influence to introduce "dangerous" ideas to their pupils. For many anticommunists, any book, lecture, or curriculum that criticized the United States in any way or that portrayed the Soviets or Chinese in a positive light was subversive. Teachers who refused to kowtow to external or internal examinations of their backgrounds or classes frequently paid a steep price. In New York City alone, 400 teachers lost their jobs during the 1950s as a result of security issues. Dismissals occurred throughout the country, in areas from Philadelphia to Los Angeles. University professors as well felt the pressure to follow the American line unquestioningly or risk losing their tenure.[65]

Librarians also came under close watch. Controversy divided a quiet Pennsylvania community when a Quaker-controlled library refused to fire a librarian who had appeared before the Senate Subcommittee on Internal Security. Mary Knowles, the librarian in question, first appeared before the committee in 1953. FBI mole Herbert Philbrick identified Knowles as a party member who had been secretary of a school assumed to be associated with communism. After Knowles took the Fifth Amendment during her hearing, her current employer, the Merrill Memorial Library in Massachusetts, fired her. The library committee that operated the William Jeannes Memorial Library in Plymouth Meeting, Pennsylvania, hired her, first on a temporary and later on a permanent basis. Despite considerable controversy, the library committee refused to fire her. For its stand, the library received a $5,000 grant from the Fund for the Republic. Because of disagreements within the community, the money remained in an escrow account for years. Eventually, the Senate committee recalled Knowles; again, she refused to name names. This time they cited her for contempt of Congress, and a judge sentenced her to 120 days in jail.[66]

Throughout the controversy, anticommunist women worked actively to force her dismissal. Mrs. Philip Corson, as she signed her materials, led the way. As part of her "Citizens for Philbrick" campaign, she sent out flyers and pamphlets explaining the story again and again to the citizens of her community, as well as to interested parties around the country. She almost always emphasized that the majority of both the Quaker community, which had sponsored the library, and the larger group of non-Quakers living in the area did not support Knowles. Although she understood that the original hiring of this "5th Amendment User" had resulted from committee members' ignorance of "communist double dealing and trickery," she nevertheless believed they had been "unwittingly reckless and unmindful of the public welfare" in allowing Knowles to continue in the position. She followed a two-prong strategy to eliminate Knowles. First, she sent copies of letters, newspaper editorials, and pamphlets to a wide range of people who belonged to the conservative group Alerted Americans. She encouraged the members to read the material before passing it on to someone else.[67]

Her second line of attack involved a letter-writing campaign. Not trusting her readers to write the letters themselves, she made it easy for them. She wrote the note and left a blank place for them to sign. She even included a dotted line showing them where to detach the letter and send it off. The letters would eventually wind up in places ranging from the office of the Society of Friends in Plymouth Meeting to the attorney general of the United States. When Knowles was sentenced to jail, Corson wrote to the local paper. Even though she had achieved her goal, Corson issued a warning about all the talk of "so-called 'civil liberties or rights.'" This false concern, she explained, was "secretly directed" by the communists "with the deliberate intention of creating dissension and strife" among Americans.[68]

If anticommunists were worried about librarians and teachers, it followed that they would also investigate the reading material available to young people and their elders. Recognizing the potential of the written word to challenge people's perspective, many anticommunists rid libraries of any book that did not follow their narrow view of acceptable material. As one activist put it, "Books ARE to be feared! They have caused revolutions in both past and recent history."[69] Books promoting communism and socialism obviously came under attack. Anticommunists wanted to expunge from libraries anything written by someone they suspected of leftist leanings as well as books that encouraged questioning of American policy or challenged the "grand narrative" of U.S. history. Novels and monographs that cast Christianity in a bad light were also declared off-limits. Book banners scanned libraries across the country and throughout the world. Joe McCarthy held hearings to investigate the Overseas Library Program and sent two of his most trusted aides to examine the contents of American-sponsored libraries in Europe. Roy Cohn and David Schine visited libraries and searched for objectionable books, which McCarthy then pressured the State Department to remove from the shelves. Across the country, other would-be investigators followed his example.[70]

In Marin County, California, a housewife led a crusade to rid the local school of books she and other anticommunists found objectionable. Discovering that the book list circulated by English teachers at Drake High School contained some authors she found suspicious, Anne Smart sprang into action. She began by more closely examining the list. She found twenty-four authors who had been named by state or federal agencies as communists or members of communist-front organizations. To analyze the situation further, she visited the school library to see if she could check out the books. In the process, she randomly pulled off the shelves other books that shocked her further.

She went "looking for anti-government material" and found "filth and immorality." Because she believed it would be a waste of time to contact the school board directly, she made her accusations public in a letter to the local newspaper. When the school board still did not act, she contacted the local district attorney who presented the matter to the Marin County grand jury. The jury did not act on the case to her satisfaction, so she decided "that a little public noise might be helpful." Consequently, she sent copies of her own newsletter, the *Leader Sheet*, to over 200 community leaders.[71]

Smart's strategy worked, although she was not completely satisfied with the result. The grand jury heard the case and issued a report. The Special School Committee of the grand jury accepted that most of the books on Smart's list had little scholastic value and "were definitely placed in our school libraries to plant seeds of communism in the minds of our children." Although Smart found the committee's agreement with her gratifying, the recommendation to "kick the responsibility upstairs" frustrated her. The jury decided that the blame for the situation rested beyond the school board at the state level, where the reading lists for all the schools were decided. The school trustees further infuriated her by allowing some of the books to remain on the list. She was determined, however, to continue the fight. She felt it was her responsibility to make the elected officials do their jobs and prevent communism from taking hold.[72]

Several years later she was still searching for the source of the list. She remained chagrined that her "hard earned tax money" was being spent so that children could have "the privilege of reading filthy obscene books." She wanted to "teach our boys and girls . . . what our American culture is all about and then present the best in foreign culture." Smart and others like her across the country saw no good coming from denigrating anything about America. Doing so, in their view, would only open the door to seeds of doubt and then to communism.[73]

Finally, some anticommunists looked on a broader level at national organizations and the media, which they felt led parents and children astray. Distrusting outsiders in general, anticommunist activists feared the national boards of even such homey institutions as the PTA had been subverted by communistic ideas. Numerous newsletters throughout the 1950s and early 1960s warned parents of the dangers hidden in the bulletins and directives issued by the PTA's National Congress. One appalled parent argued that some of the material distributed by the

PTA would turn readers into "suitable citizen[s] for atheistic Communism's world government." Another activist called the PTA information kits "Brainwash Study groups" and applauded her community's ability to ignore the "[r]ules laid down by the National Congress." Others charged that the national PTA officers' "unorthodox and high-handed management . . . Socialist orientation in domestic and foreign affairs, and the hypocrisy of hiding PTA's political motives under the caption 'child welfare'" threatened to ruin the entire organization.[74]

To counter this threat, anticommunist leaders encouraged parents, and members of the community in general, to become more actively involved in their schools. Bella Dodd, a "truly reformed communist," according to Helen Corson of Alerted Americans, warned members of the Barren Hill, Pennsylvania, PTA that "Communists have infiltrated education at all levels." The solution, she told the parents, was to rely more on "local common sense than on advice from the top." In other words, parents had to be responsible for their children's education and guard against insidious influences even in the classroom. The Minute Women agreed. In their national newsletter they reprinted an article by John Crippen, praising his town's success in avoiding struggles with the school board. He explained that the parents "met frequently with our educators"; thus, all were of the same mind-set. He announced that "the National Education Association and many of its departments stand indicted in the court of public opinion." He implied that only the efforts of individuals acting within their communities could stall the spread of socialism.[75] Audrey Plowden, a contributor to *The Spirit*, also agreed. She encouraged parents to "start your own educational program at home." This would "counteract or neutralize the liberal education" promulgated by the public schools and turn children into mini-anticommunist crusaders. "Consider the odds," she wrote. "One teacher, 10 informed conservatives. . . . Start today to turn the tide through the leaders of tomorrow, our children."[76]

Worries about the state of education troubled both male and female anticommunists. Both genders participated in efforts to retain control of their children's education and to keep progressive and communistic ideas away from the schools. Sometimes men organized and led the crusades; sometimes women did. Women played a crucial role in the education struggles in Houston, Los Angeles, and other areas. Their strength could be measured by the level of fear they aroused. In both cities, conservative groups succeeded in unseating school officials accused of having leftist ties. These victories galvanized activists to make further attacks on teachers, newspapers, and local politicians. No one in Houston or Los Angeles doubted that these women had power. Similarly, no one seemed to doubt that they had any right to be involved in this issue.

Obviously, then, female anticommunists actively participated in the battle against the encroachment of communism at home. Believing wholeheartedly in the cause, they searched for any evidence that communists might be making headway in undermining the American way of life. They appeared not to recognize any areas as off-limits to their investigation. Like their male colleagues, they looked for Red influences in politics, economics, education, entertainment, and the arts. They might have deferred to men as spokespersons or leaders, but they also assumed that their own actions played an important role in protecting their homes and families.

Male anticommunists seemed to appreciate women's efforts for the cause. They welcomed female help in letter writing, organizing petitions, hosting fund-raisers and educational meetings, showing up at protests and demonstrations, and performing clerical duties. They sometimes condescendingly acknowledged that women's participation was essential to keep the communists away. Usually, they praised women's actions but described the women themselves as housewives or household managers or mothers. In some ways, they appeared to treat women as one more tool to be used in the crusade against communism.

What neither the men nor the women seemed to see was that women's actions shaped the way anticommunism was perceived by the general public. Through their newsletters, club memberships, rallies, and letter drives, anticommunist women succeeded in educating and then mobilizing large numbers of previously inactive citizens. Their persistence transformed suburban housewives into political operatives. They might have willingly deferred to male politicians on occasion, but in their everyday activities women made the key decisions. Club presidents and advisory boards decided on speakers and projects; individual women mounted campaigns and led letter drives to remove individuals they found suspicious. They might have appeared to accept the domestic ideal, but their actions redefined it at every turn.

In encouraging women to join their political effort, activist women utilized anticommunist rhetoric to explain many of the social challenges of the day. It was far easier for many middle-class white

Americans to think of the emerging Civil Rights Movement in terms of communist subversion than to acknowledge the persistence of racism. The ramifications of middle-class women choosing to work to increase their families' consumption of material goods appeared too frightening and far-reaching for a society that professed to hold to an ideal of female domesticity. It was better to blame the communists for seducing women into the workforce. Fearful of an education system that might invite students to challenge the existing value structure, Americans saw the Red menace rather than intellectual enlightenment. Conservative Republicans in particular found this strategy useful in their quest to gain political power. Democrats and even moderate Republicans, they argued, were, perhaps unconsciously, allowing communistic-socialistic influences to transform the U.S. government from its Christian, democratic roots into a sinister clone of the Soviet Union. Obviously, right-wingers emphasized, these fellow travelers must be stopped.

Using anticommunism to further a broader right-wing agenda proved an effective tool for conservative anticommunist women. Since the American public saw communism as a great evil, they accepted women's participation in the fight to stop it. If, then, communism posed not just a political challenge but a social one as well, this expanded the area of women's political involvement. Women could become more embedded in the political system in ways that seemed "normal" to the vast majority of the public. Additionally, women's efforts helped expose the U.S. electorate to the goals and rhetoric of the broader conservative movement. Women became key players in the evolution of the Right.

CHAPTER FIVE

"MANLY MEN AND THE LITTLE WOMAN"

GENDER AND ANTICOMMUNISM

Gendered images underlay much anticommunist rhetoric, reinforcing the idealized social structure advocated by conservatives and providing potent language for attacking their opposition. A strong man supporting and protecting his family and the little woman contentedly caring for her children and home represented a social order most Americans found desirable. Anticommunists, however, imbued those images with political meaning. In their scenario, the happy family members symbolized perfection of the American way of life and proved the superiority of democratic, capitalistic, Christian Americans over the communistic, totalitarian, atheistic Soviets and Chinese. At the same time that they reflected all that was good about America, they also served as a bulwark protecting Americans from the evil in the world. As a result, these images not only had to be recognized as the ideal, but they had to be reinforced continually to preserve the American system. If any part of these safeguards weakened, anticommunists warned, the communists would have an opening through which to poison the rest of America.

Gendered images could also serve as an effective method of attacking anticommunists' domestic political opponents. Although Democrats also utilized gendered symbols to undercut their enemies, conservative Republican anticommunists perfected the art. For these right-wingers, gendered language was a natural by-product of their political ideology. Traditionalist conservatives had always emphasized the importance of a stable family in which women were submissive to their husbands, free enterprise advocates desired a limited federal government that stayed out of local affairs and family matters, and anticommunists warned that free love instead of marriage would follow a communist takeover of society. Consequently, anticommunist activists moved easily from using gendered imagery and language in their battle against communism to utilizing the same tactics against their Democratic adversaries.

The shifting realities of the postwar world provided anticommunists with fertile ground to plant the seeds of their concerns. Various historians have pointed out that the trauma of the Depression and World War II undermined traditional familial and gender relationships, creating anxiety as people adjusted to their new roles. At war's end, a tremendous desire to reverse the changes of the previous decades encouraged an emphasis on domesticity among both men and women. Not surprisingly, although men and women worked hard to maintain the illusion that they were living up to these domestic images, they violated the rules at every turn. Many men found their new jobs boring and resented the pressure to conform. Women, even middle-class women, joined the workforce or occupied themselves outside the home with volunteer work.[1]

The apparent sexualization of U.S. society further upset the middle class. Suddenly, it seemed sex was everywhere: in the movies (Marilyn Monroe's sex kitten characters), in books (*Peyton Place*, for example), in music (Elvis Presley's gyrating hips). And it was not just "normal" sex. The government's attempt to purge gays and lesbians from holding office had the unintended consequence of causing people to talk about homosexuality in the open. Alfred Kinsey's reports on human sexuality, published in 1948 (*Sexual Behavior in the Human Male*) and 1953 (*Sexual Behavior in the Human Female*), exposed the truth that

Americans were sexually active and adventurous. Refusing to accept the reality of a transformed social order, many people emphasized the importance of the heterosexual, nuclear family. A lack of conformity to that ideal, anticommunists warned, could lead to all sorts of problematic behaviors, including experimenting with radical ideas.[2]

Confusing the situation further, some experts argued that too much domesticity could also be bad. In particular, some "authorities" followed the lead of Philip Wylie, who in his book *Generation of Vipers* blamed society's problems on what he termed "momism." Although the book was originally published in the early 1940s, the shifting gender roles of the postwar years gave Wylie's theories new validity. Wylie and his cohorts argued that mothers were smothering their sons, raising boys to be weak physically and mentally. This would explain why there were so many homosexuals and why American men seemed so weak and willing to conform. In anticommunists' view this constituted a real danger, since such men would easily succumb to the temptation of communism.[3]

An emphasis on the right balance of domestic ideals and social conformity, combined with the fear that both homosexuals and communists seemed to be increasing in numbers and influence, created what historian K.A. Cuordileone called a "crisis in American masculinity." The image of the rugged American male conquering the frontier single-handedly had given way to "the man in the gray flannel suit" doing the bidding of his wife and boss. Reinforcing this concern about weakening masculinity, Alfred Kinsey's *Sexual Behavior in the Human Male* reported that one in three men acknowledged having had at least one homosexual encounter. The confusion resulting from the mixed messages men (and women) received about their true role in society intensified the fear that America was under attack from all manner of perversion.[4] Anticommunists eagerly exploited this fear to build support for their struggle against communist infiltration by emphasizing that "real" men knew their place in the world and were determined to fight to preserve it.

Women continually heard the message that their place in the home was vitally important not just for their families but for all of society. Even as men challenged women to participate in the political system, they reemphasized the importance of women staying in their proper role as homemakers. The men failed to recognize that by inviting women to join the anticommunist cause, they were undermining the very vision of American life they were desperately trying to protect.

FBI director J. Edgar Hoover stressed the role women as homemakers and mothers—a very important career—should play in fighting communism. In 1956 he told attendees at the annual convention of the National Council of Catholic Women that women constituted "the basic source for pressures for peace and security" in America. He encouraged them to "make their contribution by raising their voices to preserve the American way of life."[5] Similar to the Republican Mothers of the early republic, women, some men argued, could best serve their country by teaching and supporting their husbands and sons.

Much of their ability to play such a role, some male anticommunists explained, resulted from the fact that women were guided by their emotions rather than their intellect. Writer and philosopher Russell Kirk stated the problem for women explicitly. Women, he wrote in *The Intelligent Women's Guide to Conservatism,* were naturally conservative in part because they knew society was "a spiritual thing, founded upon love." He hoped his book would help conservative women "defend with their minds what they already sense through their hearts." In other words, women should use their dedication to tradition, morality, and family to improve humanity as a whole. To that end, he had written his book as "simply" as he could so women could understand and use the information.[6] Once again, the image conservative anticommunists presented was one of a woman who was not as smart as a man but whose natural affinity for home and family could and should be used to work against the evil that existed in society.

Other anticommunists emphasized the threat communism posed to the important relationship among women, the home, and the American way of life. The Reverend Billy Graham warned in a 1948 sermon that communists wanted to "destroy the American home." Since "a nation is only as strong as her homes," that would spell the end of the United States. Maine senator Owen Brewster agreed that women had to do whatever was necessary to protect their homes and their way of life.[7] The authors of *Good Citizen,* a pamphlet designed to accompany the Freedom Train—a mobile exhibit of U.S. political artifacts aimed at promoting patriotism—obviously thought so. They depicted "the home as [the] cradle of Republican virtue" and placed women squarely in the middle of it. American women, the authors reassured readers, would not be tempted by such dangerous ideas as abandoning home and family for a career, as communist women had done. The housewife contentedly surrounded by the latest gadgets became a powerful symbol of America's superiority.[8]

Richard Nixon's performance in Moscow in 1959 epitomized the use of the housewife as Cold War weapon. During a debate with Nixon in a model kitchen, Soviet premier Nikita Khrushchev proclaimed the superiority of the Soviet system by comparing U.S. and Russian homes. Mocking the American claim that families could buy a new home every twenty years, Khrushchev boasted that Russians did not need to change dwellings because they constructed their homes to last: "We build for our children and grandchildren." Nixon, the anticommunist, could see no better existence for women than keeping a perfect house and pointed out the different appliances available to aid the American housewife by lessening her workload. Khrushchev, the communist, convinced that women should not be accomplices in creating successful consumer industries based on free enterprise, dismissed him with the remark, "We don't think of women in terms of capitalism. We think better of them." The rest of the argument developed along similar lines, with the two men trying to confine their competition to the family home rather than broadening it to include the nuclear arms race.[9]

Nixon continued the same theme that evening in the address that opened the first U.S. Exhibition to be held in Moscow. Hoping to capture the hearts and minds or at least the eyes of the Russian masses, as well as the votes of Americans tuning in to the broadcast, Nixon bragged about the number of U.S. families who owned their own homes, televisions, and radios. He went on and on about the amount of goods the "average American family" could buy in a year. Obviously, these facts indicated, at least to Nixon and the listening American audience, that capitalism—which provided families with such an abundance of goods—was vastly superior to communism, which did not. What the Soviet audience, much less the Soviet masses, thought about such a claim was not recorded.[10] Americans, however, clearly understood that as long as women could stay at home, caring for their families and using all the new equipment available to them, the American way of life was secure. Any change in that routine would undermine the entire structure of the country.

This image of domestic—and fully equipped—bliss contrasted sharply with the anticommunist version of life under communism. In a world under Red control, Americans would be forced to adopt a type of cooperative lifestyle that upset Americans committed to individualism. For example, in one issue of *The Spirit*, the "women's magazine men read," the editors reviewed a book by Charles Seely, who had, according to the editors, "impressive qualifications to speak to and for the Defenders of Liberty." A retired naval commander and American Legion member, Seely wrote *Russia and the Battle of Liberation* to describe the "new Russian system" in which husband and wife share the housework or have someone else do it: "Meals may be obtained from the central kitchen, or may be prepared in the family apartment, but patronage of the central kitchen is encouraged." The editors sarcastically interjected comments about the "new way of describing communal living." Even Seely's description of mothers having paid time off to nurse their infants at their jobs warranted a mocking "[t]hat's nice" from the editors.[11]

Another anticommunist newsletter reported on the Congress of American Women (CAW), a left-wing organization, and warned that it threatened to disrupt women's lives. The group noted with horror CAW's call to set up cooperative units to "'free the housewife from isolation,' [and] to set up cooperative child care committees, cooperative sewing, and canning committees on a neighborhood basis." At a time when American society treasured the image of a doting mother giving her all to her children and husband, this group activity reeked of laziness, boded ill for the children, and raised questions about what women were doing in their spare time.[12]

Anticommunists warned that communism would lure women away from their husbands, children, and domestic responsibilities and into the working world of men. A pamphlet prepared by the U.S.-backed International Confederation of Free Trade Unions explained that Soviet women were labeled "selfish," "unproductive," and lazy if they chose to stay home and care for their children.[13] Francesca Rhee, wife of President Syngman Rhee of South Korea, had one explanation for why this was the case: women had to work because all the men were in the army. Others, however, saw more devious motives. The women had chosen careers over motherhood, an idea shocking in itself. Worse, however, was the notion that the Soviet and Chinese governments forced women to assume jobs traditionally labeled "man's work." The communists deceptively called this equality and freedom for women. Catherine Caradja, an exiled Romanian princess, patiently explained to her American audience that "[t]he equality for women in a Russian controlled state is an absolute equality. . . . [T]he women . . . do not have any protection customarily reserved for the female sex by nature or by any of the gallant traditions." The Minute Women of the USA used plainer images: "Does anyone think for a minute that the Russian women under Soviet Rule want to dig ditches and work on the railroad? Could the separation from family and the indignities and hardships of communal living in Red China be by choice on the part of the women?" Obviously, the Minute Women thought they could not. Making things worse was the knowledge that the Soviets forced these women to work to increase their chances of successfully taking over the world.[14]

Communists' emphasis on working women shocked American women for a number of reasons and attracted new adherents to the anticommunist cause. The idea of women being compelled to join the workforce appalled white middle-class men and women, who cherished women's "freedom" from the world of paid labor. Anticommunists argued that although communists said they were giving women equality with men and freeing them from enslavement to their husbands, the truth was far different. Desperate for workers after the devastating losses during World War II, the Soviet government had called upon women "to fill the gap" in achieving industrial and agricultural recovery. In short, anticommunists liked to explain, "Soviet women have been freed from 'slavery' to husbands, but they have been plunged . . . into a slavery to the state." The organization of Business and Professional Women, in particular, pointed out that "this emancipation" had resulted in only a few female "minor executives." Most women laborers performed more menial and backbreaking tasks such as "bricklaying, hod carrying [sic], and street sweeping."[15]

Second, anticommunists emphasized the kind of work communist women were supposedly forced to perform. They usually described women engaged in hard, physical, monotonous drudgery such as digging ditches, cleaning streets, or working in factories or on farms. In the United States, immigrants, minorities, and working-class men and women took care of these tasks. Even the possibility that middle-class white women might be thrust into the gutters to pick up trash or driven onto the assembly line was enough to give many U.S. women nightmares. In other words, it was less the notion of women working than the kinds of jobs communist women supposedly held that horrified Americans.

When all else failed, anticommunists appealed to women's vanity. If societal and economic arguments did not convince their audiences that communism was harmful for women, some anticommunists fell back on traditional gender stereotypes. One newsletter produced under the auspices of Business and Professional Women explained that the "real expose of the communist attitude toward women's equality . . . comes in the field of fashion." The authors detailed that Russian women were so busy tending their families, their jobs, and party responsibilities that they did not have time to make themselves look feminine. In fact, the party discouraged "excessive grooming," since it might take time away from women's other duties. "The result," the newsletter concluded in dismay, was "that styles are designed more to prepare women for masculine work than to make them attractive." In fact, anticommunists emphasized, communist women risked losing whatever true femininity they had left. One historian noted the way *U.S. News and World Report* described women living under Soviet rule. Moscow, the author claimed, was a "city of women—hardworking women who show few of the physical charms of women in the West. Most couples stroll together in the parks after dark, but you see many more young women [stride] along the streets purposefully, as though marching to a Communist Party meeting." Usually portrayed as ugly and mannish, communist women seemed always to be working in a dismal factory job.[16]

Having emphasized how de-feminizing communism could be, anticommunists pointed to the example of Ana Pauker, the foreign minister of Rumania and, according to *Time*'s editors, the "most powerful woman alive." The magazine's cover portrait of Pauker reinforced the masculine nature of communist women. Stout and stern, with steely eyes and a firm chin, she appeared angry, uncompromising, and cold.[17] Stories about her past spread through anticommunist circles. The most infamous rumor was that this "brazen Communist turned her husband up to the dreaded Communist secret police and laughed as she watched him put to a cruel death." Other anticommunists focused on her ambition and greed. After she gained office in Rumania, the story went, she allowed her people to starve while she indulged her own appetites. The antithesis of a maternal figure, Pauker became for anticommunists the example they needed to show how communism destroyed women and thus the family. Everything a woman was supposed to be, Pauker was not. She was cruel rather than kind, she was greedy rather than giving, and she had assumed a position of political power that was obviously beyond her abilities. Her true nature was fully exposed when the author revealed that she had "followed the Russian armies into Rumania during the second World War." After all, what kind of women were camp followers?[18]

Ironically, anticommunists could have used the reality of Pauker's life (rather than rumor and innuendo) to emphasize their vision of communism's impact on women. Pauker did have many characteristics Americans associated with masculinity. She was intelligent, fiercely loyal to her beliefs, and ambitious. She left her children in a state-run home while she pursued her party duties. Imprisoned on numerous occasions for her political work, she was shot while trying to escape. In fact, contrary to persistent rumors, she was in prison when the Soviets rounded up her husband and exterminated him. Upon learning of his supposedly "traitorous activities," she was stunned. Rather than collapse in grief and dismay, as Americans would have expected, however, Pauker took it like a man and continued working with the party that had murdered her husband. Her loyalty paid off, as she worked her way up the bureaucratic ladder until, in 1947, she became the most powerful woman in Rumania.[19] *The New York Times* called her "the intellectual leader of the Rumanian Communist party and a key strategist in the government campaign to fix Rumania's place in the Russian orbit." Like many of her comrades, however, her reign of power was short-lived. By 1952 she had been arrested, imprisoned, and ostracized. She adamantly maintained her innocence against charges of "deviationism" until her death in 1960.[20]

Thus, based on the reality of her atypically powerful position, the word of disgruntled Rumanian exiles, and the investigations of at least one congressional committee, anticommunists turned Ana Pauker into a prime example of communism's effects on women. Pauker was a mannish-looking woman who, according to American standards, seemed to display none of the "normal" feminine virtues of kindness, humility, and softness. Both an exiled general and a former princess toured the anticommunist speech circuit, continually reinforcing Pauker's image as a dangerous leader. Her party affiliation, anticommunists explained, had stripped her of whatever femininity she had once possessed and turned her into just another communist dictator.[21] For anticommunists, Pauker represented a prime example of the evils communism visited upon women: it had destroyed her womanly virtues and turned her into a ruthless communist robot.

Just as dangerous, anticommunists argued, were American women who allowed themselves to be tricked into believing Red lies. Anticommunists feared that unless women understood the dangers of communism, they could be taken in by the slick lies and seductive tones of communist manipulators. Particularly vulnerable, they believed, was the "jaded society woman . . . looking for something different." Enticed by the novelty, she had no real political and ideological motives for joining the party, and next year she would move on to something else. In the meantime, however, she would have "parted with a heap of folding money" that could be used for evil purposes.[22]

Muriel Draper was a fine example of such a case. According to the *National Republic Lettergram,* an anticommunist newsletter, this American woman, "well known in artistic circles as a pianist, a lecturer of sorts, and . . . at times . . . as a 'patron of the arts,'" had become "bored and disgruntled" when her family lost some of its money. "Suddenly deprived of opportunities for the satisfaction of ego, condemned to the 'relative barrenness of life' in the United States—shorn of her position, her importance, and significantly of her audience, artistic cliques— she turned elsewhere for an outlet—to the pro-Soviet artistic circles in New York City." The implication is clear: Draper was a weak woman, obviously without a husband or children to care for. All of her needs would have been fulfilled if she had just stayed in her proper place. Perhaps, they seemed to be saying, if she had been a real American woman, one who knew the meaning of housework, one who had a family of her own, she would not have fallen prey to the communists, who were using her for "their own shrewdly calculated, conspiratorial purposes."[23]

As with Pauker, the truth of Draper's life differed significantly from part of the anticommunists' version. She did come from money, and she and her husband were "patrons of the arts" during their years in London. That lifestyle ended abruptly, however, because of her husband's gambling and alcohol problems. Taking matters into her own hands, Draper divorced her husband and moved back to the United States. Forced to support her children, she found work as an interior designer and freelance writer. She returned to her interest in the arts as soon as she was financially able. She also became increasingly politically active. Although she never joined the Communist Party, she greatly admired the Soviet experiment during its early years. During World War II, she served as chair of the woman's division of the National Council of American-Soviet Friendship. As such, she helped organize exchanges of information on women's hygiene, child care, and maternal health. Following the war, she participated in the Women's International Democratic Federation (WIDF) meeting in 1945. Subsequently, she helped found the Congress of American Women (CAW), the American branch of WIDF. Far from the lazy, rich woman playing at politics as described by anticommunists, Draper was a serious, hardworking single mother who fought for women all over the world. Her real story, however, played less well to middle-class and working women than the version in which her work with WIDF and CAW paved the way for communism to take over America.[24]

If, according to anticommunists, communism turned women such as Pauker and Draper into manly, unfeminine women, the Red disease would also, they warned, transform their male counterparts into "girly men." In other words, men also had to meet certain gendered expectations. Prominent anticommunists such as Senator Joe McCarthy frequently characterized male communists in very feminine terms and described themselves as ultra-masculine. For example, McCarthy and his cohort accused Secretary of State Dean Acheson, a favorite target, of fighting the communists by sending them "perfumed notes in a perfumed Harvard accent." Such "powder puff diplomacy" would not begin to defeat the enemy. McCarthy explained to a Texas American Legion branch that "you can't fight Communism with a silk handkerchief, in a delicate fashion."[25] McCarthy almost always mentioned an article of Acheson's clothing whenever he talked about him. By referring to the secretary's "striped pants" or "silk handkerchief," McCarthy treated Acheson the way the media treated women.[26] (No matter how prominent the woman, the press always commented on her clothing before stating anything else.) Democratic presidential candidate Adlai Stevenson was another favorite target. Anticommunists frequently used gendered characteristics to undermine Stevenson's legitimacy with the American public. According to historian Cuordileone, conservative anticommunists mocked Stevenson's name (calling him Adelaide), his vocabulary (he used "teacup words"), and his voice (at various times they said he "trilled" or "giggled"). Such insinuations did not help Stevenson in his presidential ambitions.[27]

These gendered characterizations took on added force because anticommunists increasingly equated homosexuality with communism. The merging of homosexuality with ideological radicalism resulted from the convergence of several factors. Defined as perverted and diseased, even by professionals, homosexuals spent much of their time hiding their true identities from their families and co-workers. The public assumed this double life made them especially vulnerable to blackmail by communists looking for pawns. In addition, homosexuals' ability to blend into heterosexual society made them seem even more capable of deceit; they were already fooling most of the people in their lives. Most important, according to scholar Barbara Epstein's study of the scandal magazines of the time, Americans equated homosexuality with communism because both were "spread through seduction." Both groups played on innocence, particularly that of young men, and lured their victims into their web of perversion. Once he had tasted the forbidden nectar, a young man "lost the will to resist." Thus, both communists and homosexuals preyed on the weak and innocent to spread their message covertly throughout an unsuspecting society.[28]

Numerous groups and individuals reinforced the connection between sexual and ideological radicalism. Leading the way, the Senate issued a report in December 1950 warning of the danger of homosexual civil servants who lacked the moral backbone to stand up for American values. Others jumped on the bandwagon. According to GOP chair Guy Gabrielson, "sexual perverts . . . have infiltrated our government." Senator Kenneth Wherry of Nebraska told one journalist that homosexuals and communists were practically the same. J. Edgar Hoover characterized those who joined the Communist Party as "maladjusted" and "neurotic" seekers of sexual pleasure.[29] The Lavender Scare, the government purge of homosexuals from federal offices, succeeded in ways the Red Scare never did. Although the FBI found few actual Soviet spies, it was able to force hundreds of men out of government service on suspicion of homosexual behavior. Because these dismissals were usually listed as "security risks," it validated the anticommunists' claim that Washington was riddled with evil and that they were successfully eliminating the problem. It did not matter to them if the evil was Red or Lavender.[30] Moreover, for politicians, equating homosexuality with communism provided the added bonus of expanding their base of support. Even those uninterested in foreign policy or who refused to worry about domestic spies might be outraged at the thought of sexual "perverts" running the government.

On the surface, utilizing gendered images suited anticommunists' purposes perfectly. It allowed them to build support for their cause, to question the Democrats' motives and actions, and to set themselves up as saviors of American values. In particular, it gave anticommunist women, portraying themselves as defenders of home and family, firm ground on which to address international, national, and local affairs since few people questioned a woman's right to be involved in such matters. Nevertheless, the use of gendered language posed complications for anticommunist conservatives. Reliance on dedicated female political workers might provide political candidates and politicians with reliable, intelligent, and committed assistants while undercutting the anticommunist ideological adherence to the women's place in the domestic sphere. Female anticommunists could be particularly vulnerable to male counterparts who used gendered language to denigrate women's political positions or contributions. Finally, the political opposition, specifically individual members of the Democratic Party, could call on these gendered images to attack their conservative, anticommunist, and Republican opponents.

Three case studies demonstrate the use of gendered images and language in specific incidents relating to the anticommunist political campaign. The first concerns Joe McCarthy, his wife, Jean, and the controversy associated with the Maryland senatorial campaign in 1950; the second details Margaret Chase Smith's Declaration of Conscience and the resulting firestorm; the last revolves around a brief statement by Doloris Bridges during the 1960 presidential campaign. Each case involved an important political challenge to committed anticommunist crusaders and the use of gendered language in either the attack or the defense of the anticommunist position. In each case the individual woman became almost incidental to the creation of the properly gendered images that clearly defined the result of the battle.

Joe and Jean McCarthy epitomized the gendered images anticommunists preached. As a former boxer and Marine, McCarthy emphasized that it might take "lumberjack tactics" to rid the world of communism, and he, for one, was not afraid to use such tactics.[31] Anticommunist women helped reinforce McCarthy's provocative image. Although they sometimes mentioned his weaknesses or flaws in his approach to fighting communism, they more often described him in very flattering terms. Sometimes, the description fit the romanticized picture McCarthy's people tried to create for him. Doloris Bridges emphasized that he was a "Marine who was decorated for heroism in World War II," yet he was "soft-spoken . . . and respected by his colleagues." She could be describing most women's dream lover. Elizabeth Churchill Brown saw him in more maternal terms; he was, she wrote in an unpublished book, "as friendly and awkward as a

St. Bernard puppy." In other words, he was someone who saved the lost and was no threat to the innocent. Both women admitted that he might be a little overzealous in his quest to root out communism, but they did not believe that diminished the good work he did.[32] These characterizations, however, did nothing to disturb the 1950s order of gender relations. Whether regarded as a lover or a friendly puppy, Joe McCarthy was still very much in charge, while Bridges and Brown dutifully played supporting roles. Thus, the women around McCarthy protected his reputation as a vigorous, heterosexual male.

Interestingly, Joe needed their support. The man who freely questioned his opponents' sexuality faced gossip concerning his own. As he became more prominent, the rumors about his sexuality intensified. Journalist Drew Pearson, a bitter McCarthy foe, kept a file of accusations and names of McCarthy's supposed homosexual partners. People all over the country sent Pearson leads on alleged witnesses and incidents. Although Pearson never published the list himself, he occasionally showed it to people who would leak word to the press. At one point Hank Greenspan, another journalist and McCarthy hater, used the material to write an article for *The Las Vegas Sun*. Implying that the senator's bachelor ways were merely "window dressing," Greenspan stated outright that "Sen. Joe McCarthy has often engaged in homosexual activities."[33]

McCarthy's association with Roy Cohn and David Schine added credibility to the accusations. Cohn and Schine traveled all over Europe together, supposedly investigating U.S. embassy libraries but also generating numerous rumors about the exact nature of their relationship. Their rude behavior and extravagant bills scandalized both Europeans and Americans. The relationship between the two helped lead to the Army-McCarthy hearings. When McCarthy attacked the army for harboring communists, the military establishment countered with accusations that Cohn had requested special favors for Schine, an army private. Connecticut senator William Benton, who led a "Stop-Joe" movement in Wisconsin, wrote an associate that "these Cohn-Schine-McCarthy rumors are everywhere." McCarthy never considered dropping his association with the two, despite all the problems they caused.[34]

McCarthy and his associates did what they could to counteract the gossip and the presumed harm Joe's alleged homosexuality would do to his carefully crafted image as a powerful male senator. He pointedly referred to the "crackpots" who spread lies about him. He told the

American Society of Newspaper Editors that "the Reds, their minions and the egg-sucking phony liberals" were responsible for the personal vilification he had suffered.[35] His speeches almost always included allusions to his masculinity, especially highlighting his military experience and his brief boxing career. Friends from Wisconsin and supporters in Washington pointedly characterized Joe as a swinging bachelor who always had a pretty woman on his arm.[36]

Increasingly in the early 1950s, that pretty woman was Jean Fraser Kerr, who worked in his office. They dated off and on after they met in 1947. Although they came from different backgrounds, they shared a love of politics and a devotion to the anticommunist cause. From all indications, their relationship was stormy; both were opinionated, strong-willed, and ambitious. Stories about their pursuit of one another at various times, as well as their arguments and breakups, achieved legendary proportions around the McCarthy office. Although there were rumors that Joe saw other women, he always came back to Jean. After five years of this pattern, friends, aides, and the press wondered why the two did not marry, especially since they appeared to be in love with one another.[37] McCarthy also had compelling reasons for getting married. Aside from the obvious political benefit of having a wife, a wedding would end, once and for all, rumors of Joe's homosexuality—or at least McCarthyites hoped it would.

Jean did more than shield her husband from gossip and innuendo. Like many other anticommunist women, Jean straddled the line between political activism and being a "normal" wife and mother. Throughout her relationship with Joe, she worked as hard as he did for the cause of anticommunism. She justified her participation, however, not just in terms of the imminent danger communism posed but more immediately in terms of helping her husband. In many ways, Jean personified the anticommunist woman who broke the stereotypical rules of feminine behavior, all the while maintaining the facade of a traditional wifely role. She even used her position as McCarthy's wife to retain her place in the movement after his death. In fact, it became her second career.[38]

Jean's willingness to assume a subordinate role and to help Joe maintain the gendered image anticommunists attached to men echoed the efforts of many anticommunist women of the time and reinforced those existing stereotypes. Such "normalcy" brought comfort to people frightened by the changes around them. Her actions seemed to prove that women who participated in the anticommunist crusade were still women, despite their political activity. Just as her marriage to Joe quashed rumors of his homosexuality, so her acceptance of a behind-the-scenes role made her political work seem normal.[39]

Gender issues in McCarthy's case, however, extended beyond the nature of his sexuality. Joe seemed to prefer utilizing committed, anticommunist females as political operatives when it suited his purposes. Of course, these women should have been at home tending to the needs of their families, but, as we have seen, dedicated anticommunist women were frequently in the public sphere defending America from the threat of communism. In one instance, the 1950 Senate election in Maryland, McCarthy's use of women was particularly effective in bringing about the defeat of a perceived weak link in the fight against the communist menace. However, in the investigation of McCarthy's tactics following the election, the Senate investigators' attitude and demeanor toward these women and McCarthy's defense of them demonstrated the various ways gendered language could be utilized in pursuing a political goal.

McCarthy's interest in the 1950 Maryland senatorial campaign originated from his antipathy for Millard Tydings, the Democratic incumbent in the race. Tydings had chaired the committee that had investigated McCarthy's earliest accusations that communists had infiltrated the federal government. The committee ultimately rejected McCarthy's indictments, leading the Wisconsin senator to claim that a Democratic whitewash had taken place and revealing Tydings to be less than a staunch anticommunist. McCarthy was determined to unseat Tydings in November. Caught between the pre- and postwar worlds, Tydings faced an uphill battle for reelection. Internal divisions within the state Democratic Party, lingering resentment about a recently imposed sales tax that threatened consumers' newfound prosperity, and a "blacklash" against Tydings's typical southern white responses to civil rights legislation put him in a difficult spot that was only made worse by the continuing hostilities in Korea. Tydings's opponent in the race was the newcomer John Marshall Butler, a McCarthy protégé.[40]

Numerous women played critical roles in McCarthy's battle to assure Tydings's defeat. One of Joe's Maryland contacts, a rich Republican woman, suggested Butler as a potential, viable opponent. From there, McCarthy consulted Ruth McCormick Miller, editor of the *Washington Times-Herald*, who, through the auspices of another woman, Bertha Adkins of the Republican National Committee, introduced Butler to Jon M. Jonkel, a public relations expert. Jonkel ended up serving as Butler's campaign manager and chief speechwriter. Facilitating these arrangements was Ruth Miller. Her office served as the original meeting place for many of the participants in the plan to unseat Tydings.[41] Additionally, Miller raised considerable funds for Butler and personally contributed money during both the primary and general campaigns.[42]

Miller's most controversial efforts for the campaign were centered around the much-discussed tabloid *From the Record*. At McCarthy's request, Miller allowed her presses to be used to publish this four-page newsletter quickly and relatively cheaply. Her staff worked on it, and her future husband, Garvin Tankersley, put together the infamous composite picture that showed Tydings apparently in intimate conversation with Communist Party chief Earl Browder. Although Miller claimed to have had no direct part in composing or creating the tabloid, she was crucial to its eventual publication and distribution.[43]

Playing an even more critical role in the senator's scheme was Jean Kerr, McCarthy's administrative assistant, speechwriter, and future wife. In many ways, Jean's role in the campaign sparked the most controversy, both because of her attitude and because it tied Joe so intimately to the Butler camp. Jean, by her own admission, worked very hard for Butler's election. She provided his staff with an endless source of anti-Tydings material; she wrote a campaign biography of Butler; she carried money from McCarthy's office and facilitated raising funds from his supporters; she worked on the tabloid, perhaps even writing some of the copy; and she helped orchestrate a postcard campaign to contact voters right before the election.[44]

In addition to these more prominent women, countless others were involved in key areas of the race. Running the office with Jonkel was Catherine Van Dyke, who began as a volunteer and ended up virtually second in command at Butler headquarters. Although, like Jonkel, she had no previous political experience, she learned so quickly and so well that she received job offers both before and after election day.[45] Wilma Lee similarly volunteered and learned her job as she went along. The wife of an associate of Joe McCarthy's, Lee accepted responsibility for running the postcard campaign after her husband suggested her for the job. Her responsibilities included assembling a large number of volunteers, organizing their efforts, providing them with supplies, and gathering their finished products. Since Butler headquarters thought this was an important project, they devoted a significant amount of money and effort to it. Thus, hundreds of women participated in the Butler campaign and shared the credit for his ultimate victory.[46]

When Tydings lost the election, he complained to the Senate that McCarthy had unethically, if not illegally, caused his defeat through his unwarranted intervention in the campaign. The Senate Subcommittee on Privileges and Elections, controlled by the Democratic majority, began an investigation and called many of the key participants in the election to testify. Interestingly, the men on the subcommittee as well as McCarthy's supporters reacted to the women's participation in much the same way. Primarily and most pervasively, they ignored evidence of the women's valuable political skills and activities and acted as if they were simply employed in "typical" female roles. For example, almost all witnesses referred to Kerr and Van Dyke as secretaries, when neither had ever served in that capacity. Van Dyke could not even type.[47]

Equally enlightening were the committee's responses to the testimony of Van Dyke and Kerr. Tremendously loyal to their bosses and their cause, both women approached the committee with a certain animosity. Committee members, who as Democrats were less ideologically wedded to the gendered images held by anticommunists, nevertheless treated the women with a level of restraint, courtesy, and tolerance that facilitated their ability to hide behind the facade of traditional female behavior. For example, after opening her testimony with a rather lengthy statement, Van Dyke chided committee counsel Edward McDermott for asking questions she claimed she had already answered. He pointed out that nothing in her remarks addressed his particular point. He continued, "I do not wish to quarrel with you. Let's just visit back and forth about this matter." Furthermore, McDermott did not challenge Van Dyke when she denied allegations made by other witnesses that she had knowingly violated election laws by failing to record contributions. Rather, he merely accepted that she thought the record was "incorrect" and went on to something else.[48] Van Dyke denied involvement in the alleged crimes and challenged the committee's political authority. Nevertheless, she had stayed within accepted parameters of female behavior, and the committee responded in traditional ways. Van Dyke played the retired school marm, chiding the sheriff, and McDermott responded by shushing her. All in all, he was very gentle with her. As a male Senate staffer, he did not want to affront Van Dyke's female sensibilities with confrontational challenges when all that was necessary from a relatively unimportant female political operative was a "visit."

The committee was less tolerant of Kerr. A dedicated believer in the evils of communism in general and of Tydings in particular, Kerr used her time before the committee to mount an offense as well as a defense. She attacked Tydings's record, repeatedly insinuating that he was "pink around the edges." Questioned about the validity of the tabloid *From the Record* and the authenticity of the composite picture of Tydings and Browder, Kerr vigorously defended both. She claimed they could have shown "much more damaging" evidence of Tydings's treachery. She challenged Oklahoma senator A. S. "Mike" Monroney's description of the tabloid as a "fabrication" and argued strenuously with Missouri senator Thomas C. Hennings about the "truth" shown in the picture. She even mocked Hennings's own reelection campaign, stating that he and his opponent "pretty much complimented each other up and down the State." Hennings's frustration and dismay with her responses was obvious. When Jean argued that the tabloid could have painted a much more sinister picture, Hennings asked her who was the "sissy in this crowd who did not want the whole story [about Tydings] told"?[49] Hennings's comment both reinforced the stereotype of tough guy anticommunists and tried to strip Jean of her femininity, since she obviously was not the "sissy."[50]

From an anticommunist woman's perspective, Jean was doing what she had to do to fight evil. While committee members saw a woman who did not fit their stereotypical image of females, confronting male senators as peers, Jean saw herself as continuing in her normal pattern of fighting communism. Just as the editors of the American Woman's Party newsletter and Elizabeth Churchill Brown had chided men for shirking their responsibilities, Jean chastised members of the committee for questioning her actions in the name of standing up to communism. Just as Brown and Schlafly willingly employed harsh language usually reserved for men, Jean adopted a belligerent attitude toward both Tydings and the committee.

Her performance, however, had mangled the gendered image of anticommunist women, even publicly active female anticommunists such as Catherine Van Dyke. She was not acting like a proper lady. She argued, she fought, she mocked, she refused to back down. Perhaps most shocking, she proudly supported what the senators perceived to be unethical, if not illegal, behavior. In fact, she boldly stated that she had wanted harsher treatment of Tydings. When Hennings pushed, she pushed back. He got angry with her but did not seem to know what to do when she not would retreat from her stance or appear apologetic. Ultimately, he had met his match, and he stopped questioning her. It was left to Margaret Chase Smith, the only woman on the committee, to calm the situation by returning Jean to her proper feminine role. Reminding everyone that Jean had an injured hip and would need to be protected from the press as she left the room, Smith restored Jean's feminine vulnerability and reinforced her status as a "good little woman." Nevertheless, the senators on the committee had clearly failed either to bully Jean into submission or denigrate her responses to irrelevancy.

The committee members used Jean's involvement to tie Joe to the Butler campaign. In their final report, they stated that in participating in the Maryland race, she had "acted at his request." This statement contradicted Kerr's testimony. She had stated that she "was very, very much interested in the Maryland campaign and . . . had given the Butler headquarters research material that . . . [she] had assumed he would be using in speeches." McCarthy might have approved and encouraged her, but Kerr acted of her own volition. That fact negated one crucial piece of evidence in the war against McCarthy. It was far better to assume that Jean, both as a woman and as an assistant in Joe's office, could not and would not have acted except under his direct order.[51]

Jean's actions in the campaign, her testimony before the committee, and the reactions of both her supporters and her detractors exemplified the complexity of the situation surrounding anticommunist women. From all indications, Jean was an avid anticommunist and a willing participant in the Butler campaign. Although Joe might have instigated the involvement of those in his office, her zealousness in working for Tydings's defeat went beyond routine duty. Jean wanted to take action. As an anticommunist woman, she felt she had not only the right but also the responsibility to defeat Tydings. Her behavior before the committee reinforced this version of her actions. She was proud of what she had done to further the anticommunist cause. In the end, Jean Kerr had destroyed the stereotypical image of the female political operative and even the gendered image anticommunist women preferred in defense of America's greatest opponent of the communist menace: Joe McCarthy.

The language of male committee members reflected their basic assumptions about women. Throughout the hearings, men on both sides of the table referred to women, no matter how old or capable, as "girls." This language, while demeaning of women's role in the campaign, was not always used with political purpose, as it often reflected both colloquial usage and general stereotypes of female employees. Sometimes, this choice of nouns made the women seem less like young females and more like pieces of office equipment. McCarthy aide Don Surine dictated his statement to "the girl"; he then instructed "the girl" to make photostats of the statement, and then "the girl" got Butler's address—all this despite the fact that he proved in his later testimony that he knew the names of all the women stenographers in the office.[52] Surine appeared almost enlightened, however, compared to Jon Jonkel, the campaign manager. When questioned about the paid staff in his office, he admitted that he had trouble with the part-time stenographer's name (he could not remember the exact pronunciation or spelling of her last name). The campaign later hired a second stenographer. He could not remember her name either, so he simply called her "cupcake." Jonkel also could not figure out the responsibilities of his staff: he said Catherine Van Dyke, the woman who was his second in command, was a "taker-carer of almost anything that required any follow-through."[53] Playing down her political influence, he turned her into a glorified secretary.

In contrast, McCarthy, who had encouraged his female supporters in their actions on his behalf, employed with clear political purpose the same gendered language as his opponents to undermine the committee. McCarthy used the committee's treatment of Kerr as an excuse to go after its members. "What I resent most in this report is the reference to a *little girl* who works in my office [emphasis added]," he ranted. "There are a lot of small, evil-minded people in this town, who are trying [to] smear this girl just because she works for me." In the tradition of 1950s westerns, Joe turned himself into Gary Cooper protecting Grace Kelly from the evil gunslingers. How could anyone believe this "child," in his words, was capable of doing the things they insinuated she had done?[54]

McCarthy was probably unaware of the ideological contradictions embedded in the Tydings affair. Like many anticommunist men, Joe accepted the support of his female compatriots. He willingly allowed them—in fact, encouraged them—to do the grunt work that needed to be done to achieve what he saw as the higher purpose—defeating Tydings. In many ways, however, he treated his female associates just like Surine and Jonkel did. His "girls" were one more piece of equipment to be used in the crusade. He was clever enough to realize that he could employ the gendered language so integral to the anti-communist message to pursue his own agenda. However, it was only a small step from gendered language to actually turning Jean into the child he had portrayed as threatened by the committee. He seemed not to recognize that his words diminished her as an anticommunist crusader, at the very time she was proving to be an admirable defender of him and his cause.

The response to Margaret Chase Smith's Declaration of Conscience offers another example of the complex relationship between anticommunism and the language and image of gender. Although Smith tended to be more moderate than many of her fellow anticommunists, like most of her colleagues on the Hill she believed communism was evil and "must be rooted out." She worried that the Democratic administration was not doing enough about the problem. She explained to one constituent that she was "disturbed with the smug complacency that exists towards the growing threat of communism."[55] To counter that apparent indifference, she recommended that various steps be taken to mount an offensive against the enemy. At one point, for example, she "proposed the creation of a non-partisan commission to investigate communism in government." She also introduced legislation to outlaw the Communist Party in March 1953; opposition from the Eisenhower administration, however, killed her bill in committee. When a colleague introduced a new internal security bill, Smith helped attach and steer through the floor debate an amendment outlawing the Communist Party. Recognizing the controversial nature of such an action, Smith defended her position in letters to her constituents and through her newspaper column. "Why talk about the evils of communism," she asked, "if we are not willing to outlaw its sponsors?" The Communist Party, she argued, was not just a political party that deserved constitutional protection. It was instead an organization that sought "to overthrow our government by the use of violence and force and certainly by subversion."[56] She considered the danger very real.

Smith's dedication to anticommunism involved a brief verbal altercation with Khrushchev himself. In response to her perception of President John F. Kennedy's attempts to slow the growth of the nuclear arsenal, Smith gave a rare speech on the Senate floor castigating the Kennedy administration for downgrading the U.S. nuclear deterrent. She accused the president of doing exactly what the Soviets wanted, since the Reds could possibly win a conventional war with the United States. Questioning his courage, she condensed his move into simple terms: "In short, we have the nuclear capability, but not the nuclear credibility."[57] As reported in *Time* magazine, Nikita Khrushchev responded "shrilly' to Smith:

> Who can remain calm and indifferent to such provocative statements made in the United States senate by this woman, blinded by savage hatred toward the community of Socialist countries? . . . It is hard to believe how a woman, if she is not the devil in disguise, can make such a malicious man-hating appeal. She should understand that in the fire of nuclear war millions of people would perish, including her own children, if she has any. Even the wildest of animals, a tigress even, worries about her cubs, licks and pities them.

Time commented, "Back home in Maine, Senator Smith, a childless widow, shrugged off the blast."[58]

Smith's steadfast anticommunism did not blind her to the way some abused the issue for personal and political purposes. Concerned that investigations into anticommunist activities should be conducted as impartially and fairly as possible, she suggested that former President Herbert Hoover lead a new nonpolitical commission. She advocated letting the Constitution be the guiding principle in the investigation, lest the "American concept that a man is innocent until proven guilty" be "perverted" into its opposite.[59] In particular, she was increasingly appalled by McCarthy's behavior. Initially shocked by his accusations, she waited and waited for proof of his charges. She was disappointed that it never arrived. When his statements increased in number and his aim spread widely across the political spectrum, she waited for someone to do something to stop him. Knowing she was just a freshman senator and a woman, she felt certain that someone with more experience and power should and would challenge him. Democrats waited for the Republicans to rein him in; Republicans relished his attacks on the Truman administration and looked the other way at his abuses of his position.[60]

Smith finally decided something had to be done.[61] After consulting with a select group of senators she felt she could trust, she wrote her "Declaration of Conscience," which she read on the Senate floor on 1 June 1950. Announcing that she wanted to speak about a "serious national condition," she articulated her concern that America was headed for "national suicide and the end of everything that we Americans hold dear." She spoke, she explained, as a Republican, a woman, a senator, and an American. Chastising legislators for abusing their privileges and ignoring their responsibilities to the Constitution and the American people, she called on her colleagues to "do some soul-searching" and examine their behavior. Smith bluntly addressed what she saw as the heart of the matter.

> Those of us who shout the loudest about Americanism in making character assassinations are all too frequently those who, by our own words and acts, ignore some of the basic principles of Americanism:
>> The right to criticize;
>> The right to hold unpopular beliefs;
>> The right to protest;
>> The right to independent thought.

She worried that if people feared to "speak their minds" lest they be "politically smeared as 'Communists' or 'Fascists,'" Americans' freedom of speech would be destroyed.

She mostly blamed the Democrats for the situation. The Democratic administration had "failed pitifully to provide leadership" and thus had left Americans confused and fearful. Knowledge about cases of real spies frightened the public and left citizens with valid questions for the administration. When Truman and associates did not provide answers and seemed "complacen[t] to the threat of communism at home," Americans became suspicious and paranoid. This attitude left them vulnerable to those who would use the real danger of communism for political and personal gain. She feared the nation would "continue to suffer as long as it [was] governed by the present ineffective Democratic Administration."

The Republican Party, despite its own flaws, should, she stated, provide the necessary leadership to save America and American freedoms. Drawing on images from Civil War days, Smith called on her colleagues to reunite the country as it had in the past. She wanted a Republican victory, but not at the cost of "political integrity and intellectual honesty." There were enough real issues on which to attack the Democrats, she cautioned, without resorting to innuendo and false accusations. Resorting to smear tactics would ultimately lead to the end of the two-party system and the American way of life. "Shocked at the way Republicans and Democrats alike" had played into "the Communist design of 'confuse, divide and conquer,'" she longed to see Americans "recapture" their strength and unity. They needed, she explained, to fight the enemy, not one another.

Interestingly for a woman who rarely mentioned her gender in her role as politician, Smith directly addressed the women of America: "As a woman, I wonder how the mothers, wives, sisters, and daughters feel about the way in which members of their families have been politically mangled in Senate debate—and I use the word 'debate' advisedly." She obviously hoped to draw women into the debate by making them feel they were part of the situation. Her word choices, however, presented them as outsiders. Despite the fact that numerous women had been directly confronted by both McCarthy and other congressional investigatory bodies, she spoke only to women in their traditional role as homemakers who created a support system for men, the true political actors.

Smith's speech posed a problem for anticommunist women. Although her speech attacked communism's greatest opponent, McCarthy, there could be little doubt about Smith's own anticommunist credentials. The speech itself reinforced the importance of fighting communism. In particular, she encouraged women—as wives and mothers—to join the battle to defeat the enemy. She was doing what anticommunist women were supposed to do: take a firm stand against the spread of communistic ideas abroad and at home. If they criticized her for giving the speech, they would seem to undermine the very role they had chosen for themselves.

McCarthy, clearly the target of the speech even though his name was never mentioned, had listened in silence and left as soon as it was over. However, he soon made clear in gendered language that Smith's speech was without value. According to one Maine newspaper, he refused to comment on the "spanking" he had received from Smith. "I don't fight with women senators," he sneered. At another point he labeled Smith and her co-signers "Snow White and the Six Dwarves."[62] In typical McCarthy fashion, he said one thing but acted in an entirely different manner. His condescending and sarcastic remarks about Smith's speech were typical of his usual response to criticism. His restraint implied that her declaration was not worth commenting on and barely caused him a moment's pause. She was a woman, after all, his words implied; what do you expect? In fact, however, his revenge, taken months later, proved that he was very angry at Smith. He had her removed from his Investigations Subcommittee without the courtesy usually accorded fellow party members and senators. The GOP, responding to pressure from McCarthyites, also tinkered with her committee assignments; in essence, she was demoted and exiled to "minor" committees.[63]

Some of Smith's constituents, as well as interested parties across the country, responded to the declaration in gender-neutral language. *Newsweek* editors noted that the senator's colleagues "disapproved of her action on strategic grounds." One constituent warned that Smith's anti-McCarthy stance might force voters to retire her to a "nice warm corner next to the hearth." Others were even more blunt. "Moscow must be very proud of you," wrote constituent James H. Carroll. "No doubt," he continued, "you will be disappointed if a citation is not forthcoming from the Kremlin." An article in the *Saturday Evening Post* characterized her as part of the "Soft Underbelly of the Republican Party."[64] All these comments could as easily have been made about a male politician.

Most commentators, however, could not separate Smith's actions from her gender. Her speech, according to constituent W. M. Jeffers, had obviously been written by a "schoolmam [sic] who used too much language." How else, he seemed to imply, could she have said what she did? Carl T. Smith, another constituent, also seemed shocked that "a nice lady" like Senator Smith could be caught up in such a "dirty mess."[65] Journalist Elizabeth Churchill Brown, a friend of McCarthy's as well as a fervent anticommunist, wrote condescendingly of "the little lady from Maine" who spoke "her piece" and "delighted" anti-McCarthyites. In a book she drafted but never completed, Brown continued her scornful treatment of Smith. "No one ever knew," she wrote, "precisely how . . . or exactly why" Smith gave the speech, since she was "unquestionably anti-Communist." Referring to Smith as "Senator Maggie," Brown turned her from a duly elected federal representative into a caricature. Brown further undermined Smith's credibility by stating that she was "sensitive to attack—even sometimes anticipating an attack when none was intended." Thus, Brown described Smith as a flighty, irresponsible woman who did not deserve the respect accorded "real" senators.[66] Constituent Margaret Smith agreed with Brown. She found Senator Smith "too flighty—too gabby—too showofish [sic]" to represent Maine. Constituent Smith wondered who the senator was "trying to cover for" and thought she was "a complete flop as a senator." In a letter to *Newsweek* in response to its story on Smith, Paul Clement likewise emphasized the senator's feminine weaknesses. He accused Smith of thinking "that the business of the Republicans is to drink tea and play Pollyanna."[67]

Other critical commentators made Smith representative of all women. Viola Blumenstock, head of the Women's Republican Club of

Lancaster County, Pennsylvania, scolded the senator for "acting like a spoiled child" and, in the process, "hurting all Republican women." Because Smith reacted badly when she was feeling "dejected by what some man" had done to her, Blumenstock argued, she was making it more difficult for other women to win election to office. As Blumenstock explained, Smith was "Republican womanhood personified in Congress." In other words, Blumenstock implied, Smith should expect this kind of treatment from men and ignore it, as most women did. Clara Aiken Speer, a member of the Federated Women's Republican Clubs of Missouri, also felt Smith was setting a poor example. Claiming she had "always been an advocate of more women in government," Speer found herself "grieved that you [Smith] represent your sex, your party, your state, and your American heritage so poorly."[68]

Male co-signers of the declaration found their manhood questioned. An article in the *Saturday Evening Post* labeled the signers "sensitive" souls who were looking for something "to get mad about." The author suggested that they do something more constructive with their anger than attack McCarthy. A pro-McCarthy pamphlet took a similar approach. The author, Kenneth Colegrove, called the declaration a "curious [display] of self-righteousness" and an "act of affectation." He postulated that the male signers had acted "at the behest of a lady Senator" and would soon regret their endorsement of her speech. Further impugning their masculinity, Colegrove described the participants as "too nice-minded" to "attack the problem" as a man would.[69]

The voices in support of Smith's speech were almost as numerous as those in opposition. According to her biographer, Janann Sherman, Herman Wouk summed up the opinion of many when he wrote, "by one act of political courage, you have justified a lifetime in politics." Many others were equally enthusiastic. *The Chicago Sun-Times* wrote her into the lexicon of American heroes, comparing her courage to that of the men who fought at Lexington and Concord. Margaret Frakes, in the *Christian Century*, claimed that if Smith "had done nothing in the Senate" but give her speech, "her claim on the gratitude of the American people would be secure." Some constituents also wrote in support. Jim Glover congratulated her on saying "what a lot of people have been thinking."[70]

Like Smith's opponents, many supporters could not separate her words from her gender. *Time* titled its article about the declaration

"A Woman's Conscience" rather than "A Senator's Conscience," as Frakes had done in *Christian Century*. *Newsweek* followed the same pattern, titling its article "The Lady from Maine." In the article the author continually referred to Smith as "a woman" or "the diminutive lady" rather than as senator or simply "Smith," as might have been done in discussing a man. Moreover, the author compared her rhetoric to "a broom sweeping out a mess," further emphasizing her femininity. Both publications supported Smith's speech, but their words indicated to readers that her actions should be viewed in terms of her gender rather than her political principles. Years later, *Time* referred back to the declaration as "Maggie's most righteous indignation (and her finest hour in public life)." Even after she was nominated for president in 1964, the national newsmagazine still treated her in a condescending manner.[71]

Other supporters simply acknowledged her gender in offering congratulations. Elizabeth Cushing wrote that "women all over the United States . . . are proud of the fine record you are making in the Senate [and] . . . particularly proud of you since last Thursday when you had the courage to speak out" against McCarthyism. Taking his cue from her own characterizations in the declaration, Will Beale mentioned all her labels: woman, Republican, senator, American. He thought it was a "brave, precarious," and important speech that brought "uplift and re-encouragement" to people looking for leadership. In typical Yankee fashion, Maine resident Roland McDonald put the matter simply: "I think you are a god fearing honest woman."[72] These letters, and many others like them, mentioned her gender but did not emphasize her feminine characteristics.

Some people could not help but recognize that Senator Smith had done what no man had been willing to do. Maine constituent Jack Cottrell wrote to "congratulate" her on the declaration. He also wondered, "[W]hy do some of these things that wear trousers have to be so timid for so long?" He seemed to assume that a man should have been the one to take the principled stand. Former Roosevelt aide Harold Ickes similarly recognized that while men had "caviled and equivocated and slandered," a woman had led "the way back to the homely and decent Americanism we used to take . . . for granted." Smith's speech, he announced, "fully justified" women's participation in politics. Ickes's article, which appeared in *The New Republic*, certainly praised Smith. The need to justify women's political participation thirty years after passage of the Nineteenth Amendment, however, reinforced the fact that women were still outsiders in politics. Financier Bernard Baruch acknowledged this outright when he commented that if Smith had been a man and had made that speech, she would have been touted as the next presidential candidate.[73]

Smith's speech sparked a variety of contradictory gendered responses. On the one hand, some people, including McCarthy, used her gender as an excuse to ignore her declaration publicly. Others used gender stereotypes to undermine the significance and importance of the address. Many anticommunist women searched for a way to disagree with the speech without undermining Smith's duty, as an anticommunist woman, to act. They found the answer by concentrating on Smith as a particular kind of woman. She was weak, flighty, and too emotional. She did not have what it took to be a real anticommunist. On the other hand, men such as Connecticut senator William Benton, who had also spoken out against McCarthy, were ignored. Smith's declaration at least received a national hearing, perhaps because she was a woman, the only woman in the Senate at the time. In a sense, the popular image of women as morally superior to men also gave her a credence a man might not have had. If McCarthy was a macho fighter, Smith was a stern mother. Above all, the episode illustrates the role of gender, gendered images, and gendered language in the political language of the early Cold War era.

One last example of the relationship between gendered language and anticommunist politics involves Doloris Bridges, the wife of Senator Styles Bridges. During the 1960 presidential campaign, Doloris Bridges chastised John F. Kennedy for his stand on communism. She did not say he was a communist; in fact, she thought that was an "absurd" notion. Instead, using his record as evidence, she cited his lack of intense feeling on the subject to condemn him. Comparing him unfavorably with Republican candidate Richard Nixon, who had "distinguished himself as an outstanding anti-Communist," Bridges set out to prove that JFK was "very soft on Communism." "Even when the issue was hot," she explained, "Kennedy was absent and apparently uninterested when sound anti-Communist legislation reached the [Senate] Floor."[74] Senator Henry Jackson quickly accused Nixon of orchestrating the attack on his opponent. According to Jackson's tortured logic, Mrs. Bridges would not have made the comment without clearing it with her husband; since her husband was one of Nixon's top strategists, the accusation must really have come from the candidate himself, using his friend's wife as a decoy.

Jackson's reaction to Mrs. Bridges's speech was immediate and again reflected the difficult position in which anticommunist women found themselves. She had said nothing she and numerous other anticommunist women had not said before. She was speaking to a group of women, making a typical argument. JFK and his staff ignored the situation. Her disapproval hardly constituted a threat to JFK's candidacy.

Both Democratic national chair Senator Henry Jackson and Democratic state chair J. Murray Devine ignored Doloris and instead used the incident to indict Nixon and accuse him of weakness. Devine saw "tactics of desperation" in the speech; Styles Bridges did not dare make such "wild, reckless charges" himself, so he had his wife do it for him. Jackson was astounded that the Republicans had resorted to "hiding behind a woman's skirts to launch the most vicious underhanded attack imaginable." Neither man gave Doloris a role in the act; she was simply the unthinking mouthpiece for her husband and his colleague. Both assumed that she, merely the wife of a senator, could not possibly have made the accusation on her own. According to their way of thinking, the men were using her to do their dirty work. Since the Democrats, as gentlemen, would not dare attack a lady as they would a male political opponent, Nixon could make the accusation public without negative political consequences.[75]

Most ingeniously, the Democrats had been able to insert their own use of gendered language, so frequently associated with their anticommunist opponents, into the affair by using Bridges's statement to denigrate the GOP candidate's masculinity. Both men insinuated that Nixon was too frightened or weak to do his own fighting. The Republicans, Jackson and Devine charged, hid behind their women to win the campaign. By taking this approach, the Democrats attempted to turn Doloris Bridges's charge of softness back onto the Republicans. Ironically, some of Doloris's supporters took the same approach. Using Senator Jackson's remarks as further proof of Democrats' "softness," William Loeb of the *Manchester Union Leader* castigated the senator for "fighting with women." The "viciousness" of his statement, Loeb felt, indicated just how worried Democrats were by the truth. The way Loeb worded his editorial, however, inferred more than just agreement with Bridges's statement. Loeb seemed to imply that Jackson was less than a real man because he was attacking a woman rather than waging war against the truly dangerous enemy.[76]

An editorial in the *Washington Evening Star* took Loeb's insinuations a step further. The author offered one reason for Jackson's "irrational reasoning": he was a bachelor. Implying that most "normal" men had wives, the editor hinted that Jackson was somehow less than healthy. Perhaps, he suggested, the senator's statements might also have resulted from the "fevered imagination of a man who has no first-hand knowledge of married life." The editorial not only called Jackson's manhood into doubt but also, by implication, his dedication to the fight against communism.[77]

Thus, conservative journalists who supported Mrs. Bridges's actions employed gendered language to make their point even if that language also belittled her and women in general. The *Star* editorial assumed that everyone would know that wives cannot be controlled by their husbands; the joke was that wives, and women in general, said whatever they wanted to and men had to put up with it. Loeb, however, went beyond gender stereotypes by praising her for having the courage to expose JFK's "horrible voting record" when Nixon had been "tip-toeing" around the issue. Hinting that Nixon had been too easy on Kennedy, Loeb used Bridges's statement to attack Nixon from the Right. "The tragedy" of the campaign was that Nixon had not directly confronted JFK on what Loeb thought was the truly important issue: the presence of communism in the United States and around the world. Instead, "it remained for Mrs. Bridges to point to the [voting] record." Echoing Jackson's remarks, Loeb implied that Nixon had not been "man enough to fight his own battles."[78]

Male reactions to Bridges's statements revealed much about the gendered nature of the political system. The Democrats, represented by Jackson and Devine, fell back on the traditional relationship between men and women as well as the accepted role of women in election campaigns. Assuming she could not or would not have spoken her own mind, Jackson and Devine attributed her remarks to her husband and his associate. This assumption gave them a way to shift attention from her characterization of their candidate to the character of their political opponent. From their perspective, Nixon looked weak; he had a woman fighting his battles for him. Because this view conformed to the standard interpretation of gender characteristics—Doloris as unwitting mouthpiece—it was easy to portray and accept. Regardless of whether they actually believed Doloris was merely her husband's puppet, that image suited their purpose of undermining Nixon.

Republicans relied on traditional gender images as well in their counterattack, using the incident to their political advantage as much as possible. To that end, they also utilized accepted gender stereotypes to attack Jackson and Devine. In questioning the Democrats' masculinity and chivalry, Republicans assigned everyone traditional gender roles: real men fought only other men. Republicans could thus undercut the attack on their candidate by deflecting criticism back onto the Democrats. Conservatives like Loeb used the same strategy to prod Nixon into a more forceful stance: if a woman had bravely stated a "truth" about Kennedy, surely Nixon should be "man enough" to do so.

Both sides ignored Doloris as an active anticommunist woman. She made the decision to make the comment; she wrote and delivered the speech to a group of like-minded activist women. All of that was lost as the men with power used her efforts to their own advantage. Doloris, like Jean Kerr and numerous other anticommunist women, overlooked the insult and concentrated on the larger picture of advancing the anticommunist movement.

Jean, Margaret, Doloris, and countless other women like them across the country willingly accepted and even helped create the gendered images so important to anticommunism. Like their male counterparts, they saw them as an essential ingredient in the fight against communist forces. The image of the strong man with the helpful woman at his side reassured an American public confused and frightened by the changes around them. In the midst of a world gone mad, at least family remained the same. Referring to this ideal family was a way of encouraging others to join the anticommunist crusade and validating the importance of the fight.

For anticommunist women, however, the situation was complicated by their desire to participate actively in the movement. They believed in both the images and the cause. Much of the time, they could convince themselves and many others that no contradiction existed between the two. Their male compatriots seemed to agree. The limitations of that agreement and the shallowness of the men's respect for women's efforts quickly became apparent in the men's willingness, through their language or their actions, to undermine women as political actors if it served their political goals. Anticommunist women thus often found their work diminished and their position in the movement relegated to caricature. They accepted this because to them the movement was more important than any other consideration, but gendered images and language—however ideologically useful they might be—continued to be a two-edged sword for female anticommunists.

CONCLUSION

Anticommunism in America was a gendered affair. Those defending the American system against the menace of communist expansion understood their society to be one in which men and women had specific roles. Earning a living and running the government was the males' function. Raising families, managing households, and keeping their husbands content was the female role. Maintaining separate spheres of activity for men and women was believed to be the foundation of U.S. society and the freedoms it enjoyed, and communism directly threatened that foundation. Individuals who did not fit neatly into these gendered categories, most noticeably homosexuals, were castigated as communist sympathizers. Thus, the images and language of the anticommunist movement possessed a gendered subtext that frequently emerged in the battle in which these individuals were engaged. Nevertheless, defeating communism proved a long and arduous affair. In the course of pursing victory, the strict gender separation all true believers wanted was altered for practical reasons. Most significant, as this study has demonstrated, women began to emerge as significant contributors to the attempt to save America and its families from the communist menace, creating in the process a gendered activity uniquely suited to the women who pursued it.

When female activists appealed directly to women, they drew on a long tradition of female activism. Anticommunist women understood that sometimes even derogatory stereotypes of women could be manipulated to convince women of the importance of their participation in the cause. Journalist Elizabeth Churchill Brown explained that her book was the "result of a woman's curiosity, so often maligned by the opposit [sic] sex." Using her ignorance of foreign policy as well as her gender to her advantage, she "ask[ed] questions no intelligent man would ask." Similarly, Doloris Bridges felt women's lack of knowledge and experience in politics often made them the best warriors. As she explained, "[W]omen don't know when they are licked." Consequently, they kept on fighting and could even be downright "reckless when the fate of their loved ones is at stake." This language was echoed by grassroots activists as well. Praising Senator Margaret Chase Smith for making a "sensible speech," one constituent wondered why it had taken so long for the senator to be forthcoming about something even "a poor nitwit of a woman like me" knew. This sort of diffident language frequently undermined male critics and allowed women some voice in the debate. Of course, it also reinforced the stereotype of women as ignorant and unintelligent.[1]

For female activists, however, appealing to women as housewives and mothers provided more than just a common language with which to approach potential female converts. Talking to women about these particular concerns allowed female activists to claim a special mission of their own. Who was better equipped to convert housewives, mothers, and women in general than other housewives, mothers, and women? Frequently, female activists proudly displayed their homemaking credentials as one way of creating common ground with audiences.

In describing themselves as housewives with a mission, women with political ambitions disarmed some of their critics, built a rapport with other women, and claimed a unique role within the movement. Frequently, women like Margaret Chase Smith and Phyllis Schlafly would allow themselves to be photographed performing typical homemaking tasks. They emphasized their ability to combine work for the cause with their family responsibilities. Often, the press helped bolster this image. One reporter referred to Senator Smith as "the very picture of the American housewife up in arms." Since at the time the senator was "hammer[ing]" a fellow senator with "her implacable questions," this characterization made Smith seem less threatening and more "properly" feminine.[2]

Activist women, proudly wearing the housewife mantle, also empowered housewives in general. If Smith, Schlafly, and the others could juggle families, husbands, and political work, then other women could as well. Moreover, by emphasizing the importance of household labor, these activists transformed drudgery into something requiring skill and intelligence and deserving of respect. Margaret Chase Smith, for example, frequently suggested that a housewife would know how to run the government "on a strict budget" better than the men in Washington. While such language was intended to shame the over-spending bureaucrats, it also boosted the egos of homemakers.

Such appeals convinced women that they could have an impact on the political process, particularly at the local level. Through writing letters, attending meetings, and voicing public disapproval, women let their leaders know they were concerned and interested. In addi-tion, the number of women voting increased by 40 percent between 1948 and 1956.[3] Elected officials could ill afford to ignore these voters. From Houston to Los Angeles, groups such as the Minute Women and the General Federation of Women's Clubs succeeded in turning out record numbers of their supporters at polling places. Although women had never voted as a bloc, the fear that they would haunted male politicians. Women's potential power turned their votes into a force that could not be ignored. Moreover, as an author in *National Business Woman* argued, "on local and state issues, wives probably influence their husbands because women usually take a more active community interest."[4]

In addition, during the 1950s, political organizers increasingly turned to suburban women for help with the day-to-day operations of party machinery. The booming economy made it easy for men to find work without relying on party patronage, thus creating a need for new volunteers. Middle-class housewives had both the time and the desire to participate. As a result, men found themselves dealing with women not just as a large voting constituency but also as political allies who needed to be informed, motivated, and appreciated. This was especially true within the Republican Party, where the Federation of Republican Women's Clubs provided essential volunteers during campaign seasons.[5]

Women who did not join formal political organizations still played a role in shaping the overall movement. From the informal groups that sprang up in response to a local crisis to the newsletters printed on mimeograph machines in someone's garage, countless women participated in some aspect of the anticommunist crusade. Their actions may not have directly affected national foreign or domestic policy, but in challenging a school board decision or trying to get a librarian fired or picketing a visiting foreign leader, their efforts provided concrete examples of proper anticommunist activity for many Americans. Regardless of whether people agreed with the action, the public associated it with the broader movement. The newsletters served a similar function. For women who did not have the time or the energy to read a newspaper, newsletters provided a window to understanding what was happening in their country and their local communities. Many of the newsletters and pamphlets promoting local events were written in an informal tone, so they provided their readers with a language for translating national issues and ideological arguments into everyday concerns.

Women did not, however, limit themselves to addressing local issues or even an exclusively female public. A number contributed directly to the national debate over communism. Freda Utley, Margaret Chase Smith, and Phyllis Schlafly participated in the ongoing discussion about the meaning, purpose, and direction of anticommunism. Utley attempted to use her own experiences to teach U.S. foreign policy makers about the dangers inherent in Chinese communism and foreign policy in general. Smith took a more moderate but no less intense stance on controlling communism's impact in America. Schlafly's work in educating the public about the threat of communism succeeded in paving the way for conservative anticommunist Barry Goldwater to win the Republican presidential nomination.

All of these women, whether they were active on a national or a local level, as well as the women they encouraged to join them in their crusade, espoused an anticommunism that went beyond political or diplomatic concerns. At the heart of anticommunism for many American women was the defense of their idealized vision of the United States. In this perfect world, all Americans lived happy lives in well-equipped homes. Everyone believed in God and the flag and got along with one another. There was no racism or poverty or crime. If there were problems, they were minor flaws that the constitutional system would eventually correct. The linchpin in this entire image was the family, with Mom, Dad, and children. Anticommunists feared communism would destroy that family picture. If that happened, they worried, everything else would fall apart as well. To that end, the family must be maintained in its current form.

Anticommunist women thus found themselves making two contradictory arguments. On the one hand, many middle-class suburban women fought communism to protect their children, their families, and their way of life. That "way of life" meant women ruled the home while men ruled the world. Many women believed, as Margaret Chase Smith stated, that "the first and original governor in our democracy is the woman. Woman administers the home. . . . [T]here is not a finer role that you can play in the defense of democracy and our American way of life than that of wife, mother, and homemaker."[6] On the other hand, as many discovered, defending that way of life expanded the notion of "wife, mother, and homemaker" to include not just husbands and children but their communities and country as well. In fact, anticommunists were encouraging women to leave the very homes and families they had declared sacrosanct to get involved in political activity. In their minds, their actions were both legitimate and consistent. Because communism was so dangerous, women had to join the political fight to protect their families. Anticommunist women assumed that once the battle had been won, women would go back home willingly and eagerly.

Men as well seemed to accept this female behavior as a temporary expedient. Male anticommunists eagerly accepted the help of their female counterparts when it suited their purpose. They expected that women would perform the mundane clerical duties involved in a political campaign; they appreciated women's volunteer efforts in gathering signatures on petitions, organizing teas and fund-raisers, and getting voters to the polls. They were willing to use women when there was a job a man could not do, even if it meant risking the women's freedom or reputations. Joe McCarthy encouraged Jean and numerous other members of his staff to help defeat his political enemy. He, like many anticommunist men, even acknowledged that the women's work was valuable to the overall movement. He was equally willing, however, to ignore the work the women had done and focus instead on their role as wives, mothers, or victims of their opponents' unchivalrous behavior. Rather than equal partners working toward a common goal, men sometimes treated their female teammates as pawns to be moved at will. The men gave no indication that their dismissal of their associates' effort would cause problems or even be challenged.

Most of the time, they were correct. Women seemed not to notice boorish male behavior and to overlook the insults directed toward their efforts. The cause, they implied, was more important. If, as some women argued, men had fallen down on the job of protecting American families from communism or did not appreciate what women had accomplished, that just meant the women had more work to do. They should roll up their sleeves and get to it. After all, that was what mothers had done.

In the end, what does it all mean? Most middle-class white women did not join anticommunist clubs, write letters, give speeches, or run for offices. Most of those who did participate in some way were less extreme in their views than several of the women described in this study. Clearly, most women supported the existing gender structure and did little to challenge the authority of men. Nevertheless, although the anticommunist crusade did not drastically change women's everyday lives in terms of household responsibilities, equity issues, or power relationships, it did have an impact on the anticommunist movement and on gender relations.

In ways both subtle and obvious, the actions of anticommunist women weakened rigid stereotypes of female behavior. Although they paid homage to female domesticity, they continually encouraged women to expand their horizons beyond housekeeping and cooking. They demanded that women participate more actively in the political system. Perhaps more significant, despite their white gloves and frilly hats, these women were warriors who wanted the complete destruction of their communist opponents. These were not nice little old ladies telling everyone to calm down before someone got hurt or suggesting some kind of peaceful dialogue. No, anticommunist women disparaged compromise as a weakness and spoke of the need for their enemies to be annihilated. They might have looked like "girls," but they talked like men. Distracted by the fact that these activists looked like respectable women, most Americans missed their adoption of masculine behavior. By the time anyone noticed, it was too late to rebuild the old mold of femininity.

The traditional story of the postwar years has largely ignored anticommunist women. In picturing anticommunism solely as a male crusade, historians and contemporaries have slighted the efforts of women, misinterpreted public feelings about communism, and reinforced conventional stereotypes about women. In some ways, this is symptomatic of the larger society's failure to recognize women's contributions during this period and throughout American history. It is the same tendency that has caused historians to focus on Martin Luther King Jr. while ignoring Ella Baker, that made Cesar Chavez a household name while leaving Deloris Huerta in the dust, or that analyzed Adlai Stevenson's politics while turning Eleanor Roosevelt into a caricature. Historians have tended to focus on male actors while ignoring the women who made political movements viable operations.

In a larger sense, then, this study reinforces a historiography that challenges long-held views of postwar American women. Neither the hopeless victims of Friedan's *Feminine Mystique* nor the happy *Stepford Wives* of television sitcoms, women of the 1950s and 1960s lived complex lives that defied simplistic categories like "housewife" or "career woman." The public might have expected a leftist woman to ignore the rules; they would have been shocked to find that conservative women also acted as though limitations on their behavior did not exist.

Were these women feminists? The answer would seem to be no. As historian Kim Nielsen has pointed out, "[E]mpowered women do not necessarily feminists make." In fact, to label them as such does them a disservice by treating them as the anticommunist men of their time did. These women said they believed in the patriarchal system; they were working to support and protect it by fighting communism. To interpret other meanings from their actions would discount their own statements to the contrary; it would imply that these women did not know their own minds. Moreover, to call these conservative, anticommunist women feminist is to make "feminism" so elastic a term as to be almost meaningless. They were women acting as political agents for a conservative agenda that included the belief that a woman's first responsibility was to her family. They did not find that notion limiting, since they believed it demanded their political involvement when necessary.[7]

In the midst of a world beset by communism, conservative women believed all Americans should fight to preserve the American way of life. Significantly, anticommunist rhetoric condemned not only the actions of the Soviets and the Chinese but of anyone who threatened the stability of the rapidly changing postwar world. The U.S. public had dealt with a tremendous amount of change in the two decades prior to the end of World War II: the Depression, the New Deal, Hitler, the Holocaust, the war, the bomb, population shifts, labor unrest, and a Civil Rights Movement. The onset of hostilities with the Soviet Union and China increased the pressure on an already stressed population. Although there was legitimate fear of what the communists might do abroad, at home the anxiety became entangled with the multiplicity of other changes taking place. Frequently, it was hard to tell whether conservatives truly feared a "communist" force at work or, more broadly, the transformation of U.S. society threatened by political and social change.

Without recognizing the key role women played in the anticommunist crusade, the social and political landscape of postwar society remains obscured. Only in seeing how intimately women were involved with all aspects of anticommunism can we see the true nature of the movement and the way it was intertwined with larger concerns about the shifting American landscape. Anticommunism was a tool used by men and women to express their fears and anxieties about their changing world. The irony, of course, was that in joining the battle, women were furthering the transformation they so feared.

NOTES

INTRODUCTION

1. *Red Nightmare,* Department of Defense, Directorate for Armed Forces Information and Education, Warner Brothers Studios, 1962, distributed by National Audiovisual Center, Capitol Heights, Maryland.

2. George Nash, *The Conservative Intellectual Movement in America* (New York: Basic Books, 1976).

3. Linda K. Kerber, "The Republican Mother and the Woman Citizen: Contradictions and Choices in Revolutionary America," in *Women's America: Refocusing the Past,* 5th ed., ed. Linda K. Kerber and Jane Sherron De Hart (New York: Oxford University Press, 2000), 112–120; Mary Beth Norton, *Liberty's Daughters: The Revolutionary Experience of American Women, 1750–1800* (Boston: Little, Brown, 1980).

4. Barbara Welter, "The Cult of True Womanhood," *American Quarterly* (Summer 1966): 151–174; Jeanne Boydston, *Home and Work: Housework, Wages,*

and the Ideology of Labor in the Early Republic (New York: Oxford University Press, 1991).

5. Paula Baker, "The Domestication of Politics: Women and American Political Society, 1780–1920," *American Historical Review* 89 (June 1984): quotes on 631, 625. See also, Kathryn Kish Sklar, *Catharine Beecher; A Study in American Domesticity* (New Haven: Yale University Press, 1973); Elizabeth Jacoway, *Yankee Missionaries in the South* (Baton Rouge: Louisiana State University Press, 1980).

6. Baker, "Domestication of Politics," 644. See also, Katheryn Kish Sklar, *Florence Kelley and the Nation's Work: The Rise of Women's Political Culture, 1830–1900* (New Haven: Yale University Press, 1995); Victoria Bissell Brown, *The Education of Jane Addams* (Philadelphia: University of Pennsylvania Press, 2004); Felice D. Gordon, *After Winning: The Legacy of the New Jersey Suffragists, 1920–1947* (New Brunswick, NJ: Rutgers University Press, 1986), 20–21.

7. Karen J. Blair, *The Clubwoman as Feminist: True Womanhood Redefined, 1868–1914* (New York: Holmes & Meier, 1980), 4–5, 105–106, 114–115.

8. Elaine Tyler May, *Homeward Bound: American Families in the Cold War Era* (New York: Basic Books, 1988), 37–91. For an interesting comparison with Nazi women, see Claudia Koonz, *Mothers in the Fatherland: Women, the Family and Nazi Politics* (New York: St. Martin's, 1987), 122.

CHAPTER 1

1. For a discussion of this phenomenon, see Elaine Tyler May, *Homeward Bound: American Families in the Cold War Era* (New York: Basic Books, 1988).

2. For a quick overview of the breadth of women's activities during these years, see Joanne Meyerowitz, *Not June Cleaver: Women and Gender in Postwar America, 1945–1960* (Philadelphia: Temple University Press, 1994); Eugenia Kaledin, *Mothers and More* (Boston: Twayne, 1984).

3. For background on the relationship between the United States and Russia, see M. J. Heale, *American Anticommunism: Combating the Enemy Within, 1830–1970* (Baltimore: Johns Hopkins University Press, 1990), 3–122.

4. The complexity of the origins of the Cold War has led to a long-standing historiographical debate on the subject. Historians who blame the Soviets for the conflict are referred to as traditionalists. See, for example, William H. McNeill, *America, Britain and Russia: Their Co-operation and Conflict, 1941–1946* (New York: Oxford University Press, 1953); Herbert Feis, *Churchill-Roosevelt-Stalin: The War They Waged and the Peace They Sought* (New York: Oxford University Press, 1953). Other historians, often referred to as revisionists, emphasize the U.S. role in the hostilities. See, for example, Walter La Feber, *America, Russia and the Cold War 1945–1990*, 6th ed. (New York: McGraw-Hill, 1991); Thomas J. McCormick, *Half-Century: United States Foreign Policy in the Cold War* (Baltimore: Johns Hopkins University Press, 1989); Gabriel Kolko and Joyce Kolko, *The Limits of Power: The World and United States Foreign Policy,*

1945–1954 (New York: Harper & Row, 1972). In more recent years, a post-revisionist school has emerged. These historians recognize the role both sides played in the development of the Cold War but still cast the Soviets as the true bad guys. The best example of this type of scholarship is John Lewis Gaddis, *We Now Know: Rethinking Cold War History* (New York: Oxford University Press, 1998). The opening of Eastern European and former Soviet archives has led to more interesting debates. Much of the new evidence directly contradicts the traditionalist view. See Ronn Pineo, "Recent Cold War Studies," *The History Teacher* (November 2003): 79–86. For the Soviet side of the story, see Vladislav Zubok and Constantine Pleshakov, *Inside the Kremlin's Cold War: From Stalin to Khrushchev* (Cambridge, MA: Harvard University Press, 1996).

5. J. Edgar Hoover, *Masters of Deceit: The Story of Communism in America and How to Fight It* (New York: Henry Holt, 1958; paperback, Pocket Books, 1961), vi.

6. J. Edgar Hoover, Testimony before HUAC, 26 March 1947, in Ellen Schrecker, *The Age of McCarthyism*, 2nd ed. (New York: Bedford/St. Martin's, 2002), 127.

7. J. Edgar Hoover, "The Twin Enemies of Freedom: Crime and Communism," speech to the National Council of Catholic Women, 9 November 1956, in *Vital Speeches* (1 December 1956) 23, no. 4: 106; Hoover, *Masters of Deceit*, 8.

8. David McCullough, *Truman* (New York: Simon & Schuster, 1992), 539–549, quote on 548.

9. James F. O'Neil, "How You Can Fight Communism," *American Legion Magazine* (August 1948), 16–17, cited in Schrecker, *Age of McCarthyism*, 122–123.

10. National Security Council Paper No. 68, in *Foreign Relations of the United States 1950*, vol. 1 (Washington, D.C.: U.S. Government Printing Office, 1977), 234–312.

11. James T. Patterson, *Grand Expectations: The United States, 1945–1974* (New York: Oxford University Press, 1996), 207–242.

12. Joseph R. McCarthy, speech, 9 February 1950, Wheeling, West Virginia, reprinted in Schrecker, *Age of McCarthyism*, 238; Richard Nixon quoted in Stephen E. Ambrose, *Nixon: The Education of a Politician, 1913–1962* (New York: Simon & Schuster, 1987), 243; Hoover, *Masters of Deceit*, 310.

13. Bridges quoted in "Foreign Relations, *Time* (1 December 1952): 10.

14. Quoted in Charles C. Alexander, *Holding the Line: The Eisenhower Era, 1952–1961* (Bloomington: Indiana University Press, 1975), 289.

15. See, for example, Lewis Mumford to editor, *The New York Times,* 28 March 1954, 10.

16. Charles Grutzner, "Gain in 'Cold War' Seen by Stevenson after World Tour," *The New York Times*, 21 August 1953, 1.

17. Richard Gid Powers, *Not without Honor: The History of American Anti-communism* (New York: Free Press, 1995), 1–40.

18. Ibid., 43–116.

19. Ibid., 117–154.

20. Allen Weinstein, *Perjury: The Hiss-Chambers Case* (New York: Random House, 1978); Ronald Radosh and Joyce Milton, *The Rosenberg Rile: A Search for the Truth* (New York: Random House, 1983); Allen Weinstein and Alexander Vassiliev, *The Haunted Wood: Soviet Espionage in America—The Stalin Era* (New York: Random House, 1999).

21. For background on McCarthy, see Thomas C. Reeves, *The Life and Times of Joe McCarthy* (New York: Stein and Day, 1982); David Oshinsky, *A Conspiracy So Immense* (New York: Free Press, 1983). For a general discussion of the differences between liberal and conservative anticommunists, see Powers, *Not without Honor*, 214.

22. Arthur M. Schlesinger Jr., *The Vital Center* (Boston: Houghton Mifflin, 1949), 129.

23. Internal Security Act, 1950, Veto Message from President of the United States, 22 September 1950, in *Congressional Record*, 81st Cong. 2nd sess., 15629–32.

24. Powers, *Not without Honor*, 214.

25. A classic description of the partisan use of anticommunism can be found in Robert Griffith, *The Politics of Fear: Joseph R. McCarthy and the Senate* (Lexington: University Press of Kentucky, 1970).

26. For an overview of foreign policy during this era, see Stephen E. Ambrose, *Rise to Globalism: American Foreign Policy since 1938*, 7th rev. ed. (New York: Penguin Books, 1993), 127–189; John Lewis Gaddis, *Strategies of Containment: A Critical Appraisal of Postwar American National Security Policy* (New York: Oxford University Press, 1982), 127–273. For Eisenhower's views, see Stephen Ambrose, *Eisenhower*, vols. 1 and 2 (New York: Simon & Shuster, 1983); Robert Divine, *Eisenhower and the Cold War* (New York: Oxford University Press, 1981). For Kennedy's foreign policy, see Michael Beschloss, *The Crisis Years: Kennedy and Khrushchev, 1960–1963* (New York: Edward Burlingame Books, 1991); Herbert Parmet, *JFK: The Presidency of John F. Kennedy* (New York: Penguin Books, 1984). For Johnson and Vietnam, see George Herring, *America's Longest War* (New York: Alfred A. Knopf, 1986).

27. William H. Chafe, *The Unfinished Journey: America since World War II*, 4th ed. (New York: Oxford University Press, 1999), 112–114; Robert M. Collins, *More: The Politics of Economic Growth in Postwar America* (New York: Oxford University Press, 2000), 24; Kirkpatrick Sale, *Power Shift: The Rise of the Southern Rim and Its Challenge to the Eastern Establishment* (New York: Vintage Books, 1975), 23–33; Patterson, *Grand Expectations*, 312, 314.

28. Patterson, *Grand Expectations*, 380–406. See also, Taylor Branch, *Parting the Waters* (New York: Simon & Shuster, 1988); JoAnne Robinson, *The Montgomery Bus Boycott and the Women Who Started It* (Knoxville: University of Tennessee Press, 1987).

29. Patterson, *Grand Expectations*, 314–317, 341–342; Chafe, *Unfinished Journey*, 119.

30. Patterson, *Grand Expectations*, 71–76; Chafe, *Unfinished Journey*, 117–118.

31. Patterson, *Grand Expectations*, 321–326.

32. Ibid., 76-81; May, *Homeward Bound*, 20–27, 37–91.

33. Adlai Stevenson, "Women, Husbands and History," Commencement Address, Smith College, 6 June 1955, in Adlai Stevenson, *What I Think* (New York: Harper & Brothers, 1956), 182–189; Chafe, *Unfinished Journey*, 130; Karal Ann Marling, *As Seen on TV: The Visual Culture of Everyday Life in the 1950s* (Cambridge, MA: Harvard University Press, 1994), 217–240.

34. Betty Friedan, *The Feminine Mystique* (New York: W. W. Norton, 1963).

35. Eva Moskowitz, "It's Good to Blow Your Top: Women's Magazines and a Discourse of Discontent, 1945–1965," *Journal of Women's History* 8, no. 3 (Fall 1996): 66–98; Patterson, *Grand Expectations*, 364–365.

36. See, for example, Meyerowitz, *Not June Cleaver*.

37. Robinson, *Montgomery Bus Boycott*; Margaret Rose, "Gender and Civic Activism in Mexican American Barrios in California," in ibid., 175–200.

38. Dennis A. Deslippe, " 'We Had an Awful Time with Our Women': Iowa's United Packinghouse Workers of America, 1945–75," *Journal of Women's History* 5, no. 1 (Spring 1993): 10-32; Lisa Kannenberg, "The Impact of the Cold War on Women's Trade Union Activism: The UE Experience," *Labor History* 34 (Spring-Summer 1993): 309–323; Dorothy Sue Cobble, "Recapturing Working-Class Feminism: Union Women in the Postwar Era," in Meyerowitz, *Not June Cleaver*, 57–83.

39. Kate Weigand, *Red Feminism: American Communism and the Making of Women's Liberation* (Baltimore: Johns Hopkins University Press, 2001); Leila J. Rupp and Verta Taylor, *Survival in the Doldrums: The American Women's Rights Movement, 1945 to the 1960s* (New York: Oxford University Press, 1987); Amy Swedlow, *Women Strike for Peace: Traditional Motherhood and Radical Politics in the 1960s* (Chicago: University of Chicago Press, 1993).

40. Patterson, *Grand Expectations*, 367–369.

41. Nancy Rubin, *The New Suburban Woman: Beyond Myth and Motherhood* (New York: Coward, McCann & Geoghegan, 1982), 65.

42. Jo Freeman, *A Room at a Time: How Women Entered Party Politics* (New York: Rowman & Littlefield, 2000), 176–177.

CHAPTER 2

1. The literature examining right-wing women has been growing in recent years. For a sampling, see Jane Jerome Camhi, *Women against Women: American Anti-Suffragism, 1880–1920* (Brooklyn, NY: Carlson, 1994); Kim E. Nielsen, *Un-American Womanhood: Antiradicalism, Antifeminism and the First Red Scare* (Columbus: Ohio State University Press, 2001); June Melby Benowitz, *Days of Discontent: American Women and Right-Wing Politics, 1933–1945* (Dekalb: Northern Illinois University Press, 2002); Rebecca Klatch, *Women and the New*

Right (Philadelphia: Temple University Press, 1987), 144; Susan E. Marshall, *Splintered Sisterhood: Gender and Class in the Campaign against Woman Suffrage* (Madison: University of Wisconsin Press, 1997); Marshall, "Ladies against Women: Mobilization Dilemmas of Antifeminist Movements," *Social Problems* 32 (April 1985): 357–358 for other examples of this type of behavior. For examples from abroad, see Claudia Koonz, *Mothers in the Fatherland: Women, the Family and Nazi Politics* (New York: St. Martin's, 1987); Elizabeth Harvey, "Visions of the Volk: German Women and the Far Right from Kaiserreich to Third Reich," *Journal of Women's History* 16, no. 3 (2004): 152–167; Margaret Power, "More Than Mere Pawns: Right-Wing Women in Chile," *Journal of Women's History* 16, no. 3 (2004: 138–151; Julie V. Gottlieb, "Women and British Fascism Revisited: Gender, the Far-Right and Resistance," *Journal of Women's History* 16, no. 3 (2004): 108–123.

2. Camhi, *Women against Women*, 213.

3. George Nash, *The Conservative Intellectual Movement in America* (New York: Basic Books, 1976), 131–153.

4. Camhi, *Women against Women*, 218.

5. For a general description of women working for anticommunism, especially at the grassroots level, see Don E. Carleton, *Red Scare! Right-Wing Hysteria, Fifties Fanaticism and Their Legacy in Texas* (Austin: Texas Monthly Press, 1985), 125–134. For new works exploring conservative women's activities, see, among others, Michelle Nickerson, "Moral Mothers and Goldwater Girls," in *The Conservative Sixties*, ed. David Farber and Jeff Roche (New York: Peter Lang, 2003), 51–62; Sylvie Murray, "Suburban Citizens: Domesticity and Community Politics in Queens, New York, 1945–1960" (Ph.D. diss., Yale University, 1994); David Laurence O'Connor, "Defenders of the Faith: American Catholic Lay Organizations and Anticommunism, 1917–1975" (Ph.D. diss., State University of New York at Stony Brook, 2000); Christine Kimberly Erickson, "Conservative Women and Patriotic Maternalism: The Beginnings of a Gendered Conservative Tradition in the 1920s and 1930s" (Ph.D. diss., University of California, Santa Barbara, 1999); Lisa McGirr, *Suburban Warriors: The Origins of the New American Right* (Princeton, NJ: Princeton University Press, 2001), 81–98.

6. Kim E. Nielsen, "Doing the 'Right' Right," *Journal of Women's History* 16 (August 2004): 171; Nielsen, *Un-American Womanhood*, 63; Benowitz, *Days of Discontent*, 175–176; Catherine E. Rymph, *Republican Women: Feminism and Conservatism from Suffrage through the Rise of the New Right* (Chapel Hill: University of North Carolina Press, 2006), 125–130.

7. Nielsen, *Un-American Womanhood*, 63.

8. Rymph, *Republican Women*, 125–130.

9. McGirr, *Suburban Warriors*, 81–98.

10. Mildred White Wells, *Unity in Diversity: The History of the General Federation of Women's Clubs* (Washington, D.C.: General Federation of Women's Clubs, 1953), 21. For more information, see Karen J. Blair, *The Clubwoman as*

Feminist: True Womanhood Redefined, 1868–1914 (New York: Holmes & Meier, 1980), 93–115.

11. Paula Baker, "The Domestication of Politics: Women and American Political Society, 1780–1920," *American Historical Review* 89 (June 1984): 640; Kathryn Anderson, "Evolution of a Partisan: Emily Newell Blair and the Democratic Party, 1920–1932," in *We Have Come to Stay: American Women and Political Parties, 1880–1960,* ed. Melanie Gustafson, Kristie Miller, and Elisabeth I. Perry (Albuquerque: University of New Mexico Press, 1999), 109, 113; Eric Rauchway, "A Gentlemen's Club in a Woman's Sphere: How Dorothy Whitney Straight Created the *New Republic,*" *Journal of Women's History* 11 (Summer 1999): 61–62.

12. Blair, *Clubwoman as Feminist*, 98–104, 114.

13. Laura McEnaney, *Civil Defense Begins at Home: Militarization Meets Everyday Life in the Fifties* (Princeton, NJ: Princeton University Press, 2000), 91–93.

14. Esther M. Guilfoy, "Clubwomen Hear Talk by Mrs. Bridges," *Morning Union*, 15 January 1948; "Mrs. Styles Bridges 1947–49," Case 4, Doloris Bridges Papers, New Hampshire Records and Archives, Concord, NH [hereafter DB papers].

15. Quotations are from these editions of the newsletter, in the order listed: "Why Clubs," *Texas Clubwoman* 34, no. 3 (April 1958): 4; "Plan Your Course of Study," *Texas Clubwoman* 27, no. 14 (March 1950): 5–7; Sara A. Whitehurst, "World Cooperation," *Texas Clubwoman* 28, no. 30(1) (January 1952): 6–7; all in Texas Woman's Collection, Texas Woman's University, Denton, Texas [hereafter TWU Collection].

16. See, for example, Mrs. J. Howard Hodge, "This Is Our World," keynote address, 13 May 1951, Texas Federation of Women's Clubs Annual Convention, transcript in TWU Collection.

17. See newsletters of the Minute Women of the USA, Inc., Reel 76 M19, Right-Wing Collection, University of Iowa, Iowa City [hereafter Right-Wing Collection]. Quotations from January 1954, November 1952, and October-November 1953 editions. For general background, see Carleton, *Red Scare*, 111–125.

18. See, for example, *The Minute Women of the USA, Inc.,* newsletters, June 1957 and March 1956.

19. The best source for information on Republican women in general and the source for most of the information in this paragraph is Rymph, *Republican Women*, especially chapters 3–5.

20. Ibid., chapter 5. The observer was Elizabeth Churchill Brown. See Brown to Raissa Browder, 20 September 1954, "Browder, Earl (and Mrs.), 1954–1965," Box 1; Constantine Brown to William Knowland, 28 May 1959, "Knowland, William F. (Senator), 1959–1963," Box 2, both in Elizabeth Churchill Brown Papers, Hoover Institute on War, Revolution and Peace, Stanford University, Palo Alto, CA [hereafter ECB Papers].

21. Rymph, *Republican Women*, chapter 6.

22. Phyllis Schlafly to Henry Regnery, 29 April 1957 and 2 March 1957, in "Schlafly, Phyllis," Box 67, Henry Regnery Papers, Hoover Institute on War, Revolution and Peace, Stanford University, Palo Alto, CA [hereafter Regnery Papers].

23. See, for example, All American Conferences to Combat Communism, *Freedom's Facts* 3, no. 5 (May 1955), Reel 56 F40, Right-Wing Collection.

24. See series of letters between Mrs. Arthur Peterson and Mrs. Kathryn Rave, 1960–1961, Mss. 40, American Association of University Women–Texas, the Woman's Collection, Blagg-Huey Library, Texas Women's University, Denton, TX.

25. Alfred Kohlberg to Joe McCarthy, 29 January 1951, in "Senator Jos. R. McCarthy, 1951," Box 122, Alfred Kohlberg Papers, Hoover Institution on War, Revolution and Peace, Stanford University, Palo Alto, CA [hereafter Kohlberg Papers]; Mrs. Philip L. Corson, "Alerted Americans," January 1964, Reel 13 A73, Right-Wing Collection.

26. Isabel Kinnear Griffin, "Politics without Pulling Punches," *The Evening Gazette* [Worcester, MA], 9 June 1952, Scrapbook #1, DB Papers; Mrs. Philip L. Corson, "Alerted Americans," January 1964, Reel 13 A73, Right-Wing Collection; Florence Lyons to ECB, 6 December 1960, in "Lyons, Florence Fowler, 1960–1962," Box 2, ECB Papers.

27. All these newsletters are available through the Right-Wing Collection at the University of Iowa, Iowa City. The series is available on microfilm and is arranged alphabetically. Quotation from *New Mexico Women Speak!* 1, no. 1 (November 1955), Reel 86 N39, Right-Wing Collection.

28. Mrs. Clarence Uhl, *The Farmer's Voice* 2, no. 2 (November 1958), Reel 48 F13; *New Mexico Women Speak!* (November and December 1955), Reel 86 N39; "We Are Dedicated To," *The Spirit* (March 1964), Reel 8 A49; all in Right-Wing Collection.

29. Phyllis Schlafly is the exception to this rule. She has both extensive archives and several studies of her life. See, for example, Carol Felsenthal, *The Sweetheart of the Silent Majority: The Biography of Phyllis Schlafly* (New York: Doubleday, 1981); Donald T. Critchlow, *Phyllis Schlafly and Grassroots Conservatism* (Princeton, NJ: Princeton University Press, 2005); Critchlow, "Conservatism Reconsidered: Phyllis Schlafly and Grassroots Conservatism," in *The Conservative Sixties*, ed. David Farber and Jeff Roche (New York: Peter Lang, 2003), 108–126; Catherine E. Rymph, "Neither Neutral nor Neutralized: Phyllis Schlafly's Battle against Sexism," in *Women's America: Refocusing the Past*, 5th ed., ed. Linda K. Kerber and Jane Sherron De Hart (New York: Oxford University Press, 2000), 501–507.

30. Obviously, there could have been a number of other examples. Mary Mundt, wife of South Dakota senator Karl Mundt, had a reputation as a fervent anticommunist. Unfortunately, all of her papers were destroyed in a fire.

31. For complete biographical information, see Patricia L. Schmidt, *Margaret Chase Smith: Beyond Convention* (Orono: University of Maine Press, 1996), chapters 1–5; Patricia Ward Wallace, *Politics of Conscience: A Biography of Margaret Chase Smith* (Westport, CT: Praeger, 1995), chapters 1–2; Janann Sherman, *No Place for a Woman: A Life of Senator Margaret Chase Smith* (New Brunswick, NJ: Rutgers University Press, 2000).

32. Schmidt, *Beyond Convention*, 60–66, 68–74; Wallace, *Politics of Conscience*, 22–25.

33. Schmidt, *Beyond Convention*, 31–49, 74–75; Wallace, *Politics of Conscience*, 22–23, 31–33.

34. Schmidt, *Beyond Convention*, 86–102; Wallace, *Politics of Conscience*, 33–41.

35. Ed Walsh, "Will Mrs. McCarthy Run for Congress?" [Newark, NJ] *Star-Ledger Every Week* Magazine, 3 August 1958; *The George Washington University Annual*, 1946; Marshall Field Ad, *Daily Northwestern*, 23 April 1948; all in Joseph R. McCarthy Papers, Marquette University, Milwaukee, WI [hereafter McCarthy Papers, Marquette]; " 'Politics My Hobby,' Declares Jean Kerr," *The Evening Star* [Washington, DC], 18 September 1953, in "August–Dec 1953 McCarthy Clips," Box 3, Thomas C. Reeves Research Files [hereafter Reeves Files], Wisconsin State Historical Society, Madison, WI [hereafter WSHS].

36. Margaret Kernodle, "McCarthy to Wed Girl Who 'Stood Him Up,'" *LaCrosse Tribune*, 27 September 1953; Ruth Young Watt, Senate Historical Office, Oral History Project, 94–96, Lyndon Baines Johnson Library, Austin, TX.

37. Their relationship is discussed in greater detail in Chapter 5.

38. Thomas C. Reeves, *The Life and Times of Joe McCarthy* (New York: Stein and Day, 1982), 152–159, 417. Reeves based this biography on extensive interviews that he has donated to the Wisconsin State Historical Society. These interviews are extremely helpful to scholars, especially since some of the interviewees are deceased. See also, Jean Kerr to Wayne Hood, 30 November 1951, 3 December [1951]; Wayne Hood to Jean Kerr, 6 December 1951, all in Reel 7 microfilm, Wayne Hood Papers, WSHS [hereafter Hood Papers]; Jean Kerr to Tom Korb, 27 October 1951; Tom Korb to Jean Kerr, 29 October 1951, both in "Korb, Tom Papers," Box 2, Reeves Files.

39. Reeves, *Life and Times*, chapter 10.

40. "Brown, Elizabeth Churchill," *Who's Who of American Women*, 7th ed., 1972–1973 (Wilmette, IL: Marquis Who's Who, 1971); "Troth Announced of Miss Churchill," *The New York Times*, 13 February 1939, 18.

41. *Who's Who*; "Social Notes," *The New York Times*, 14 May 1925, 19; "Notes of Social Activities in New York and Elsewhere," *The New York Times*, 11 July 1929, 23.

42. "Elizabeth Churchill Has Bridal at Home," *The New York Times*, 10 August 1939, 21; "Changes in Firms Effective Today," *The New York Times*, 2 January 1935, 45; "Dinner Parties Given at Republican Dance," *The New York*

Times, 15 March 1940, 20; "Renting of Suites Takes on Volume," *The New York Times*, 9 September 1941, 40; *Who's Who.*

43. Elizabeth Churchill Brown, draft of "Prologue," n.d., *Joe McCarthy and Other Anti-Communists, Fragments, 8.2*, in Box 8, Speeches and Writings, ECB Papers.

44. Ibid.

45. There are no biographies of Doloris. Information about her early life has therefore been gathered from the public record and newspaper accounts. Most of the following information is from Irene Corbally Kuhn, "12 Senate Wives," *American Mercury* (August 1955): 52–58. There is one biography of her husband, Styles. See James J. Kiepper, *Styles Bridges: Yankee Senator* (Sugar Hill, NH: Phoenix, 2001).

46. Alice Kessler-Harris, *Out to Work: A History of Wage-Earning Women in the United States* (New York: Oxford University Press, 1982), 252–266; Ruth Milkman, *Gender at Work: The Dynamics of Job Segregation by Sex during World War II* (Chicago: University of Illinois Press, 1987), 28–29.

47. Kuhn, "12 Senate Wives," 54; Sara M. Evans, *Born for Liberty: A History of Women in America* (New York: Free Press, 1989), 224.

48. Kuhn, "12 Senate Wives," 54; "Mrs. Bridges Is Improved at Hospital," *Concord Monitor*, 8 October 1956, in "Misc. Clippings & Campaign Materials," Case 1, DB Papers.

49. "Politics: Lady in the Race," *Time* (19 January 1962): 22; Kuhn, "12 Senate Wives," 54; *American National Biography*, 1999 ed., s.v. "Bridges, Styles," by Gary Reichard. Reichard points out in this biography that Doloris was Bridges's third wife. He married Ella Mae Johnston when he was young and quickly divorced her. They had one child. He then married Sally Clement, and they had two children. She died ten years after their marriage. During most of his political life, Bridges acknowledged his second wife but completely ignored his first. In fact, most people believed Sally Bridges was the mother of all three of his sons.

50. Marie Smith, "Washington Now Looks Like Fun," *The Washington Post*, 14 January 1961, in "Tuesday 11 July 1961 Dinner at Mount Vernon," Case 1, DB Papers; Kuhn, "12 Senate Wives," 54.

51. Kuhn, "12 Senate Wives," 54.

52. Doloris Bridges to Elizabeth Coleman, 31 July 1953; Doloris Bridges to Mrs. Howard Thompson Ball, 20 September 1954 (source of quotation); Doloris Bridges to Robert McCook, 23 October 1957, all in large envelope, "Doloris Speaking Engagements in Mid-'50s," Box 6, DB Papers.

53. Elizabeth L. Hatch to Doloris Bridges, 2 October 1959, in large envelope, "Doloris Speaking Engagements in Mid-'50s," Box 6; Esther M. Guilfoy, "Clubwomen Hear Talk by Mrs. Bridges," *Manchester Union Leader* [morning edition], 15 January 1948, in "Mrs. Styles Bridges, 1947–49," Case 4; "Mrs. Bridges Quits Reception," *Manchester Union Leader*, 7 March 1961; Ruth Montgomery, "Never Underestimate the Power of Sen. Bridges' Pretty Wife," n.d., in "Tuesday 11 July Dinner at Mount Vernon," Case 1, all in DB Papers.

54. Critchlow, "Conservatism Reconsidered," 112–116.

55. For Schlafly's battles, see Rymph, "Neither Neutral nor Neutralized," 504–505; Rymph, *Republican Women*, chapter 6.

56. Freda Utley, *The Dream We Lost* (New York: John Day, 1940), 3; Michael Florinsky, "The Background of the Russian Fiasco and Where It Led," *The New York Times*, 6 October 1940, 95.

57. Utley, *The Dream We Lost*, 120.

58. Freda Utley, *Odyssey of a Liberal* (Washington, DC: Washington National Press, 1970), 126–127. For copies of letters sent to her son, Jon, regarding his father's arrest and execution, see A. P. Cherepkov to V. G. Krasnow, 5 February 2004, available on-line at http://fredautley.com/Berdichevsky.htm.

59. Utley, *The Dream We Lost*, 94–123, 218–275; Florinsky, "Background."

60. Freda Utley, *China at War* (New York: John Day, 1939); Utley, *Last Chance in China* (Indianapolis: Bobbs-Merrill, 1947); Utley, *The China Story* (Chicago: Henry Regnery, 1951); Utley, *The High Cost of Vengeance* (Chicago: Henry Regnery, 1949); Utley, *Will the Middle East Go West?* (Chicago: Henry Regnery, 1957); Utley, *The Dream We Lost*.

61. Utley, *Odyssey of a Liberal*, 302–311, quote on 304.

62. Ibid., 133.

CHAPTER 3

1. Robert D. Dean, *Imperial Brotherhood: Gender and the Making of Cold War Foreign Policy* (Amherst: University of Massachusetts Press, 2001), 10–36; Richard J. Barnet, *Roots of War: The Men and Institutions Behind U.S. Foreign Policy* (New York: Atheneum, 1972), 48–75.

2. Janann Sherman, *No Place for a Woman: A Life of Senator Margaret Chase Smith* (New Brunswick, NJ: Rutgers University Press, 2000), 101, 117, 127.

3. Extensive correspondence between Brown and Francesca Rhee is in Box 3, ECB Papers. Quotation from Francesca Rhee to ECB, 21 January 1960, in "Rhee, Syngman and Francesca, Correspondence with the Browns, 1960 Jan–July," Box 3, ECB Papers.

4. Joseph R. McCarthy, *America's Retreat from Victory: The Story of George Catlett Marshall* (New York: Devin-Adair, 1951), 41.

5. John F. Cronin quoted in Richard Gid Powers, *Not without Honor* (New York: Free Press, 1995), 174–175, 194–197, quote on 196.

6. For information on the China Lobby, see Michael Miles, *The Odyssey of the American Right* (New York: Oxford University Press, 1980), 94–120; ibid., 228–229; Gayle B. Montgomery and James W. Johnson, *One Step from the White House: The Rise and Fall of Senator William F. Knowland* (Berkeley: University of California Press, 1998), 90–98.

7. George Sokolsky quoted in M. J. Heale, *American Anticommunism: Combating the Enemy Within, 1830–1970* (Baltimore: Johns Hopkins University Press, 1990), 155.

8. For a full discussion of the situation, see David McCullough, *Truman* (New York: Simon & Schuster, 1992), 813–856, quote on 838.

9. Ibid., 844.

10. Powers, *Not without Honor*, 264–265; Stephen E. Ambrose, *Eisenhower*, vol. 2 (New York: Simon & Schuster, 1983), 328–334, 354–356.

11. For Eisenhower's campaign promises, see Stephen E. Ambrose, *Eisenhower*, vol. 1 (New York: Simon and Schuster, 1983), 546–548. For his willingness to meet with Soviets, see Ambrose, *Eisenhower*, vol. 2, 257–265, 535–537. For background on the John Birch Society, see Miles, *Odyssey of the American Right*, 246–250. Quote from Welch's *The Politician*, which he circulated in manuscript form in the late 1950s and privately published in the early 1960s. Here taken from Miles, *Odyssey*, 249.

12. Miles, *Odyssey*, 82.

13. Frank Holman quoted in Duane Tananbaum, *The Bricker Amendment Controversy: A Test of Eisenhower's Political Leadership* (Ithaca, NY: Cornell University Press, 1988), 9.

14. Miles, *Odyssey*, 81–83; George Nash, *The Conservative Intellectual Movement in America* (New York: Basic Books, 1976), 263–265.

15. Tananbaum's *The Bricker Amendment* is the most complete study of the incident. For Eisenhower's reactions, see Ambrose, *Eisenhower*, vol. 2, 68–70, 151–152, 154–155.

16. Amy Swerdlow, *Women Strike for Peace: Traditional Motherhood and Radical Politics in the 1960s* (Chicago: University of Chicago Press, 1993).

17. Frances P. Bolton, address, reprinted in Summary of Proceedings, 22nd Women's Patriotic Conference on National Defense, 15–17 January 1948 [Washington, DC], Reel 153 W59, Right-Wing Collection.

18. *New Mexico Women Speak!* newsletter, November 1955, Reel 86 N39, Right-Wing Collection.

19. American Woman's Party, "Our Country Needs Its Mother," n.d. (source of quotation); American Woman's Party, "War at Its Worst," n.d.; Leona Scannell to Dear Americans, n.d.; American Woman's Party, "MEN . . . Let us call to your attention . . . THESE FACTS," n.d., all on Reel 13 A100, Right-Wing Collection.

20. American Woman's Party, "MEN . . . Let us call to your attention . . . THESE FACTS"; June Melby Benowitz, *Days of Discontent: American Women and Right-Wing Politics, 1933–1945* (Dekalb: Northern Illinois University Press, 2002), 175–176.

21. Mrs. M. Conan, *What Do You Think?* November 1947, Reel 36 C133, Right-Wing Collection.

22. "Senator's Wife Discusses Effect of Khrushchev Visit," *Manchester Union Leader*, 15 October 1959, in "Clippings—esp. 1959," File Drawer no. 4, DB Papers; Margaret Chase Smith, speech to Rumford Rotary-Lions Ladies noon meeting, 22 October 1951, in "Statements and Speeches," vol. 8, Margaret Chase Smith Library [hereafter MCS Library], Skowhegan, ME.

23. Margaret Chase Smith to Leslie B. Johnson, 19 November 1954, in "Maine Support for McCarthy," McCarthy, Joseph Raymond Correspondence, McCarthy File, MCS Library; Elizabeth Churchill Brown to Francesca Rhee, 5 January 1958, in "Rhee, Syngman and Francesca, Correspondence with the Browns, 1958," Box 3, ECB Papers; Elizabeth Churchill Brown to A. C. Wedemeyer, n.d., in "Brown (Mrs. Constantine)," Box 28, A. C. Wedemeyer Papers, Hoover Institute on War, Revolution and Peace, Stanford University, Palo Alto, CA [hereafter Wedemeyer Papers].

24. Mrs. Philip Corson to Bud, 5 October 1955, *Alerted Americans*, Reel 13 A73, Right-Wing Collection.

25. Clare Boothe Luce to A. C. Wedemeyer, 1 March 1947, in "Luce, Clare Boothe," Box 93, Wedemeyer Papers; Conan, *What Do You Think?*; Esther M. Guilfoy, "Clubwomen Hear Talk by Mrs. Bridges," *Manchester Union Leader* [morning edition], in "Mrs. Styles Bridges, 1947–49," Case 4, DB Papers; "Mrs. Bridges Tells Why She Keeps Sharp Eye on Government Affairs," *New Hampshire Sunday News*, 20 January 1952, Scrapbook no. 1, DB papers; Brown to Rhee, 5 January 1958.

26. Margaret Chase Smith, speech to Rumford Rotary-Lions Ladies noon meeting, 22 October 1951.

27. Women Investors Research Institute, Special Report no. 712, 2 December 1950, Reel 153 W52, Right-Wing Collection.

28. Marguerite Atterbury to Lucy Jewett Brady, 19 March 1955, reprinted in *The Minute Women of the USA, Inc.*, Houston Chapter newsletter [1955?]; Minute Women of the USA, Inc., statement, 11 April 1951, both on Reel 77 M53, Right-Wing Collection.

29. Elizabeth Churchill Brown to Francesca Rhee, 21 January 1958, in "Rhee, Syngman and Francesca, Correspondence with the Browns, 1958," and Brown to Rhee, 6 August 1959, in "Rhee, Syngman and Francesca, Correspondence with the Browns, 1959, Aug–Dec," both in Box 3, ECB Papers.

30. John J. Judis, *William F. Buckley, Jr.: Patron Saint of the Conservatives* (New York: Simon & Shuster, 1988), 175–176.

31. "Mrs. Bridges Speaks to Women in Plymouth," 30 October 1958, *Concord Monitor*, Scrapbook no. 2, DB Papers.

32. Mrs. M. Conan, *What Do You Think?* October 1953, Reel 36 C133; Florence Dean Post, "US and UN," speech before Boca Ciega chapter of the DAR, 5 October 1953, Reel 77 M53; Katharine G. Reynolds, *National Defense News*, January 1953, DAR Press Relations, Reel 89 N85, all in Right-Wing Collection.

33. Mrs. James C. Lucas, statement before Senate Judiciary Committee Hearings, February 1953, reprinted in *The New York State Minute Women of the USA, Inc.*, newsletter, July 1954, Reel 89 N85, Right-Wing Collection.

34. Florence Fowler Lyons, "Compilation of Reports on UNESCO, September 1959 to December 1960," Reel 102 R14, Right-Wing Collection.

35. Nash, *Conservative Intellectual Movement*, 86–88.

36. Ibid., 84–130.

37. Ibid., 89–91. For other examples of works critical of FDR's foreign policy, see Harry Elmer Barnes, ed., *Perpetual War for Perpetual Peace* (Caldwell, ID: Caxton, 1953); William Henry Chamberlin, *America's Second Crusade* (Chicago: Regnery, 1950); James Burnham, *The Struggle for the World* (New York: John Day, 1947).

38. Freda Utley, *Japan's Feet of Clay* (New York: Norton, 1937); Utley, *Japan's Gamble in China* (London: Secker and Warburg, 1938); Utley, *Japan Can Be Stopped!* (London: "News Chronicle" Publications Dept., 1937). The term "feet of clay" refers to Utley's theory that Japan was bluffing during the war against China because it lacked solid economic footing. If the United States had imposed economic sanctions, Japan would have collapsed and been forced to end the war against the Chinese.

39. Freda Utley to Clare Boothe Luce, 21 June 1946, in "Luce, Clare Boothe," Box 8, Correspondence, Freda Utley Papers, Hoover Institute on War, Revolution and Peace, Stanford University, Palo Alto, CA [hereafter Utley Papers]; Freda Utley, *The China Story* (Chicago: Henry Regnery, 1951), 239–240.

40. Utley, *China Story*, 223, vii.

41. For a more general description of the acceptance of anticommunist theories during this period, see Powers, *Not without Honor*, 230–231.

42. Richard L. Walker, "Smoke—and Red Fire," *The New York Times*, 13 May 1951, BR4; "A Checklist for Vacation Readers," *The New York Times*, 10 June 1951, BR18.

43. Freda Utley, *China at War*; Utley, *Last Chance in China* (Indianapolis: Bobbs-Merrill, 1947); Utley, *The China Story* (Chicago: Henry Regnery, 1951); Utley, *The High Cost of Vengeance* (Chicago: Henry Regnery, 1949); Utley, *Will the Middle East Go West?* (Chicago: Henry Regnery, 1957); Utley, *The Dream We Lost* (New York: John Day, 1940). Quotations from Utley, *Will the Middle East Go West?*, xiii, and Utley, The *High Cost of Vengeance*, 310.

44. Freda Utley, *Odyssey of a Liberal* (Washington, DC: Washington National Press, 1970), 278–279, 298–299.

45. Freda Utley to Albert C. Wedemeyer, 20 October 1957, in "Wedemeyer, Albert C.," Box 13, Utley Papers. For more evidence of her financial struggles, see the correspondence between Utley and Wedemeyer concerning her work on his memoirs.

46. Powers, *Not without Honor*, 273–274; James T. Patterson, *Grand Expectations: The United States, 1945–1974* (New York: Oxford University Press, 1996), 299–301. For a description of the economic boom, see Patterson, *Grand Expectations*, 311–312. For a discussion of race relations, see Taylor Branch, *Parting the Waters* (New York: Simon & Shuster, 1988).

47. Judis, *William F. Buckley, Jr.*, 113–158; Nash, *Conservative Intellectual Movement*, 147–153; Powers, *Not without Honor*, 273–274.

48. ECB to Henry Regnery, 18 April 1954; ECB, "Introduction," n.d., both in "Brown, Constantine (Mrs.)," Box 10, Regnery Papers.

49. Ibid.

50. Elizabeth Churchill Brown, *The Enemy at His Back* (New York: Devin-Adair, 1956), xiii.

51. Ibid., xiv.

52. George Sokolsky, "History in the Making," n.d. [no paper given]; "From Yalta to Yalu," *Sunday News* [New York], 16 September 1956, both in "Brown, Mr. & Mrs. Constantine," File 42, Styles Bridges Papers, New Hampshire Records and Archives, Concord, NH [hereafter Styles Bridges Papers].

53. ECB to Henry Regnery, 20 August 1954, and Henry Regnery to ECB, 23 May 1955, both in "Brown, Constantine (Mrs.)," Box 10, Regnery Papers.

54. ECB to Alfred Kohlberg, 15 June 1955, in "Constantine Brown," Box 20, Kohlberg Papers. She held on to some animosity; see ECB to Henry Regnery, 15 February 1957, in "Brown, Constantine (Mrs.)," Box 10, Regnery Papers; Lee Mortimer, column, *Daily Mirror*, 17 August 1955, attached to Richard Wels to William C. Lewis, 17 August 1955, in "Brown, Constantine," Smith, Margaret Chase Correspondence, Margaret Chase Smith Papers, MCS Library, Skowhegan, ME [hereafter MCS Papers].

55. "From Yalta to Yalu"; Sokolsky, "History in the Making"; Walter Jaskievicz, "Who Was Responsible?" *Herald Tribune Book Review*, 30 September 1956, in "Brown, Mr. and Mrs. Constantine," File 42, Styles Bridges Papers; Robert Welch to ECB, 15 August 1956, in "Welch, Robert, 1956–1959," Box 4, ECB Papers; *Chicago Sunday Tribune,* 7 October 1956, 8; ECB to Barry Goldwater, 28 March 1957, in "Goldwater, Barry (Senator), 1957–1966," Correspondence, Box 2, ECB Papers.

56. ECB to Alfred Kohlberg, 7 January 1957, in "Constantine Brown," Box 20, Kohlberg Papers.

57. For an example of a review of Brown's book, see "Book Event," *Human Events*, 4 August 1956. For a review of Utley's book, see Dana Adams Schmidt, "The Warning Is Timely," *The New York Times*, 8 December 1957, BR22.

58. Richard M. Fried, "The Rise and Fall of Electoral Redbaiting," paper presented at the annual meeting of the Organization of American Historians, 25 April 1999, Toronto.

59. Elizabeth Churchill Brown to Henry Regnery, 17 October 1963, in "Brown, Constantine (Mrs.)," Box 10, Regnery Papers; Elizabeth Churchill Brown to Francesca Rhee, 3 December 1963, in "Rhee, Syngman and Francesca Correspondence with the Browns, 1963–1966," Box 3, ECB Papers.

60. For a discussion of the Goldwater phenomenon, see Mary C. Brennan, *Turning Right in the Sixties* (Chapel Hill: University of North Carolina Press, 1995); F. Clifton White, *Suite 3505* (New Rochelle, NY: Arlington House, 1967); Robert Goldberg, *Barry Goldwater* (New Haven: Yale University Press, 1995), 149–239.

61. Donald T. Critchlow, "Conservatism Reconsidered: Phyllis Schlafly and Grassroots Conservatism," in *The Conservative Sixties,* ed. David Farber and Jeff Roche (New York: Peter Lang, 2003), 120–121; Catherine E. Rymph,

Republican Women: Feminism and Conservatism from Suffrage through the Rise of the New Right (Chapel Hill: University of North Carolina Press, 2006), 174–175.

62. Donald T. Critchlow, *Phyllis Schlafly and Grassroots Conservatism* (Princeton, NJ: Princeton University Press, 2005), 439–441.

63. Ibid., 119.

64. Phyllis Schlafly, *A Choice Not an Echo* (Alton, IL: Pere Marquette, 1964), 8–22, quotes on 8, 21.

65. Critchlow, *Phyllis Schlafly*, 125; Rymph, *Republican Women*, 175–176.

66. Lewis Nichols, "In and Out of Books," *The New York Times*, 4 October 1964, BR8.

67. Critchlow, *Phyllis Schlafly*, 128.

68. Phyllis Schlafly and Chester Ward, *The Gravediggers* (Alton, IL: Pere Marquette, 1964), 65–66, 5.

69. Ibid., 21–42.

70. Freda Utley to Clare Boothe Luce, 21 June 1946, in "Luce, Clare Boothe," Correspondence, Box 8, Utley Papers.

71. Rymph, *Republican Women*, 174.

CHAPTER 4

1. Mrs. Ben W. Boyd, "Women's Role in the Scene Today," *Texas Clubwoman* 36, no. 2 (May 1960): 21–22, TWU Collection.

2. *Brown v. Board of Education, Topeka, Kansas*, 347 U.S. 483 (1954). For a discussion of the time period, see James T. Patterson, *Grand Expectations: The United States, 1945–1974* (New York: Oxford University Press, 1996), 61–68, 270–275, 313–322, 361–369, 374–406.

3. M. J. Heale, *American Anticommunism: Combating the Enemy Within, 1830–1970* (Baltimore: Johns Hopkins University Press, 1990), 145–190.

4. For a discussion of McCarthy, see Thomas C. Reeves, *The Life and Times of Joe McCarthy* (New York: Stein and Day, 1982); David Oshinsky, *A Conspiracy So Immense* (New York: Free Press, 1983). For a discussion of Eisenhower's view of the situation, see Fred Greenstein, *The Hidden-Hand Presidency* (New York: Basic Books, 1982); Stephen E. Ambrose, *Eisenhower*, vol. 2 (New York: Simon & Schuster, 1983), 56–60, 160–168, 219–221.

5. Heale, *American Anticommunism*, 168–171, 183–189.

6. J. Edgar Hoover, *Masters of Deceit: The Story of Communism in America and How to Fight It* (New York: Henry Holt, 1958; Pocket Books, 1961), 80 [1961 ed.].

7. Elizabeth Fones-Wolf, *Selling Free Enterprise: The Business Assault on Labor and Liberalism* (Chicago: University of Illinois Press, 1994), 204–205.

8. Heale, *American Anticommunism*, 183; Richard Fried, *The Russians Are Coming! The Russians Are Coming! Pageantry and Patriotism in Cold-War America* (New York: Oxford University Press, 1998), 67–81.

9. Mrs. M. Conan, *What Do You Think?* October 1947, Reel 36 C133; Doloris Bridges, "A Statement on the John Birch Society and the ADA," n.d., attached to Jack Beall to Doloris Bridges, 7 June 1962, in "Letters, Releases, re/Campaign 1962," File Drawer no. 4, DB Papers; "What's in a Party?" *The Spirit*, February 1964, Reel 8 A49, all in Right-Wing Collection.

10. American Woman's Party, "Open Letter to American Men Voters," n.d., Reel 13 A100; *New Mexico Women Speak!* newsletter, December 1955, Reel 86 N39, both in Right-Wing Collection; Phyllis Peck, "Senator's Wife Gives Warning to Clubwomen," 19 February 1956 [no paper listed], Scrapbook no. 1, DB Papers.

11. *The Minute Women of the USA, Inc.,* newsletter, June-July 1953, Reel 76 M19; Florence Dean Post, "Metro Network," *The Spirit*, March 1964, Reel 8 A49, both in Right-Wing Collection.

12. Post, "Metro Network"; American Woman's Party, "Open Letter to American Men Voters"; "Mrs. Bridges Scores Again," editorial, *Manchester Union Leader*, 28 November 1957, in "Mrs. Bridges Editorials, 1957," File Drawer no. 4, DB Papers; Doloris Bridges, "Excerpts from Address at NE College Commencement Exercise," 18 June 1962, in "New England College," File Drawer no. 1, DB Papers; Mrs. Philip L. [Helen Payson] Corson, letter to editor, *Evening Bulletin*, 17 May 1962, *Alerted Americans,* summer 1962, Reel 13 A73, Right-Wing Collection.

13. *New Mexico Women Speak!* November 1955.

14. *The Minute Women of the USA, Inc.,* newsletter, November-December 1960, Reel 76 M19, Right-Wing Collection; Peck, "Senator's Wife Gives Warning to Clubwomen"; American Woman's Party, "Open Letter to American Men Voters," n.d., Reel 13 A100, Right-Wing Collection.

15. American Woman's Party, "Open Letter"; Elizabeth Churchill Brown to Francesca Rhee, 28 June 1959, in "Rhee, Syngman and Francesca, Correspondence with the Browns, 1959, May–August." Rhee and Brown discussed their frustration with male leaders on numerous occasions. See also, Elizabeth Churchill Brown to Francesca Rhee, 9 November 1963, in "Rhee, Syngman and Francesca, Correspondence with the Browns, 1963–1966," Box 3, ECB Papers.

16. Christine Sadler, "Congresswoman Urges Distaff Side to Save Feuding GOP," *The Washington Post*, 9 July 1952, MCS Scrapbook 114, no. 185, MCS Library; *New Mexico Women Speak!* January 1956, 1, Reel 86 N39, Right-Wing Collection; Margaret Chase Smith, speech to American Woman's Association, 15 November 1948, in "Statements and Speeches," vol. 5, MCS Library.

17. Anne Firor Scott, *Natural Allies: Women's Associations in American History* (Chicago: University of Illinois Press, 1991), 141–158; Sarah A. Leavitt, *From Catharine Beecher to Martha Stewart: A Cultural History of Domestic Advice* (Chapel Hill: University of North Carolina Press, 2002), 76.

18. Margaret Chase Smith, "No Place for a Woman?" *Ladies Home Journal* (February 1952): 50+; Leona Scannell to "Dear American," n.d., Reel 13 A100, Right-Wing Collection; Kristina Zarlengo, "Civilian Threat, the Suburban

Citadel, and Atomic Age American Women," *Signs: A Journal of Women in Culture and Society* 24 (Summer 1999): 941.

19. Laura McEnaney, *Civil Defense Begins at Home: Militarization Meets Everyday Life in the Fifties* (Princeton, NJ: Princeton University Press, 2000), 68–101.

20. Ibid, 100.

21. Smith, "No Place for a Woman," 83.

22. Dee Garrison, "'Our Skirts Gave Them Courage' The Civil Defense Protest Movement in New York City, 1955–1961," 201–226, and Ruth Feldstein, "'I Wanted the Whole World to See': Race, Gender, and Constructions of Motherhood in the Death of Emmett Till," 263–303, both in Joanne Meyerowitz, ed., *Not June Cleaver: Women and Gender in Postwar America, 1945–1960* (Philadelphia: Temple University Press, 1994).

23. "Democrat and Republican Women United for MacArthur for President," pamphlet, 1952, Reel 13 A100; Maryland Chapter, the Minute Women of the USA, Inc., "What Kind of Country Are You Leaving Us?" pamphlet [1955?], Reel 77 M53, both in Right-Wing Collection.

24. Katharine St. George, address, reprinted in Summary of Proceedings, 22nd Women's Patriotic Conference on National Defense, 15–17 January 1948 [Washington, DC], Reel 153 W59, Right-Wing Collection.

25. *The Minute Women of the USA, Inc.,* newsletter, March 1962, Reel 76 M19; "Dear Member," newsletter, New York State Minute Women, Inc., July 1954, Reel 89 N85; Frances P. Bolton, address, reprinted in Summary of Proceedings, 22nd Women's Patriotic Conference on National Defense, 15–17 January 1948 [Washington, DC], Reel 153 W59, all in Right-Wing Collection.

26. Typed notes, n.d., in "Releases 1966," File Drawer no. 4, DB Papers; All American Conferences to Combat Communism, *Freedom's Facts*, no. 3, December 1952, Reel 56 F40, Right-Wing Collection.

27. Susan E. Marshall, "Ladies against Women: Mobilization Dilemmas of Antifeminist Movements," *Social Problems* 32 (April 1985): 356–357; *The Minute Women of the USA, Inc.,* newsletter, June–July 1953, Reel 76 M19; "Fedicare," *The Spirit*, February 1964, Reel 8 A49, both in Right-Wing Collection.

28. For examples, see ECB to Everett Dirksen, 4 September 1951, in "Brown (Mrs. Constantine)," Box 28, Wedemeyer Papers; ECB to Roy Howard, 14 September 1959, in "Howard, Roy W., 1950–1959," Box 2; correspondence between ECB and Barry Goldwater, 1963, Box 2; both in ECB Papers.

29. ECB to Roy Howard, 14 September 1959, in "Howard, Roy W., 1950–1959," Box 2, ECB Papers; ECB to Everett Dirksen, 4 September 1951, in "Brown (Mrs. Constantine)," Box 28, Wedemeyer Papers; correspondence between ECB and Barry Goldwater, 1963, Box 2, ECB Papers. For her correspondence with Butler, see ECB to John Marshall Butler, 12 November 1951, and John Marshall Butler to ECB, 18 December 1951, both in "Communism, Anti-Communism," McCarthy, Joseph, Correspondence, 1951–1952, Box 17, ECB Papers. She also described the exchange in the draft of her book *Joe*

McCarthy and Other Anti-Communists, "Draft #2 Chap. 4," 43–44, Box 10, ECB Papers.

30. ECB to Henry Regnery, 18 January 1964, in "Brown, Constantine (Mrs.)," Box 10, Regnery Papers; correspondence between ECB and Barry Goldwater, 1963, Box 2; correspondence between ECB and Roy Howard, in "Howard, Roy W., 1950–1959," Box 2, both in ECB Papers.

31. ECB, "Woman's Place Is Under the Dome," *Human Events* 2, 13 January 1958, 1–4.

32. "A Number of Readers . . ." notice, *Human Events,* 3 February 1958, 6; ECB to Francesca Rhee, 21 January, 5 March, and 11 February 1958 (dates match order of quotes in text), in "Rhee, Syngman and Francesca, Correspondence with the Browns, 1958," Box 3, ECB Papers.

33. Smith, "No Place for a Woman?" 50; Dorothy B. Frankton to "Minute Women," *The Minute Women of the USA, Inc.,* newsletter, December 1952, Reel 76 M19; American Woman's Party, "MEN . . . Let us call to your attention . . . THESE FACTS," n.d., Reel 13 A100, both in Right-Wing Collection.

34. "The Lady from Maine," *Newsweek,* 12 June 1950, 24–26; S&H Green Stamps Ad, *National Business Woman,* October 1960, 1; "As Maine Goes . . ." *Time,* 5 September 1960, 13–16; Doloris Bridges to ?, sample letter, 31 August 1966, in "Sample Letters–Flexowriter 1966," File Drawer no. 4, DB Papers.

35. "International Affairs Department," *The Texas Clubwoman* 35, no. 6 (October 1959): 15; Mrs. John J. Perry, "Texas Clubwomen Get-Out-the-Vote," *The Texas Clubwoman* 29, no. 1 (January 1953): 6; both in TWU Women's Collection.

36. Jo Freeman, *A Room at a Time: How Women Entered Politics* (New York: Rowman & Littlefield, 2000), 228; Catherine E. Rymph, *Republican Women: Feminism and Conservatism from Suffrage through the Rise of the New Right* (Chapel Hill: University of North Carolina Press, 2006), 131–159; Jacqueline R. Braitman, "Legislated Parity: Mandating Integration of Women into California Political Parties, 1930s–1950s," in *We Have Come To Stay: American Women and Political Parties, 1880–1960,* ed. Melanie Gustafson, Kristie Miller, and Elisabeth I. Perry (Albuquerque: University of New Mexico Press, 1999), 181–182; Sandra Baxter and Marjorie Lansing, *Women and Politics: The Visible Majority,* rev. ed. (Ann Arbor: University of Michigan Press, 1983), 21–22.

37. Freeman, *A Room at a Time,* 22–24, quote on 23.

38. Bolton, address; Margaret Frakes, "One Senator's Conscience," *Christian Century,* 13 May 1953, 570–571.

39. Janann Sherman, *No Place for a Woman: A Life of Senator Margaret Chase Smith* (New Brunswick, NJ: Rutgers University Press, 2000), 43–57.

40. Ibid., 73–89. For information on women following their husbands into office, see Karen Foerstel and Herbert N. Foerstel, *Climbing the Hill: Gender Conflict in Congress* (Westport, CT: Praeger, 1996), 1–2.

41. ECB, "Mrs. Smith Comes to Washington," *The American Mercury,* 1953, 73–76, MCS Scrapbook 129, no. 194, MCS Library; Sherman, *No Place for a*

Woman, 97–98. The controversy surrounding the Declaration of Conscience is discussed more fully in Chapter 5.

42. "After Styles," *Time*, 31 August 1962, 18–19.

43. Ibid., 19.

44. May Craig, "No Machinery for Snow Removal," *The Washington Star*, 25 January 1961, in "Bridges, Styles," New Hampshire Congressional Delegation, MCS Papers; Doloris Bridges to "Dear Friend," n.d., campaign brochure no. 2, in "Misc. Clippings and Campaign Materials," DB Papers; "Widow Will Run for Bridges Seat," *The New York Times*, 11 January 1962, 22; Doloris Bridges to Norman J. Tremaine, 6 February 1962, in "Correspondence on Past Engagements," Case 1; Doloris Bridges to voter, campaign brochure no. 1, Doloris Bridges for Senate, 1962, in "Misc. Clippings and Campaign Materials," Case 1, both in DB Papers; John H. Fenton, "New England Has Five Senate Races," *The New York Times*, 17 December 1961, 60.

45. "After Styles," 19; "New Hampshire Contests," *The New York Times*, 9 September 1962, 58; Bridges to "Dear Friend," campaign brochure no. 2.

46. Charles N. Dale quoted in campaign brochure no. 2; "Guest Editorial," *Monadnock Ledger* [Jaffrey, NH], reprinted in *Hillsborough Messenger* [NH], 23 August [1962]; Drew Pearson, "The Influence of Women in U.S. Politics" [Gannett Publishers], 18 December 1961, in "Bridges, Styles," New Hampshire Congressional Delegation, MCS Papers.

47. William Loeb to Margaret Chase Smith, 18 January 1962; Doloris Bridges to Margaret Chase Smith, 31 January 1962, both in "Bridges, Styles," New Hampshire Congressional Delegation, MCS Papers; William Loeb to Doloris Bridges, 11 May 1962; William Loeb to Doloris Bridges, 4 May 1962; William Loeb to Doloris Bridges, 13 June 1962, all in "William Loeb 1962," Case 1, DB Papers.

48. "New Hampshire Picks Moderates," *The New York Times*, 13 September 1962, 21; Barry Goldwater to Doloris Bridges, 13 September 1962, envelope, in "Letters/re/campaign," Case 4, DB Papers; "Bass Wins in Recount," *The New York Times*, 3 October 1962, 27; "G.O.P. Feuds Stir Democratic Hopes for New Hampshire Upset," *The New York Times*, 3 October 1962, 27; "2 in New Hampshire Upheld in Vote Case," *The New York Times*, 11 October 1962, 27.

49. "War Issue Minor in New England," *The New York Times*, 21 August 1966, 63.

50. Phyllis Schlafly to Henry Regnery, 25 July 1967, in "Schlafly, Phyllis," Box 67, Regnery Papers.

51. Mrs. Warren J. Le Vangin, letter to editor, *Newsweek*, 3 July 1950, 2.

52. *The Minute Women of the USA, Inc.*, newsletter, December 1952, Reel 76 M19, Right-Wing Collection.

53. Mrs. M. Conan, *What Do You Think?* May 1947, Reel 36 C133, Right-Wing Collection.

54. Ibid., November 1947.

55. See all issues of *The Farmer's Voice*, particularly vol. II, no. 2, November 1958, Reel 48 F13, Right-Wing Collection.

56. Ibid, vol. II, no. 2.

57. "Mrs. Bridges Tells Why She Keeps Sharp Eye on Government Affairs," *New Hampshire Sunday News*, 20 January 1952, Scrapbook no. 1, DB Papers; "Mrs. Corson Asks Support of Liberty Amendment Which Would Repeal Income Tax Regulation," *Times Herald* [Morristown, PA], 21 June 1962, in *Alerted Americans,* Summer 1962, Reel 13 A73, Right-Wing Collection.

58. Bridges for Senator Headquarters, press release, 16 August 1966, in "Releases 1966," File Drawer no. 4, DB Papers.

59. Ibid.; Margaret Chase Smith, speech to American Woman's Association, 15 November 1948, in "Statements and Speeches," vol. 5, MCS Library; American Woman's Party, "Platform Issues," pamphlet, 1952, Reel 13 A100, Right-Wing Collection.

60. Elaine Tyler May, *Homeward Bound: American Families in the Cold War Era* (New York: Basic Books, 1988), 162–167; S&H Green Stamps Ad; J. Warren Kinsman quoted in Ruth Rosen, *The World Split Apart: How the Modern Women's Movement Changed America* (New York: Penguin Books, 2000), 11.

61. Heale, *American Anticommunism*, 184–185.

62. Don E. Carleton, *Red Scare! Right-Wing Hysteria, Fifties Fanaticism and Their Legacy in Texas* (Austin: Texas Monthly Press, 1985), 154–178.

63. Ibid., 179–223.

64. Lisa McGirr, *Suburban Warriors: The Origins of the New American Right* (Princeton, NJ: Princeton University Press, 2001), 56–60, 71–74.

65. Heale, *American Anticommunism*, 185–186. For a discussion of the Red Scare's impact on higher education, see Ellen Schrecker, *No Ivory Tower* (New York: Oxford University Press, 1986).

66. C. P. Trussell, "Librarian Disputes Panel's Right to Question Her on Communism," *The New York Times*, 16 September 1955, 1; Luther A. Huston, "6 Indicted by US in Senate Inquiry," *The New York Times*, 27 November 1956, 22; [no author], "Librarian Jailed in Contempt Case," *The New York Times*, 19 January 1957, 18.

67. See items in *Alerted Americans,* in particular, Mrs. Philip Corson, "The Gist of the Jeanes Library Controversary [sic]," March 1955; "Mrs. Knowles Is Jailed 120 Days," *Times Herald* [Norristown, PA], 18 January 1957, both in Reel 13 A73, Right-Wing Collection.

68. "Mrs. Knowles Is Jailed 120 Days." For a version of the detachable letter, see Corson, "The Gist of the Jeanes Library Controversary [sic]."

69. Anne Smart, "Report of the Tamalpais Union High School District Trustees on Library Books," 13 September 1954, Reel 127 S65, Right-Wing Collection.

70. Heale, *American Anticommunism*, 185; McGirr, *Suburban Warriors*, 74–75; David Oshinsky, *A Conspiracy So Immense* (New York: Free Press, 1983), 279–282.

71. See various letters and speeches, Anne Smart, June–September 1954, Reel 127 S65, Right-Wing Collection. For a more straightforward account, see

"Book Purge Fails in Coast Schools," *The New York Times*, 19 September 1954, 127.

72. "Book Purge Fails in Coast Schools"; Anne Smart, "Special School Committee Report," 7 September 1954, Reel 127 S65, Right-Wing Collection.

73. Anne Smart letter, 18 May 1956, printed in Mrs. Clarence Uhl, *The Farmer's Voice* II, no. 10 (December 1959), Reel 48 F13, Right-Wing Collection.

74. To editor, n.d., reprinted in *The Farmer's Voice* II, no. 3 (December 1958), Reel 48 F13; "PTA," and "Should PTA Be Abolished?" Special Education Supplement, *The Spirit*, July–August 1964[?], Reel 8 A49, both in Right-Wing Collection.

75. Mrs. Philip Corson, "How to Fight Communism," April 1955, *Alerted Americans*, Reel 13 A73; John K. Crippen, "And Now 'McCallism,'" *The Minute Women of the USA, Inc.*, newsletter, November 1952, Reel 76 M19, both in Right-Wing Collection.

76. Audrey Plowden, "As the Twig Is Bent," *American Spirit*, February–March 1965, Reel 8 A49, Right-Wing Collection.

CHAPTER 5

1. K. A. Cuordileone, " 'Politics in an Age of Anxiety': Cold War Political Culture and the Crisis in American Masculinity," *Journal of American History* (September 2000): 515–545; John D'Emilio, "The Homosexual Menace: The Politics of Sexuality in Cold War America," in *Making Trouble: Essays on Gay History, Politics, and the University* (New York: Routledge, 1992), 57–73; Elaine Tyler May, *Homeward Bound: American Families in the Cold War Era* (New York: Basic Books, 1988), 20–27, 37–91.

2. Alfred C. Kinsey, Wardell B. Pomeroy, and Clyde E. Martin, *Sexual Behavior in the Human Male* (Philadelphia: W. B. Saunders, 1948); Kinsey, Pomeroy, and Martin, *Sexual Behavior in the Human Female* (Philadelphia: W. B. Saunders, 1953). For a discussion of the impact of the Kinsey reports and the sexualization of America, see K. A. Cuordileone, *Manhood and American Political Culture in the Cold War* (New York: Routledge, 2005), 83–87; David Halberstam, *The Fifties* (New York: Villard Books, 1993), 272–281.

3. Philip Wylie, *Generation of Vipers* (New York: Rinehart, 1942). For a discussion of the book's impact, see Barbara Ehrenreich, *For Her Own Good* (New York: Doubleday, 1978), 237–238; Cuordileone, *Manhood*, 126–129; May, *Homeward Bound*, 74–75, 116–117.

4. Cuordileone, "Politics in an Age of Anxiety"; Barbara Epstein, "Anticommunism, Homophobia, and the Construction of Masculinity in the Postwar U.S.," in *Cold War Culture and Society: The Cold War*, vol. 5, ed. Lori Lynn Bogle (New York: Routledge, 2000).

5. J. Edgar Hoover, "The Twin Enemies of Freedom," speech delivered to the annual convention of the National Council of Catholic Women, 9 November 1956, in *Vital Speeches* 23, no. 4 (1 December 1956): 104–107.

6. Adlai Stevenson, "Women, Husbands and History," Commencement Address, Smith College, 6 June 1955, in Adlai Stevenson, *What I Think* (New York: Harper & Brothers, 1956), 182–189; Russell Kirk, *The Intelligent Women's Guide to Conservatism* (New York: Devin-Adair, 1957), 6, 8.

7. Billy Graham quoted in Cuordileone, *Manhood*, 82; Owen Brewster quoted in Catherine E. Rymph, *Republican Women: Feminism and Conservatism from Suffrage through the Rise of the New Right* (Chapel Hill: University of North Carolina Press, 2006), 117–118.

8. Richard Fried, *The Russians Are Coming! The Russians Are Coming! Pageantry and Patriotism in Cold-War America* (New York: Oxford University Press, 1998), 37–38.

9. Stephen E. Ambrose, *Nixon: The Education of a Politician 1913–1962* (New York: Simon & Schuster, 1987), 524.

10. Ibid., 524–526.

11. "Patriotic Societies Alert!" *The Spirit*, October-November 1964, Reel 8, A49, Right-Wing Collection.

12. "Turning the Searchlight on the Feminine Field," *National Republic Lettergram*, no. 211, n.d. [1949?], in "Congress of American Women," Box 40, Kohlberg Papers.

13. Helen Laville, *Cold War Women* (Manchester: Manchester University Press, 2002), 52.

14. Francesca Rhee to Elizabeth Churchill Brown, 23 April 1959, in "Rhee, Syngman and Francesca, Correspondence with the Browns, 1959, Jan.–April," Box 3, ECB Papers; "Communists to Women," *The Spirit*, November 1964, Reel 8, A49; "Minute Women Hear Princess," *The Minute Women of the USA, Inc.,* newsletter, June 1957, Reel 76 M19; *The Minute Women of the USA, Inc.,* newsletter, November-December 1960, Reel 76 M19, all in Right-Wing Collection.

15. All American Conferences to Combat Communism, *Freedom's Facts* 3, no. 5 (May 1955), Reel 56 F40, Right-Wing Collection.

16. BPW quoted in ibid.; also see May, *Homeward Bound*, 19.

17. "The Most Powerful Woman Alive," cover and story, *Time*, 20 September 1948.

18. All American Conferences to Combat Communism, *Freedom's Facts* 3, no. 5 (May 1955), Reel 56 F40, Right-Wing Collection.

19. Robert Levy, *Ana Pauker: The Rise and Fall of a Jewish Communist* (Berkeley: University of California Press, 2001), 53–54, 64–67.

20. W. H. Lawrence, "'Aunty Ana,'" *The New York Times*. 12 October 1947; ibid., 194–221.

21. "Gen. Radescu Here, Warns of Soviet," *The New York Times*, 9 November 1947; "Princess Relates Red Plot for U.S.," *The New York Times*, 8 May 1954.

22. Veterans of Foreign Wars, "Why People Go Communist," *Guardpost for Freedom* 3, no. 2 (15 February 1956), in Committee on Un-American Activities, U.S. House of Representatives, *The Communist Conspiracy*, Part 1, Section 3, 84th Congress, 2nd session, 1956, 15.

23. "Women's Front Attempts to Dodge Law of U.S.A.," *National Republic Lettergram,* no. 217, n.d., Box 40, Kohlberg Papers.

24. Background on Muriel Draper (1886–1952), in "Finding Aid," Muriel Draper Papers, Yale Collection of American Literature, Beinecke Rare Book and Manuscript Library, Yale University, New Haven, CT; available on-line at *http://webtext.library.yale.edu/xm12html/beinecke.DRAPER.con.html*; accessed January 3, 2005.

25. Joseph R. McCarthy, speech to the Young Republican State Convention, 7 May 1950, quoted in the *Milwaukee Journal,* 8 May 1950; McCarthy, speech to American Legion, 18 September 1950, quoted in the *Houston Post,* 19 September 1950, both in "*McCarthy and the Press,* Research Notes," Box 12, Edwin Bayley Papers, Wisconsin State Historical Society, Madison, WI [hereafter Bayley Papers].

26. McCarthy, speech to the American Legion, 18 September 1950.

27. Cuordileone, *Manhood,* 88–92, quotes on 88. See also David K. Johnson, *The Lavender Scare* (Chicago: University of Chicago Press, 2004), 121–123.

28. Epstein, "Anticommunism," 21–44; Johnson, *Lavender Scare.*

29. U.S. Congress, Senate, Committee on Expenditures in the Executive Departments, "Employment of Homosexuals and Other Sex Perverts in Government," 81st Congress, 2nd session, 27 November, 1950; quotes from Cuordileone, "Politics," 532–533; D'Emilio, "Homosexual Menace," 59.

30. Johnson, *Lavender Scare,* 5–10, 76–77.

31. McCarthy, speech to the Young Republican State Convention, 7 May 1950; McCarthy, speech to the American Legion, 18 September 1950.

32. "Mrs. Styles Bridges Speaker as Unity Club Season Opens," *Coos County* [NH] *Democrat,* 8 October 1952, Scrapbook no. 1, DB Papers; Elizabeth Churchill Brown, *Joe McCarthy and Other Anti-Communists,* unpublished manuscript, "Draft #2 Chap. 1," Box 10, ECB Papers.

33. For Pearson's files, see "33. McCarthy General II [folders 1–3]," Box g222, Personal Papers of Drew Pearson, Lyndon Baines Johnson Library, Austin, TX; Hank Greenspan, "Where I Stand," 25 October 1952, in "Communism: Anticommunism, McCarthy, Joseph, Non-printed Material, General, Printed Material, General," Box 17, ECB Papers.

34. William Benton to John Howe, memo, 23 March 1954, in "General: Jan–March 1954," Box 4, William Benton Papers, Wisconsin State Historical Society, Madison, WI. See also David Oshinsky, *A Conspiracy So Immense* (New York: Free Press, 1983), 310–311.

35. Edwin Bayley, research notes, n.d., in "*McCarthy and the Press,* Research Notes," Box 12, Bayley Papers.

36. Oshinsky, *Conspiracy,* 311. Thomas Reeves did a significant number of interviews for his book on McCarthy. Those interviews are available in the Reeves Files, WSHS.

37. Ed Nellor, interview by Thomas Reeves, 1 January 1980, in "McCarthy Interviews III"; Francis A. Werner, interview by Thomas Reeves, 18 August

1975, in "McCarthy Interviews I," both in Box 1, Reeves Papers; Willard Edwards, interview by Edwin Bayley, 27 June 1977, in "Interviews, 1976–1980," Box 11, Bayley Papers; Eleanor Harris, "The Private Life of Senator McCarthy," *The American Weekly*, 16 and 23 August 1953, in "Aug–Dec 1953 McCarthy Clips," Box 3, Reeves Files.

38. While grieving his death, Jean vowed to continue her crusade as primary repository of information about McCarthy. As his widow, Jean claimed to be the only person who really understood Joe and what he stood for. She made certain that people knew she was the rightful source of knowledge about her husband. See, for example, Jean McCarthy to Lyndon Johnson, 3 June 1957, in "[McCarthy, Joseph R.]," Box 48, Lyndon Baines Johnson Congressional File, LBJ Library; "Huge Sorting Task Faces Mrs. McCarthy," Appleton *Post-Crescent*, 16 August 1957, in "July 1955–1957 + Beyond," Box 4, Reeves Files. Despite Jean's marriage to Democrat Joe Minetti, in 1961, she continued to try to control Joe's memory and reputation. She promised to send Joe's papers to Marquette University but then held on to them. See Jean Minetti to Raphael N. Hamilton, S.J., 14 June 1972, in "Administrative Files for the Joseph R. McCarthy Papers," McCarthy Papers, Marquette. She expressed her anger when derogatory images of Joe appeared in the media by writing letters to the editors of major newspapers and venting to fellow conservatives. See "McCarthy's Widow Denounces TV Show," *The Milwaukee Journal*, 13 February 1977, in "McCarthy Interviews I," Box 1, Reeves Files.

39. For evidence of her willingness to give Joe the credit for her work, see Jean Kerr to Wayne Hood, 30 November 1951, 3 December [1951]; Wayne Hood to Jean Kerr, 6 December 1951, all in Reel 7 microfilm, Hood Papers; Jean Kerr to Tom Korb, 27 October 1951; Tom Korb to Jean Kerr, 29 October 1951, both in "Korb, Tom Papers," Box 2, Reeves Papers; Thomas C. Reeves, *The Life and Times of Joe McCarthy* (New York: Stein and Day, 1982), 417; Thomas Korb, 6 September 1975, in "McCarthy Interviews I"; Ed Nellor, 7 May 1977, in "McCarthy Interviews III"; Jean McCarthy Minetti, 14 March 1977, in "McCarthy Interviews I," all in Reeves Interviews, Box 1, Reeves Files.

40. Oshinsky, *Conspiracy*, 174–176; Reeves, *Life and Times* , 336, 344–345; Caroline H. Keith, *"For Hell and a Brown Mule": The Biography of Senator Millard E. Tydings* (New York: Madison Books, 1991), 418. Despite evidence that Tydings lost because of internal factors, the common belief was that he lost because of McCarthy's influence. This helped create the myth of infallibility that surrounded the Wisconsin senator. See Robert Griffith, *The Politics of Fear* (Lexington: University Press of Kentucky, 1970), 131.

41. Reeves, *Life and Times*, 335–336; U.S. Senate, Jon Jonkel testimony, Subcommittee on Privileges and Elections, *Maryland Senatorial Election of 1950: Hearings before the Subcommittee on Privileges and Elections*, 82nd Cong., 1st sess., 2 March 1951, 184–188, 236, 425–427 [hereafter *Maryland Hearings*].

42. *Maryland Hearings*, 425–457.

43. Ibid., 257–260, 394–398, 431–435.

44. Ibid., 1103–1128.

45. Ibid., 194–195, 734–738.

46. Ibid., 428–495.

47. See, for example, ibid., 156, 476, 773.

48. Ibid., 737–739.

49. Ibid., 1121–1125.

50. For a discussion of McCarthy's use of gendered images, see Geoffrey S. Smith, "National Security and Personal Isolation: Sex, Gender, and Disease in the Cold War United States," *International History Review* 14 (May 1992): 307–337. For discussions of other groups that similarly use gendered references to advance their causes, see Carol Cohn, "Sex and Death in the Rational World of Defense Intellectuals," *Signs* 12 (Summer 1987): 717; Laura McEnaney, "He-Men and Christian Mothers: The America First Movement and the Gendered Meanings of Patriotism and Isolationism," *Diplomatic History* 18 (Winter 1994): 47–57; Frank Costigliola, "The Nuclear Family: Tropes of Gender and Pathology in the Western Alliance," *Diplomatic History* 21 (Spring 1997): 183.

51. U.S. Senate, Subcommittee on Privileges and Elections, *Maryland Senatorial Election of 1950, Report of the Committee on Rules and Administration*, 82nd Congress, 1st sess., 20 August 1950, Government Printing Office, in "Maryland Senatorial Election of 1950, Report of the Committee on Rules and Administration," Mc JR MD Senatorial Election, McCarthy File, MCS Library, Skowhegan, ME; *Maryland Hearings*, 1105.

52. *Maryland Hearings*, 695.

53. Ibid., 192, 195.

54. Quoted in Reeves, *Life and Times*, 365.

55. Margaret Chase Smith to Robert E. Wood, 23 June 1950, in "Out-of-State Reactions 3 of 4"; quote to constituent from MCS to Prescott Dennett, 8 March 1950, in "Correspondence 3 of 10," both in MCS Library.

56. MCS to Elzada Frost, 10 August 1950, in "Correspondence 5 of 10," Communism Folders. For explanations of her anticommunism bill, see MCS to Mrs. Elif A. Johnson, 1 October 1954, in "Anti-Communist Propaganda 1 of 2"; [William Lewis?], memo, 18 August 1953, in "Bill to Outlaw the Communist Party 1 of 3"; MCS, "Washington and You" [1953], in "Anti-Communist Propaganda 1 of 2," all in MCS Library.

57. "Capability v. Credibility," *Time*, 29 September 1961, 16

58. "Nikita, the Devil & the Ballplayer," *Time*, 20 October 1961, 29.

59. MCS to Wood (source of the quote); MCS to Frost, MCS Library.

60. Janann Sherman, *No Place for a Woman: A Life of Senator Margaret Chase Smith* (New Brunswick, NJ: Rutgers University Press, 2000), 108–109.

61. All quotations from the Declaration of Conscience speech are from the MCS Library Web site: *http://www.mcslibrary.org/program/library/declaration.htm;* accessed February 15, 2005.

62. Quoted in Sherman, *No Place for a Woman*, 111.

63. Ibid., 117–120.

64. "Periscope," *Newsweek*, 12 June 1950, 15; Berenice Smalley to MCS, 29 August 1953, in "Criticism of Senator Smith"; James H. Carroll to MCS, 3 December 1954, in "Maine Support for McCarthy," both in McCarthy, Joseph Raymond Correspondence, McCarthy File, MCS Library; "Smearing Is Evil, but Whitewashing Reds Is Worse," *Saturday Evening Post*, 15 July 1950, 10.

65. W. M. Jeffers to MCS, 5 June 1950, telegram, in "Out-of-State Reactions 2 of 4"; Carl T. Smith to MCS, 2? August 1954, in "Maine Support for McCarthy," both in McCarthy, Joseph Raymond Correspondence, McCarthy File, MCS Library; Sherman, *No Place for a Woman*, 112.

66. Elizabeth Churchill Brown, "Mrs. Smith Comes to Washington," *The American Mercury*, 1953, MCS Scrapbook 129, no. 194, MCS Library; Elizabeth Churchill Brown, *Joe McCarthy and Other Anti-Communists*, "Draft #2 Chap. 4," Box 10, ECB Papers.

67. Margaret S. Smith to MCS, 12 September 1953, in "Criticism of Senator Smith," McCarthy, Joseph Raymond Correspondence, McCarthy File, MCS Library; Paul Clement, letter to editor, *Newsweek*, 3 July 1950, 2.

68. Viola M. Blumenstock to MCS, 30 January 1951, in "Out of State Support for McCarthy," McCarthy, Joseph Raymond Correspondence, McCarthy File; Clara Aiken Speer to MCS, 8 June 1950, in "Out-Of-State Reactions 2 of 4," both in MCS Library.

69. "Smearing Is Evil, but Whitewashing of Reds Is Worse," *Saturday Evening Post*, 15 July 1950; Kenneth Colegrove, "Senator McCarthy," pamphlet, published by Freedom Clubs, Inc.,[1951?], in "Colegrove, 'Senator McCarthy,'" both in McCarthy, Joseph Raymond Correspondence, McCarthy File, MCS Library.

70. Wouk and *Chicago Sun-Times* quoted in Sherman, *No Place for a Woman*, 112; Margaret Frakes, "One Senator's Conscience," *Christian Century*, 13 May 1953, 570–571; Jim Glover to MCS, telegram, 2 June 1950, in "Maine Reactions 12 of 13," MCS Library.

71. "A Woman's Conscience," *Time*, 12 June 1950, 19; "The Lady from Maine," *Newsweek*, 12 June 1950, 24–26; "As Maine Goes . . ." *Time*, 5 September 1960, 13–16.

72. Elizabeth Z. Cushing to MCS, 6 June 1950, in "Out-of-State Reactions 4 of 4"; Will Beale to MCS, 2 June 1950; Roland McDonald to MCS, 1 June 1950, both in "Maine Reactions 13 of 13," all in MCS Library.

73. Jack Cottrell to MCS, 21 June 1950, in "Maine Opposition to McCarthy," McCarthy, Joseph Raymond Correspondence, McCarthy File, MCS Library; Harold L. Ickes, "And a Woman Shall Lead Them," *The New Republic*, 19 June 1950, 16; Bernard Baruch quoted in Sherman, *No Place for a Woman*, 112.

74. Doloris Bridges, questionnaire, n.d., in "Kennedy-Re: Mrs. Bridges—Soft on Communism," Case 1, DB Papers.

75. "Kennedy Is Called Soft on Communism," *The New York Times*, 26 October 1960, 30.

76. William Loeb, "Mrs. Bridges Was Oh, So Right!" *Manchester Union Leader,* 1 November 1960, in "Kennedy-Re: Mrs. Bridges—Soft on Communism," Case 1, DB Papers.

77. Editorial, *Washington Evening Star,* 27 October 1960, attached to Neil to Doloris Bridges, 27 October 1960, in "Pro," Case 1, DB Papers.

78. Ibid.; Loeb, "Mrs. Bridges Was Oh, So Right!"

CONCLUSION

1. Maureen A. Flanagan, "Anna Wilmarth Ickes: A Staunch Republican Woman," in *We Have Come to Stay: American Women and Political Parties, 1880–1960,* ed. Melanie Gustafson, Kristie Miller, and Elisabeth I. Perry (Albuquerque: University of New Mexico Press, 1999), 147–148; Elizabeth Churchill Brown, "Introduction," n.d., in "Brown, Constantine (Mrs.)," Box 10, Regnery Papers; Doloris Bridges [unlabeled notes], n.d., in "Speech Materials/Background Papers and Notes, 1962," File Drawer no. 1, DB Papers; Belinda Jelliffe to Margaret Chase Smith, 4 June 1950, in "Out-of-State Reactions 2 of 4," MCS Papers.

2. Photo, St. Louis *Globe-Democrat,* 1952, reprinted in Catherine E. Rymph, "Neither Neutral nor Neutralized: Phyllis Schlafly's Battle against Sexism," in *Women's America: Refocusing the Past,* 5th ed., ed. Linda K. Kerber and Jane Sherron De Hart (New York: Oxford University Press, 2000), 503; Richard L. Strout, "Margaret Smith Speaks on Joe McCarthy," *The Milwaukee Journal,* 20 April 1952, in "General Material," McCarthy, Joseph Raymond Maryland Senatorial Election, McCarthy File, MCS Library. See also, Laura McEnaney, *Civil Defense Begins at Home: Militarization Meets Everyday Life in the Fifties* (Princeton, NJ: Princeton University Press, 2000), 78.

3. S&H Green Stamps Ad, *National Business Woman,* October 1960, 1.

4. Mrs. Robert J. Phillips, "On the Importance of Voting," *National Business Woman,* October 1960, 6–7.

5. Catherine E. Rymph, *Republican Women: Feminism and Conservatism from Suffrage through the Rise of the New Right* (Chapel Hill: University of North Carolina Press, 2006), 131–149.

6. Margaret Chase Smith, "Woman, the Key Individual of Our Democracy," Commencement Address, delivered 7 June 1953, in *Vital Speeches,* 15 August 1953, 657–659.

7. Kim Nielsen, "Doing the 'Right' Right," *Journal of Women's History* 16 (August 2004): 169. The entire issue of the journal discusses conservative women around the world.

BIBLIOGRAPHY

PRIMARY SOURCES

Unpublished

A. C. Wedemeyer Papers. Hoover Institute on War, Revolution and Peace, Stanford University, Palo Alto, CA.

Alfred Kohlberg Papers. Hoover Institute on War, Revolution and Peace, Stanford University, Palo Alto, CA.

American Association of University Women—Texas. The Woman's Collection, Blagg-Huey Library, Texas Woman's University, Denton, TX.

Doloris Bridges Papers. New Hampshire Records and Archives, Concord, NH.

Edwin Bayley Papers. Wisconsin State Historical Society, Madison, WI.

Elizabeth Churchill Brown Papers. Hoover Institute on War, Revolution and Peace, Stanford University, Palo Alto, CA.

Freda Utley Papers. Hoover Institute on War, Revolution and Peace, Stanford University, Palo Alto, CA.

G. Joseph Minetti Collection. American Heritage Center, University of Wyoming, Laramie, WY.

Henry Regnery Papers. Hoover Institute on War, Revolution and Peace, Stanford University, Palo Alto, CA.

J. B. Matthews Papers. Special Collections Library, Duke University, Durham, NC.

Joseph R. McCarthy Papers. Marquette University, Milwaukee, WI.

Joseph R. McCarthy Papers. Wisconsin State Historical Society, Madison, WI.

Lyndon Baines Johnson Congressional File. Lyndon Baines Johnson Library, Austin, TX.

Margaret Chase Smith Papers. Margaret Chase Smith Library, Skowhegan, ME.

Personal Papers of Drew Pearson. Lyndon Baines Johnson Library, Austin, TX.

Right-Wing Collection, University of Iowa, Iowa City, IA.
  Alerted Americans [Reel 13 A73]
  American Spirit [Reel 8, A49]
  American Woman's Party [Reel 13 A100]
  The Farmer's Voice [Reel 48 F13]
  Freedom's Facts [Reel 56 F40]
  The Minute Women of the USA, Inc. [Reel 77 M53]
  New Mexico Women Speak! [Reel 86 N39]
  The Spirit [Reel 8, A49]

22nd Women's Patriotic Conference on National Defense [Reel 153 W59]

Styles Bridges Papers. New Hampshire Records and Archives, Concord, NH.

Thomas C. Reeves Research Files. Wisconsin State Historical Society, Madison, WI.

Wayne Hood Papers. Wisconsin State Historical Society, Madison, WI.

William Benton Papers. Wisconsin State Historical Society, Madison, WI.

Printed

Brown, Elizabeth Churchill. *The Enemy at His Back.* New York: Devin-Adair, 1956.

———. *Joe McCarthy and Other Anti-Communists.* Unpublished manuscript, Elizabeth Churchill Brown Papers, n.d.

Committee on Un-American Activities, U.S. House of Representatives. *The Communist Conspiracy,* Part 1, Section 3. 84th Congress, 2nd session, 1956.

Friedan, Betty. *The Feminine Mystique.* New York: W. W. Norton, 1963.

Hoover, J. Edgar. *Masters of Deceit: The Story of Communism in America and How to Fight It.* New York: Henry Holt, 1958; paperback, Pocket Books, 1961.

Kirk, Russell. *The Intelligent Women's Guide to Conservatism.* New York: Devin-Adair, 1957.

Kuhn, Irene Corbally. "12 Senate Wives." *American Mercury* (August 1955): 52–58.

Lundberg, Ferdinand, and Marynia Farnham. *Modern Women, the Lost Sex.* New York: Harper & Brothers, 1947.

Schlafly, Phyllis. *A Choice Not an Echo.* Alton, IL: Pere Marquette, 1964.

Schlafly, Phyllis, and Chester Ward. *The Gravediggers.* Alton, IL: Pere Marquette, 1964.

U.S. Senate, Subcommittee on Privileges and Elections. *Maryland Senatorial Election of 1950: Hearings before the Subcommittee on Privileges and Elections,* 82nd Cong., 1st sess., 2 March 1951.

U.S. Senate, Subcommittee on Privileges and Elections. *Maryland Senatorial Election of 1950, Report of the Committee on Rules and Administration,* 82nd Congress, 1st sess., 20 August 1950, Government Printing Office. In "Maryland Senatorial Election of 1950, Report of the Committee on Rules and Administration," Mc JR MD Senatorial Election, McCarthy File, MCS Library, Skowhegan, ME.

Utley, Freda. *China at War.* New York: John Day, 1939.

———. *The China Story.* Chicago: Henry Regnery, 1951.

———. *The Dream We Lost.* New York: John Day, 1940.

———. *The High Cost of Vengeance.* Chicago: Henry Regnery, 1949.

———. *Japan Can Be Stopped!* London: "News Chronicle" Publications Dept., 1937.

———. *Japan's Feet of Clay.* New York: W. W. Norton, 1937.

———. *Japan's Gamble in China.* London: Secker and Warburg, 1938.

———. *Last Chance in China* (Indianapolis: Bobbs-Merrill, 1947.

———. *Odyssey of a Liberal.* Washington, DC: Washington National Press, 1970.

———. *Will the Middle East Go West.* Chicago: Henry Regnery, 1957.

Valeo, Francis R. Oral History Interviews. Senate Historical Office. Washington, DC, n.d.

Watt, Ruth Young. Oral History Interviews. Senate Historical Office. Washington, DC, n.d.

Wylie, Philip. *Generation of Vipers.* New York, Rinehart, 1942.

SECONDARY SOURCES

Alexander, Charles C. *Holding the Line: The Eisenhower Era, 1952–1961.* Bloomington: Indiana University Press, 1975.

Ambrose, Stephen E. *Eisenhower.* Vols. 1 and 2. New York: Simon & Shuster, 1983.

———. *Nixon: The Education of a Politician 1913–1962.* New York: Simon and Schuster, 1987.

———. *Rise to Globalism: American Foreign Policy Since 1938,* 7th rev. ed. New York: Penguin Books, 1993.

Baker, Paula. "The Domestication of Politics: Women and American Political Society, 1780–1920." *American Historical Review* 89 (June 1984): 620–647.

Barnes, Harry Elmer, ed. *Perpetual War for Perpetual Peace.* Caldwell, ID: Caxton, 1953.

Barnet, Richard J. *Roots of War: The Men and Institutions behind U.S. Foreign Policy.* New York: Atheneum, 1972.

Baxter, Sandra, and Marjorie Lansing. *Women and Politics: The Visible Majority*, rev. ed. Ann Arbor: University of Michigan Press, 1983.

Benowitz, June Melby. *Days of Discontent: American Women and Right-Wing Politics, 1933–1945.* Dekalb: Northern Illinois University Press, 2002.

Beschloss, Michael. *The Crisis Years: Kennedy and Khrushchev, 1960–1963.* New York: Edward Burlingame Books, 1991.

Blair, Karen J. *The Clubwoman as Feminist: True Womanhood Redefined, 1868–1914.* New York: Holmes & Meier, 1980.

Boydston, Jeanne. *Home and Work: Housework, Wages, and the Ideology of Labor in the Early Republic.* New York: Oxford University Press, 1991.

Branch, Taylor. *Parting the Waters.* New York: Simon & Shuster, 1988.

Brennan, Mary C. *Turning Right in the Sixties.* Chapel Hill: University of North Carolina Press, 1995.

Brown, Victoria Bissell. *The Education of Jane Addams.* Philadelphia: University of Pennsylvania Press, 2004.

Burnham, James. *The Struggle for the World.* New York: John Day, 1947.

Byrdsall, Thomas, and Mary Byrdsall. *Chain Reaction: The Impact of Race, Rights, and Taxes on American Politics.* New York: W. W. Norton, 1991.

Camhi, Jane Jerome. *Women against Women: American Anti-Suffragism, 1880–1920.* Brooklyn, NY: Carlson, 1994.

Carleton, Don E. *Red Scare! Right-Wing Hysteria, Fifties Fanaticism and Their Legacy in Texas.* Austin: Texas Monthly Press, 1985.

Chafe, William H. *The Unfinished Journey: America since World War II*, 4th ed. New York: Oxford University Press, 1999.

Chamberlin, William Henry. *America's Second Crusade.* Chicago: Regnery, 1950.

Cohn, Carol. "Sex and Death in the Rational World of Defense Intellectuals." *Signs* 12 (Summer 1987): 687–718.

Collins, Robert M. *More: The Politics of Economic Growth in Postwar America.* New York: Oxford University Press, 2000.

Cook, Fred. *The Nightmare Decade: The Life and Times of Senator Joe McCarthy.* New York: Random House, 1971.

Costigliola, Frank. "The Nuclear Family: Tropes of Gender and Pathology in the Western Alliance." *Diplomatic History* 21 (Spring 1997): 163–183.

Cott, Nancy F. *The Grounding of Modern Feminism.* New Haven: Yale University Press, 1987.

Critchlow, Donald. "Conservatism Reconsidered: Phyllis Schlafly and Grassroots Conservatism," in *The Conservative Sixties*, ed. David Farber and Jeff Roche. New York: Peter Lang, 2003.

————. *Phyllis Schlafly and Grassroots Conservatism.* Princeton, NJ: Princeton University Press, 2005.

Cuordileone, K. A. *Manhood and American Political Culture in the Cold War.* New York: Routledge, 2005.

————. "'Politics in an Age of Anxiety': Cold War Political Culture and the Crisis in American Masculinity." *Journal of American History* (September 2000): 515–545.

Dean, Robert D. *Imperial Brotherhood: Gender and the Making of Cold War Foreign Policy.* Amherst: University of Massachusetts Press, 2001.

D'Emilio, John. *Making Trouble: Essays on Gay History, Politics, and the University.* New York: Routledge, 1992.

Deslippe, Dennis A. "'We Had an Awful Time with Our Women': Iowa's United Packinghouse Workers of America, 1945–75." *Journal of Women's History* 5, no. 1 (Spring 1993): 10–32.

Divine, Robert. *Eisenhower and the Cold War.* New York: Oxford University Press, 1981.

Ehrenreich, Barbara. *For Her Own Good.* New York: Doubleday, 1978.

Epstein, Barbara. "Anticommunism, Homophobia, and the Construction of Masculinity in the Postwar U.S.," in *Cold War Culture and Society: The Cold War,* vol. 5, ed. Lori Lynn Bogle. New York: Routledge, 2000.

Erickson, Christine Kimberly. "Conservative Women and Patriotic Maternalism: The Beginnings of a Gendered Conservative Tradition in the 1920s and 1930s." Ph.D. diss, University of California, Santa Barbara, 1999.

Evans, Sara M. *Born for Liberty: A History of Women in America.* New York: Free Press, 1989.

Feis, Herbert. *Churchill-Roosevelt-Stalin: The War They Waged and the Peace They Sought.* New York: Oxford University Press, 1953.

Felsenthal, Carol. *The Sweetheart of the Silent Majority: The Biography of Phyllis Schlafly.* New York: Doubleday, 1981.

Flanagan, Maureen A. "Anna Wilmarth Ickes: A Staunch Republican Woman," in *We Have Come to Stay: American Women and Political Parties, 1880–1960,* ed. Melanie Gustafson, Kristie Miller, and Elisabeth I. Perry. Albuquerque: University of New Mexico Press, 1999.

Foerstel, Karen, and Herbert N. Foerstel. *Climbing the Hill: Gender Conflict in Congress.* Westport, CT: Praeger, 1996.

Fones-Wolf, Elizabeth. *Selling Free Enterprise: The Business Assault on Labor and Liberalism.* Chicago: University of Illinois Press, 1994.

Freeman, Jo. *A Room at a Time: How Women Entered Politics.* New York: Rowman & Littlefield, 2000.

Fried, Richard. *The Russians Are Coming! The Russians Are Coming! Pageantry and Patriotism in Cold-War America.* New York: Oxford University Press, 1998.

Gaddis, John Lewis. *Strategies of Containment: A Critical Appraisal of Postwar American National Security Policy.* New York: Oxford University Press, 1982.

———. *We Now Know: Rethinking Cold War History.* New York: Oxford University Press, 1998.

Goldberg, Robert. *Barry Goldwater.* New Haven: Yale University Press, 1995.

Gordon, Felice D. *After Winning: The Legacy of the New Jersey Suffragists, 1920–1947.* New Brunswick, NJ: Rutgers University Press, 1986.

Gottlieb, Julie V. "Women and British Fascism Revisited: Gender, the Far-Right and Resistance." *Journal of Women's History* 16, no. 3 (2004): 108–123.

Greenstein, Fred. *The Hidden-Hand Presidency.* New York: Basic Books, 1982.

Griffith, Robert. *The Politics of Fear: Joseph R. McCarthy and the Senate.* Lexington: University Press of Kentucky, 1970.

Gustafson, Melanie, Kristie Miller, and Elisabeth I. Perry, eds. *We Have Come to Stay: American Women and Political Parties, 1880–1960.* Albuquerque: University of New Mexico Press, 1999.

Halberstam, David. *The Fifties.* New York: Villard Books, 1993.

Harvey, Elizabeth. "Visions of the Volk: German Women and the Far Right from Kaiserreich to Third Reich." *Journal of Women's History* 16, no. 3 (2004): 152–167.

Heale, M. J. *American Anticommunism: Combating the Enemy Within, 1830–1970.* Baltimore: Johns Hopkins University Press, 1990.

Herring, George. *America's Longest War.* New York: Alfred A. Knopf, 1986.

Hoover, J. Edgar. "The Twin Enemies of Freedom: Crime and Communism." Speech to the National Council of Catholic Women, 9 November 1956, *Vital Speeches* (1 December 1956) 23, no. 4: 106.

Jacoway, Elizabeth. *Yankee Missionaries in the South.* Baton Rouge: Louisiana State University Press, 1980.

Johnson, David K. *The Lavender Scare.* Chicago: University of Chicago Press, 2004.

Judis, John J. *William F. Buckley, Jr.: Patron Saint of the Conservatives.* New York: Simon & Shuster, 1988.

Kaledin, Eugenia. *Mothers and More.* Boston: Twayne, 1984.

Kannenberg, Lisa. "The Impact of the Cold War on Women's Trade Union Activism: The UE Experience." *Labor History* 34 (Spring-Summer 1993): 309–323.

Keith, Caroline H. *"For Hell and a Brown Mule": The Biography of Senator Millard E. Tydings.* New York: Madison Books, 1991.

Kerber, Linda K. "The Republican Mother and the Woman Citizen: Contradictions and Choices in Revolutionary America," in *Women's America: Refocusing the Past,* 5th ed., ed. Linda K. Kerber and Jane Sherron De Hart. New York: Oxford University Press, 2000.

Kessler-Harris, Alice. *Out to Work: A History of Wage-Earning Women in the United States.* New York: Oxford University Press, 1982.

Kinsey, Alfred C., Wardell B. Pomeroy, and Clyde E. Martin. *Sexual Behavior in the Human Female.* Philadelphia: W. B. Saunders, 1948.

Kinsey, Alfred C., Wardell B. Pomeroy, and Clyde E. Martin. *Sexual Behavior in the Human Male*. Philadelphia: W. B. Saunders, 1953.

Klatch, Rebecca. *Women and the New Right*. Philadelphia: Temple University Press, 1987.

Kolko, Gabriel, and Joyce Kolko. *The Limits of Power: The World and United States Foreign Policy, 1945–1954*. New York: Harper & Row, 1972.

Koonz, Claudia. *Mothers in the Fatherland: Women, the Family and Nazi Politics*. New York: St. Martin's, 1987.

La Feber, Walter. *America, Russia and the Cold War 1945–1990*, 6th ed. New York: McGraw-Hill, 1991.

Laville, Helen. *Cold War Women*. Manchester: Manchester University Press, 2002.

Leavitt, Sarah A. *From Catharine Beecher to Martha Stewart: A Cultural History of Domestic Advice*. Chapel Hill: University of North Carolina Press, 2002.

Levy, Robert. *Ana Pauker: The Rise and Fall of a Jewish Communist*. Berkeley: University of California Press, 2001.

Marling, Karal Ann. *As Seen on TV: The Visual Culture of Everyday Life in the 1950s*. Cambridge, MA: Harvard University Press, 1994.

Marshall, Susan E. "Ladies against Women: Mobilization Dilemmas of Anti-feminist Movements." *Social Problems* 32 (April 1985): 348–362.

———. *Splintered Sisterhood: Gender and Class in the Campaign against Woman Suffrage*. Madison: University of Wisconsin Press, 1997.

May, Elaine Tyler. *Homeward Bound: American Families in the Cold War Era*. New York: Basic Books, 1988.

McCarthy, Joseph R. *America's Retreat from Victory: The Story of George Catlett Marshall*. New York: Devin-Adair, 1951.

McCormick, Thomas J. *Half-Century: United States Foreign Policy in the Cold War*. Baltimore: Johns Hopkins University Press, 1989.

McCullough, David. *Truman*. New York: Simon & Schuster, 1992.

McEnaney, Laura. *Civil Defense Begins at Home: Militarization Meets Everyday Life in the Fifties*. Princeton, NJ: Princeton University Press, 2000.

———. "He-Men and Christian Mothers: The America First Movement and the Gendered Meanings of Patriotism and Isolationism." *Diplomatic History* 18 (Winter 1994): 47–57.

McGirr, Lisa. *Suburban Warriors: The Origins of the New American Right*, Princeton, NJ: Princeton University Press, 2001.

McNeill, William H. *America, Britain and Russia: Their Co-operation and Conflict, 1941–1946*. New York: Oxford University Press, 1953.

Meyerowitz, Joanne. *Not June Cleaver: Women and Gender in Postwar America, 1945–1960*. Philadelphia: Temple University Press, 1994.

Miles, Michael. *The Odyssey of the American Right*. New York: Oxford University Press, 1980.

Milkman, Ruth. *Gender at Work: The Dynamics of Job Segregation by Sex during World War II*. Chicago: University of Illinois Press, 1987.

Montgomery, Gayle B., and James W. Johnson. *One Step from the White House: The Rise and Fall of Senator William F. Knowland.* Berkeley: University of California Press, 1998.

Moskowitz, Eva. "It's Good to Blow Your Top: Women's Magazines and a Discourse of Discontent, 1945–1965." *Journal of Women's History* 8, no. 3 (Fall 1996): 66–98.

Murray, Sylvie. "Suburban Citizens: Domesticity and Community Politics in Queens, New York, 1945–1960." Ph.D. diss., Yale University, 1994.

Nash, George. *The Conservative Intellectual Movement in America.* New York: Basic Books, 1976.

Nickerson, Michelle. "Moral Mothers and Goldwater Girls," in *The Conservative Sixties,* ed. David Farber and Jeff Roche. New York: Peter Lang, 2003.

Nielsen, Kim E. "Doing the 'Right' Right." *Journal of Women's History* 16 (August 2004): 168–172.

———. *Un-American Womanhood: Antiradicalism, Antifeminism and the First Red Scare.* Columbus: Ohio State University Press, 2001.

Norton, Mary Beth. *Liberty's Daughters: The Revolutionary Experience of American Women, 1750–1800.* Boston: Little, Brown, 1980.

O'Connor, David Laurence. "Defenders of the Faith: American Catholic Lay Organizations and Anticommunism, 1917–1975." Ph.D. diss, State University of New York, Stony Brook, 2000.

Oshinsky, David. *A Conspiracy So Immense.* New York: Free Press, 1983.

Parmet, Herbert. *JFK: The Presidency of John F. Kennedy.* New York: Penguin Books, 1984.

Patterson, James T. *Grand Expectations: The United States, 1945–1974.* New York: Oxford University Press, 1996.

Pineo, Ronn. "Recent Cold War Studies." *The History Teacher* (November 2003): 79–86.

Power, Margaret. "More than Mere Pawns: Right-Wing Women in Chile." *Journal of Women's History* 16, no. 3 (2004): 138–151.

Powers, Richard Gid. *Not without Honor.* New York: Free Press, 1995.

Radosh, Ronald, and Joyce Milton. *The Rosenberg Rile: A Search for the Truth.* New York: Random House, 1983.

Rauchway, Eric. "A Gentlemen's Club in a Woman's Sphere: How Dorothy Whitney Straight Created the *New Republic*." *Journal of Women's History* 11 (Summer 1999): 60–85.

Red Nightmare. Department of Defense, Directorate for Armed Forces Information and Education, Warner Brothers Studios, 1962. Distributed by National Audiovisual Center, Capitol Heights, MD.

Reeves, Thomas C. *The Life and Times of Joe McCarthy.* New York: Stein and Day, 1982.

Reichard, Gary. "Bridges, Styles," in *American National Biography,* ed. John A. Garraty and Mark C. Carnes. New York: Oxford University Press, 1999.

Critchlow, Donald. "Conservatism Reconsidered: Phyllis Schlafly and Grass-roots Conservatism," in *The Conservative Sixties,* ed. David Farber and Jeff Roche. New York: Peter Lang, 2003.

Robinson, JoAnne. *The Montgomery Bus Boycott and the Women Who Started It.* Knoxville: University of Tennessee Press, 1987.

Rosen, Ruth. *The World Split Apart: How the Modern Women's Movement Changed America.* New York: Penguin Books, 2000.

Rubin, Nancy. *The New Suburban Woman: Beyond Myth and Motherhood.* New York: Coward, McCann & Geoghegan, 1982,

Rupp, Leila J., and Verta Taylor. *Survival in the Doldrums: The American Women's Right Movement, 1945 to the 1960s.* New York: Oxford University Press, 1987.

Rymph, Catherine E. "Neither Neutral nor Neutralized: Phyllis Schlafly's Battle against Sexism," in *Women's America: Refocusing the Past,* 5th ed., ed. Linda K. Kerber and Jane Sherron De Hart. New York: Oxford University Press, 2000.

———. *Republican Women: Feminism and Conservatism from Suffrage through the Rise of the New Right.* Chapel Hill: University of North Carolina Press, 2006.

Sale, Kirkpatrick. *Power Shift: The Rise of the Southern Rim and Its Challenge to the Eastern Establishment.* New York: Vintage Books, 1975.

Schlesinger, Arthur M., Jr. *The Vital Center.* Boston: Houghton Mifflin, 1949.

Schmidt, Patricia L. *Margaret Chase Smith: Beyond Convention.* Orono: University of Maine Press, 1996.

Schrecker, Ellen. *The Age of McCarthyism,* 2nd ed. New York: Bedford/St. Martin's, 2002.

———. *No Ivory Tower.* New York: Oxford University Press, 1986.

Scott, Anne Firor. *Natural Allies: Women's Associations in American History.* Chicago: University of Illinois Press, 1991.

Sherman, Janann. *No Place for a Woman: A Life of Senator Margaret Chase Smith.* New Brunswick, NJ: Rutgers University Press, 2000.

Sklar, Kathryn Kish. *Catharine Beecher: A Study in American Domesticity.* New Haven: Yale University Press, 1973.

———. *Florence Kelley and the Nation's Work: The Rise of Women's Political Culture, 1830–1900.* New Haven: Yale University Press, 1995.

Smith, Geoffrey S. "National Security and Personal Isolation: Sex, Gender and Disease in the Cold War United States." *International History Review* 14 (May 1992): 307–337.

Smith, Margaret Chase. "No Place for a Woman?" *Ladies Home Journal* (February 1952): 50+.

Stevenson, Adlai. *What I Think.* New York: Harper & Brothers, 1956.

Swerdlow, Amy. *Women Strike for Peace: Traditional Motherhood and Radical Politics in the 1960s.* Chicago: University of Chicago Press, 1993.

Tananbaum, Duane. *The Bricker Amendment Controversy: A Test of Eisenhower's Political Leadership.* Ithaca, NY: Cornell University Press, 1988.

Wallace, Patricia Ward. *Politics of Conscience: A Biography of Margaret Chase Smith.* Westport, CT: Praeger, 1995.

Weigand, Kate. *Red Feminism: American Communism and the Making of Women's Liberation.* Baltimore: Johns Hopkins University Press, 2001.

Weinstein, Allen. *Perjury: The Hiss-Chambers Case.* New York: Random House, 1978.

Weinstein, Allen, and Alexander Vassiliev. *The Haunted Wood: Soviet Espionage in America—The Stalin Era.* New York: Random House, 1999.

Wells, Mildred White. *Unity in Diversity: The History of the General Federation of Women's Clubs.* Washington, DC: General Federation of Women's Clubs, 1953.

Welter, Barbara. "The Cult of True Womanhood." *American Quarterly* (Summer 1966): 151–174.

White, F. Clifton. *Suite 3505.* New Rochelle, NY: Arlington House, 1967.

Zahvi, Gerald. "Passionate Commitments: Race, Sex and Communism at Schenectady General Electric, 1932–1954." *JAH* 83 (September 1996): 514–548.

Zarlengo, Kristina. "Civilian Threat, the Suburban Citadel, and Atomic Age American Women." *Signs: A Journal of Women in Culture and Society* 24 (Summer 1999): 941.

Zubok, Vladislav, and Constantine Pleshakov. *Inside the Kremlin's Cold War: From Stalin to Khrushchev.* Cambridge, MA: Harvard University Press, 1996.

INDEX

Acheson, Dean, 125
Addams, Jane, 7, 39, 92
Adkins, Bertha, 130
Alerted Americans, 43
All American Conferences to Combat
  Communism, 41, 43
American Association of University
  Women, 38, 42
American Civil Liberties Union, 108
American Enterprise Association, 52
American Way. *See* American Way of Life
American Way of Life, 36, 115, 118, 151
American Woman's Party, 89, 90, 91, 98,
  105, 133
Anticommunism: movement defined, 4,
  20, 154; and women, 34, 147–148
Anticommunists: and Asia, 62–63, 69;
  concerns about Americans' under-

standing of communism, 69, 95; and
Europe, 61–62; gendered images,
115–117, 125–127, 143, 147–148; men
react to women, 9–10, 88, 113–114, 118,
134–135, 146, 151–152
Anticommunist Women: changes in
  communism, 80–81; concerns about
  education, 106–114; connections to
  conservatism, 32, 33, 36; defined, 5–6,
  34–36, 151, 152; emphasis on domesticity, 116, 118, 151, 152; encourage
  women to join movement, 90–92, 95–96;
  and foreign policy, 60–62, 64–84; frustration with male anticommunists, 91–
  92; as household managers, 86, 93–94,
  102–103, 104–106; involvement on local
  level, 37–41, 42–44, 86, 88, 149; involvement on national level, 44–57, 150; justi-